Undercover Cop

Undercover Cop

One man's true story of undercover
policing in Ireland, the UK and Europe

Paddy Craig

Gill & Macmillan

Gill & Macmillan Ltd
Hume Avenue, Park West, Dublin 12
with associated companies throughout the world
www.gillmacmillan.ie

978 07171 4389 4

Typography design by Make Communication
Print origination by O'K Graphic Design, Dublin
Printed by ColourBooks Ltd, Dublin

This book is typeset in 10.5/13 pt Minion.

The paper used in this book comes from the wood pulp of
managed forests. For every tree felled, at least one tree is
planted, thereby renewing natural resources.

A CIP catalogue record for this book is available from the
British Library.

5 4 3 2 1

Ode to an Undercover Officer

I've got a load of black on the plot
and a ton of shit in the boot

I think I'm half way reasonable,
nearly a proper person and certainly
not a muppet, two bob nonce,
A raspberry or a Doris

I've got my parcel wrapped around me,
I've laid my tool down and I've
called on my stash ready for
the trade

I've seen a geezer with a Hampton
who knows a bloke called J Arthur
who's got half a weight of puff
down the slaughter

There's a stewards about a Doris
with a wedge who's stamped
all over the commodity

I've Peter and Pauled it on the day
of the race. I've been rowed
out by Bert who put twenty
on the floor to turn a shilling
and then chilled out.

I'm off to Brum to blow a puff
called Charlie and hope it don't
all come on top

In this game whatever dings your
bell so if I'm happy and you're
happy we're all happy

John Carrington
Detective Superintendent, West Midlands Police
1 November 1996

Contents

Preface

In this short account of my career in the Criminal Investigation Department of the Royal Ulster Constabulary, and in particular of my time as an undercover officer operating throughout Ireland, the United Kingdom and in other European countries, I have attempted to give the reader some insight into the highs and lows, and the dangers and triumphs which working in this sphere brings with it. Undercover work is an area of police operations which by definition, I suppose, few members of the public know anything about. I certainly believe that the vast majority of the citizens of Ireland, both North and South, have no knowledge whatsoever of the dangers that were encountered on their behalf during the time I speak of by small, dedicated groups of Royal Ulster Constabulary and Garda Síochána officers, whose main purpose was to make this great little island of ours a safer place for our children to grow up in.

I am mindful that as this book is published, we are entering a new and exciting time in the future of Ireland, both North and South, and it is to be hoped that times of greater tolerance and peace for all its citizens lie ahead. In describing our trait as Irish people—and particularly as Northerners—of continually bringing up the past, the late David Ervine, Belfast City Councillor, MLA and a working-class Belfast man, coined the term 'Whataboutyouisms', and I think he observed us well. I make no apology however for reminding the people of Ireland that without the groups of officers of whom I speak, this country might not have progressed so far and our streets would be awash with drugs and other muck, poisoning our children. These forgotten few, Ireland's 'Forlorn Hope', relied above all on their own courage, guile and training and on many occasions the only acknowledgement they received for risking their lives was a slap on the back or a whispered thank-you in the corridors of power. The very nature of their work meant that they would get little or no public recognition of their achievements. Yet there have been many who suffered long-term physical damage and lasting mental scars as a result of working in the human cesspits in which they were forced to spend so much of their time, in order to achieve the successes that they did. I dedicate this book in part to their courage.

In writing this account, I have had no mind to educate either criminals or terrorists in the secret or restricted areas of the work we did, or even more importantly, to identify private citizens or agents who assisted us in our fight against the criminal fraternity. I have chosen not to mention many details regarding the tradecraft we used and the technical resources we relied upon—such as various types of restricted equipment which the security forces of all nations have at their disposal in the fight against organised crime and terrorism. My major concern has been to protect the identity of certain individuals and to obscure the full extent to which they assisted us, and with this in mind, I have, on a few very rare occasions, changed the names of certain people and places, and deliberately fed in other misinformation for the same purpose. To take such precautions is not only legally permissible but morally justified, and the very least I can do to protect those courageous people whose help has been invaluable.

Behind every operation I was involved in was a virtual army of nameless officers and backroom staff, who worked tirelessly and without testimonial. Without their help, there is no doubt that on a number of occasions I would not have survived. I trust that these colleagues and friends will also feel included in this account, which is also a testament to the crucial part they played in the war on crime. To Eleanor, Hannah and Patrick, I hope that what I relate here may go some way to explaining my long absences and my shortcomings as a husband and father. I pray that it does.

Acknowledgements

I would like to thank all my close friends, particularly Andy, Barbara and Ken and Hannah Millar; Eddie and Kim Morton, for helping me finish the manuscript by putting me up in the quietness of their beautiful apartment in Spain; my close friend and ex-colleague Jonty Brown and his wife Rebecca, who both encouraged me to write this account of my time as an undercover operative. I thank Jim McDowell and his colleague Hugh Jordan for their help, encouragement and friendship. To my friends Kelly, Bobby and Bill, I apologise for the many times when my mind was elsewhere. Particular thanks too go of course to Marshall Matchett and Fergal Tobin of Gill & Macmillan publishers, for their faith in the book and their patience, friendship and encouragement. I would like to thank their friendly staff for their assistance and perseverance, for making me feel at home on my visits to their office and for also encouraging me to finish the book. Special thanks go to my family: Eleanor, who encouraged me to start writing in the first place, and my long-suffering children, Hannah and Patrick, who had to put up with my long silences and staring at the computer for hours on end, even on holiday. Into each life a little sunshine must fall, and in conclusion I thank that special person Susan Feldstein, my literary editor, who laboured with me through the final script, encouraged me and patched it together into the form it is in today.

Terms and Abbreviations

ACC	Assistant Chief Constable
AKA	Also Known As
ASU	Active Service Unit
To Backstop	To create false companies, bank accounts and safe houses, as a means of corroborating cover stories or aliases when infiltrating a criminal conspiracy.
Blue on Blue	Refers to a situation when two agencies collide or come into conflict whilst working against the same target: the worst of all possible scenarios in an undercover context, and fraught with danger.
Chopped Down	Expression used to describe powdered drugs which have been mixed and diluted with other substances in order to add weight. Substances often used for this purpose include rat poison and baking powder.
DAAD	Direct Action Against Drugs: cover front for the IRA when they took action against anyone involved in the drug trade: such action usually took the form of an assassination.
DEA	Drug Enforcement Agency
Flash Money	Proposed upfront payment to crooks, usually carried as cash in a case or bag to be shown to the crooks for the purposes of enticing them to bring their illicit goods onto the plot (see below).
Forlorn Hope	Traditionally, a body of men, often volunteers, selected to attempt a breach, scale the wall of a fortress, or undertake some other extraordinarily perilous enterprise in the service of their country or community. Such a body of men was often regarded as expendable.
Laid On	A legal term used in undercover policing to

	define the circumstances in which intervention, including infiltration, can be undertaken by an undercover police officer. The crime must already be in motion or in progress. In such circumstances a police officer could covertly intervene. This term is more fully explained in Appendix B.
LVF	Loyalist Volunteer Force: breakaway group from the UVF, led by the notorious Loyalist gangster Billy Wright, aka 'King Rat'.
Met	London Metropolitan Police Force
Nine Bar	Refers to the form in which cannabis is usually transported. Weighing nine ounces, from whence it gets its name, a nine bar looks like a large bar of dark brown or black soap.
PIRA	Provisional Irish Republican Army
PLO	Palestine Liberation Organisation
Plot	Slang word referring to the place or location where the exchange of drugs or other illicit goods and money will happen or 'go down'.
QRF	Quick Reaction Force: usually a dedicated backup team of uniformed officers who will move in to make the arrest or arrests.
RUC	Royal Ulster Constabulary
Slaughter	Slang term for the place or location where the drugs will be divided up.
SO10; SO12	Special Operations Units at New Scotland Yard

Chapter 1
Scenes from a Life

It is June 2000. I am sitting in a Mercedes saloon, parked in a leafy lay-by just outside Newark, a small village in the middle of rural England. It is 8.00 pm, and in a few minutes I will drive into Newark and make my way to a hotel, where I will meet one of the most dangerous men in England. A man who owns not only the hotel in question, but nearly half the village.

Closing my eyes, I try to mentally run though the dozens of covert tapes I have built up on this job to date. I prepare to move back into my other self, Sean from Belfast, the gangster with Republican paramilitary links. Going through the familiar checklist in my head, I robotically run my hands through my pockets and wallet, ensuring that I have removed anything which might betray my true identity and blow my cover. One mistake at this stage of the game, and at best, months of painstaking police work by a large dedicated team of professionals will have been lost—along with hundreds of thousands, maybe even millions of taxpayers' money. At worst, for me anyway, I may end my days here as a prop for the new M8 motorway.

My mind wanders through the maze of meetings. 'You must get the scripts right…these bastards are for real…this isn't a f***ing movie. Why the hell am I doing this, anyway?' Deeper and farther back I go. What do I know? What should I not know? The facts must be in order. Apart from the intense pressure which an awareness of the dangers of this job brings, there is always the natural human fear that you might not be able to pull the job off, that you might let the side down. The operational team doesn't tell you everything, for your own good. For example, the fact that a target may have been in a certain prison, or have committed a particularly gruesome crime. A fact which may be of interest to you, not least in terms of your own safety—but if you happen to drop it into conversation with the wrong company at the wrong time, and they are switched-on people, they will probably realise that they have never mentioned it to you. It's a well-kept secret in their inner circle—so how could *you* know about it…?

I must be able to put the facts and the sequence of events together properly. How did this all start? Briggs-Price, the target, has by all accounts been a thorn in the side of the UK Crime Squad and Customs for years. The bottom line is that all attempts to lock him up to date have failed miserably. The target has run rings around every single effort to make him amenable to the law thus far. A combination of luck, his own guile and the skills of various very pricey lawyers have made sure of that.

From my initial brief, it seems that Briggs-Price has done everything from screwing the cat to robbing his granny, although very few concrete details have been given to me: you never get to know exactly what a target has done, in case you let something slip. I do know however that this evil thug is responsible for the importation of a very significant proportion of all the heroin coming into the country at the time, and so for causing untold damage to countless kids and young adults.

This is undoubtedly the most difficult time in any operation. If you lose your nerve at this point, you are, to put it bluntly, f***ed. I remind myself yet again of the fact that the intervention unit is close by, and that they are ready to storm Briggs-Price's place if the wheel comes off the plan, but the reality, I know, is that I will have my throat cut or be murdered in some equally barbaric way long before they get to me.

I look at my watch: it's time to go. I put my key into the ignition and turn. This is it: too late to turn back now…

Chapter 2
And so it Begins

Born in the Ardoyne area of North Belfast in 1954, I was the third child of the family, preceded by an elder brother, Raymond, and a sister, Gwyn. My father was a bus driver for Ulster Transport Authority, my mother worked part-time in a shop in the city centre, and I remember that we were one of the few families in the street who had a car. Although my early recollections were of five of us sharing a terrace house with no bathroom or bath and an outside toilet, I would however never have considered our family to be poor or deprived by any means. I had a reasonably happy childhood and my parents always ensured we had food on the table and clothes on our backs, even if it meant they did without themselves.

From a very early age, my mother told me that I had a guardian angel. Throughout my childhood, she would take any opportunity to relate the story of the occasion on which, on a hot summer's day, she had put me in my pram out in the backyard of our terrace house to get a breath of air. She had returned to fetch me about an hour later, only to find the thick woollen blankets in which I was wrapped peppered with air rifle slugs: some lunatic living in the street behind us, firing from an upstairs window, had been using my pram as target practice. Miraculously, not a single bullet had managed to penetrate my blankets. Although the story, and the fact that my mother enjoyed telling it so much, caused me no little embarrassment as a young boy, I was to recall it on more than one occasion later in my life and during my career as a police officer, when the prospect of death seemed imminent and my chances of survival very slim…Moments of crisis, such as at Clady Checkpoint in 1987, when a 1,000 lb car bomb was to explode literally yards from where my colleagues and myself were standing; in July 1985, when, by then a DMSU Inspector, I stood shoulder-to-shoulder with my men at the frontline on the Garvaghy Road, bearing the brunt with them of a vicious hail of stones, steel and bottles launched by a hostile mob of angry Orangemen; in 1997, working on behalf of the London Regional Crime Squad, and the moment when, in deep cover in the headquarters of a murderous gang of career criminals, the awful realisation broke over me that I was completely alone, out of range of my surveillance umbrella, and my cover about to be blown. On all of these occasions, and many others besides during my long career as a police officer, I was indeed to remember my mother's conviction that I had a guardian angel keeping me safe, and to wonder whether there might be some truth in it after all.

Even though I grew up in one of the so-called roughest areas of the city of Belfast, neither I nor my family and friends had any real awareness of the Troubles, as they would become known, until the events of 1969. Prior to that period, I cannot recall any sectarian problems whatsoever. My best mate, Danny, was a Catholic. He and I would gather the wood for the usual Eleventh Night bonfire together, while I would accompany him to Mass when his mother insisted that he go. We were blissfully unaware of the sectarian hatred which was soon to engulf the city, and our area in particular. Protestant and Catholic in the Ardoyne area had one important thing in common (and to this day, still do, although some of them won't acknowledge it)…being working class, with all the same day-to-day struggles that entails.

My mate Danny had a TV and we did not, so I used to practically live at his house. The rest of my free time I would spend at Betty Sinclair's. A close neighbour, Betty was the head of the Irish Communist Party, and a great lady who would often babysit us for my parents. It was only near election times that politicians would come out of the woodwork and communities would revert to their tribal divisions: otherwise, relations between the two communities in our area were peaceable enough. However, between the so-called Civil Rights Movement and the Paisley Brigade, street violence returned to the working class areas of the city and, locally, things would very quickly take a turn for the worse. Ardoyne was no exception in this respect, and friends became foes almost overnight. We were eventually forced out of our home at the height of the Troubles, at which point we moved to another area of North Belfast. There our family would further expand, with my long-suffering mother giving birth relatively late in life to two more daughters, Margaret and Beth. For the first time ever, we had a real back garden and, being close to the Shore Road, we could see Belfast Lough from our upstairs windows.

On leaving school at fifteen with one 'O' Level to my name, I decided I would serve my time as an electrician, and I began my apprenticeship straight away. However, I was also eager to assist my country in the face of the continuing Troubles, and from July 1973 until January 1975, I served in 'C' Company of the 10th Battalion, Ulster Defence Regiment, part-time at Girdwood Barracks, Belfast. Becoming a member of the Royal Ulster Constabulary had in fact been an ambition of mine even from an early age. Another of my late mother's favourite recollections, which she also used to recount at the most inopportune moments, was of how I as a small child of four or five would often take it upon myself to shout and yell at passing policemen on the beat. Too young to be allowed to stray too far, I would find myself locked in our small front garden while my mother busied herself with housework. On looking out of the window and seeing the police talking to me over the gate, she would often rush out in horror, wondering what on earth I could be saying to them. Apparently I was in the habit of calling them over whenever I was in the garden and saw them passing. Once I'd got their attention, I would amongst other things complain bitterly to them about being locked in the garden…

In January 1975, when I had almost completed half of my time as an apprentice electrician, I joined the Royal Ulster Constabulary Reserve. I was stationed at Oldpark RUC Station, which was very handy, as it was part of the Ardoyne neighbourhood, which of course I knew very well. I served there for nearly a year to the day, when, by that time immersed in the police family, I decided to make my full-time career in the RUC. I joined the regular Police service and signed up to begin my training at Enniskillen Depot on 7 December 1975. I can still remember the journey to the training centre well. My late father and my then girlfriend, Eleanor, who was later to become my wife, drove there with me. I was sitting in the front of the car with my arm draped back over the seat holding my girlfriend's hand. We held hands for the whole journey, and by the time we got to the Depot, my arm was numb.

My squad, the 'X' Squad, was the biggest intake of recruits in the history of the RUC (there were 104 of us altogether) and I was to spend sixteen weeks in training. There were a number of 'Principles of Policing', some of which related to simple standards of behaviour that you had to learn parrot fashion. One of the mantras which I particularly remember went something along the lines of, 'Courtesy is an essential quality. The public have a right to expect it, and with it, its complementary quality, good manners.' Something they regrettably seem to have stopped teaching the modern police recruit! As well as legal training, there was a big emphasis on drills and physical training. In addition to the regular PT classes, there were some very simple motivational exercises, guaranteed to get even the laziest recruit off his butt. If you didn't complete the five mile road run every Friday, you didn't get home—it was as simple as that. I found the training hard, but enjoyed it immensely and couldn't wait to finish and be let loose on the unsuspecting public of Northern Ireland!

I really only had one sour experience the whole time in training and it was over something relatively petty in hindsight. It was however to highlight at a very early stage in my career the fact that heeding my father's advice—to always tell the truth and stick by it—did not always pay. The incident in question occurred one Monday morning on the parade ground, when I was approached by one of the Drill Sergeants, an ex-Irish Guards instructor, who in my view still thought he was one. I had for some time been the butt of this Drill Sergeant's parade ground sarcasm. The previous weekend and entirely on my own initiative, I had got my hair cut very short. On observing this, the Sergeant screamed in my ear something to the effect that he was glad to see I'd taken his advice: had he not told me to get a haircut? As it happened, he had not done anything of the kind, and I told him so. At this, he nearly exploded with rage, so angry that his face had all the appearance of someone having a fit, down to the white spittle on his lips, which he liberally sprayed over me as he spat out, 'Are you calling me a liar, boy?' Seeing the horror on my fellow squad mates' faces, and slowly realising that I had embarked upon a dangerous road, I carefully suggested that he might have been mistaken. He was having none of it, and called me for everything: how dare I call him a liar?! He marched me off to the front of the square, and I was forced to stand there to attention whilst the rest of the squad marched off to breakfast. Later he returned, accompanied by the other Drill Sergeant. To the tune of more verbal threats, I was taken before the Camp Commandant on a charge of insubordination. I had, it was declared, called the Drill Sergeant a liar.

The Commandant asked me if I had anything to say to the charge. I asked if I could talk to him alone. The Sergeant was duly asked to retire, which he did, although I could see that he was purple with rage at my audacity. I explained the situation to the Commandant and apologised for being in front of him for such a trivial matter. It would have been quite easy, I explained, for me to agree with the Sergeant that he had indeed told me to get a haircut—but, as he hadn't actually done so, I wasn't prepared to tell lies to placate him. With all the innocence of an altar boy, I explained I had joined the police with the intention of telling the truth at all times, as this was the way I had been brought up, and so on. How naïve I was! Still, I was about to learn one of my first important lessons in life. The Commandant told me that he knew the Sergeant could be difficult and overbearing. He commended me on telling the truth—but, as the Sergeant had claimed that he had told me to get a haircut, and he was a Sergeant and I was only a Constable, he, the Commandant, had to take the word of the superior officer. He said he hoped that I understood the position he was in, and gave me two nights' extra classes.

Such was my first practical lesson in truth and justice within the police. Telling the truth doesn't always pay, unfortunately, and I would find the same principle to hold true much later in my life, when, in the twilight of my career, I would find myself morally compelled to report on more serious matters.

On the last day of our training, we all gathered in the indoor shooting range and waited with trepidation to hear where we would be stationed. I listened intently whilst the officer called out a list of names and corresponding stations. Some of my fellow recruits beamed from ear-to-ear when they heard they were going to stations such as Holywood, Bangor or Carryduff—most of these, rightly or wrongly, were perceived as cushy numbers and generally those posted there were the 'blue eyes' in the Rugby or football fraternities. Being from a working class background, I didn't play rugby or football. When my name was called out with my nominated station, Roden Street, I could see some of the old hands scratching their heads. None of my peer group had any clue where this station even was. When I inquired of one of the old hands as to where it might be, he replied, 'They've made a mistake, son, it was blown off the face of the map ages ago.' The Inspector was adamant however that Roden Street was where I was going. In West Belfast, the station proper had been decimated by a bomb and now consisted merely of a mobile hut, basically a Police report centre, situated inside Mulhouse Army barracks. The area served was the Lower Falls, regarded by most people at that time as Northern Ireland's equivalent of West Beirut.

From the start, police life was not as I had dreamed it would be. In my innocence, I had had visions of myself walking the beat and patrolling in police vehicles, but it would be nearly two years before I would get to man a police car. My first two years were spent accompanying military patrols, walking through the Lower Falls and Divis Flats areas. This activity was officially titled 'Army Liaison Duties'. The reality was, whether we liked it or not, that we were still almost completely dependent on the military any time we moved outside the camp at that time. This was still a difficult period in the Province's history, and the police were only just starting to undertake normal on-the-beat patrolling duties in the area again after the very turbulent times of the early Troubles. Years of hatred and alienation meant that our mere presence there was like a red flag to a bull, and on more than one occasion I returned to the barracks covered in brick dust and spittle, from the hail of missiles and abuse that had been directed at me. We would also come under weekly and sometimes daily sniper fire and bomb attacks. However, it would prove to be a good training ground and I would soon learn valuable lessons on how to keep alive in such a dangerous environment. Being from a working class background myself, I could in many ways understand the people of the Lower Falls and the sort of problems they had. So many saw the military as an occupying force and this wasn't helped by the fact that they sometimes acted as one. In an area such as the Falls, trust was something you had to work hard for—however, slowly but surely I managed to break through some of the prejudices and mistrust people had, rightly or wrongly, regarding the police. I was even to make good friends in that area, and some of these have become lifelong friends I still meet regularly to this very day.

It was partly down to my local knowledge of the Lower Falls area that I was subsequently, and relatively early in my career, appointed to the Hastings Street CID staff where I continued to work in the West

Belfast area and was to earn a number of commendations for good police duty. I passed the Sergeant's exam, and I reckon the powers-that-be must have mistakenly thought I had been getting it too easy or something, because in July 1979 I was given a posting on uniform section duty at Strand Road RUC Station in Londonderry. At the time, this was basically the Ulster equivalent of policing Siberia! During this period I was injured a number of times on duty and also received further commendations for good Police duty. My stint in the North Region was to be a short one, however, and within a year I was to find myself stationed back in the Falls area as Detective Sergeant. In this era in West Belfast, which spanned the Hunger Strikes crisis, I dealt with many murders and terrorist atrocities and came under terrorist fire on a number of occasions. I was subsequently to gain promotion to uniform Inspector and posted to Strabane RUC Station on 24 September 1984.

Sometimes I wished I played 'rugger' or football, like many of the other protected birds in the force, the majority of whom would find themselves given some cosseted post, such as in Special Branch or stationed in a seaside town where it would be rare to see a shot fired in anger. Nearly ten years into the job, I hadn't served a single day in a 'normal' policing environment.

Chapter 3
Turbulent Times

While stationed in Strabane, I was soon to find myself transferred to the N2 DMSU (District Mobile Support Unit), based at 'the Hump' on the border. The mid-eighties was undoubtedly one of the most turbulent periods in the Province's troubled history, and, like so many of my colleagues, I was to find myself frequently under hostile attack from mortars and sniper gunfire. One incident which always comes rushing back to me whenever I think of that period, and which is all too indicative of the perilous nature of our lives as RUC officers at the time, is the car bomb attack on Clady Checkpoint in 1984.

That night I was in fact off duty, but was still hanging around the guardroom when suddenly my friend Rabb, the Duty Inspector, burst in to say that there had been some sort of attack on Clady Checkpoint. The army personnel stationed there had abandoned the post and, as per their orders on such occasions, had dug in in the area surrounding the checkpoint so as to be in a position to repel any further attack. Unfortunately there were no details at this stage as to exactly what had happened: the men were apparently in a radio black spot.

At this point, we were joined in the guardroom by the major of the local UDR (Ulster Defence Regiment), whose men were protecting the checkpoint. The major had donned a civvies coat over his uniform and had driven straight over to the station to ask us for help to somehow get transport out there. To go openly in a police or military vehicle would have been madness, but he told us that he was determined to go out anyway. He didn't know if there had been any casualties, and felt compelled go to the aid of his men. A formal military and police response was not planned until daylight, when each road would have to be checked out for landmines or booby traps. After a brief consultation, we each grabbed a rifle from the armoury and set off for the checkpoint in Rabb's private car. Set in the centre of a small village, the checkpoint was right on the border and surrounded by narrow winding country roads in a small but deep valley. With our lights dipped, we drove as far as the outskirts of the village. Soon we started to pick up some chitchat from some of the Major's men on our radios, and we advised them immediately of our presence in the area. A short time later, we came upon some of the defenders. Dug in at the side of a ditch on the edge/outer limits of the village, they had mounted a heavy machine gun to cover the approaching roadway. All credit to them, they were as professional a bunch of soldiers as I had ever seen. Disconcertingly, we still couldn't ascertain from these men the exact details of what had happened. They were able to tell us that after a burst of heavy gunfire had been directed at the checkpoint, a bomb warning had been given, and they had then evacuated the post as per standing instructions. Due however to the radio transmissions problems, nobody seemed to know where the bomb actually was.

Thankfully, at this stage, it looked like there were no casualties, so we decided to move slowly in on the village. Wielding our semi-automatic rifles from the windows of Rabb's car, 1920s style, we edged into the outskirts of the village, which was now in total darkness. We came cautiously to a halt at the crest of a large bank which overlooked the checkpoint. The unnerving silence of the scene was suddenly pierced by the eerie wail of a peacock from the nearby and aptly named Peacock Road, warning us, it seemed, to be on our guard. If it was indeed a warning, the timing could not have been better. I had just dismounted from the rear passenger side of the vehicle and my companions from the front and rear driver's side. We were in fact facing each other across the roof of the car, when the 1,000 lb car bomb detonated from directly below us at the foot of the bank and the rear of the checkpoint. I had been in many attacks involving explosives, but none such as this. My memory of the scene is as vivid as if it had happened yesterday. I can recall hearing what sounded like a mighty roar of thunder. For a few unearthly seconds I could see Rabb's and the major's faces contort, as the air was sucked forcefully from our lungs. A millisecond later, the roar became a mighty scream and a huge orange fireball punched itself skywards, propelling most of the Ford Granada car in which the explosives had been planted right up and over our car. As I spun round, I saw the force of the blast lift the roofs off the nearby bungalows and throw them like tissues into the air. Sounding in its final stages like a sonic boom, the mighty roar tore skywards and the earth shook violently. Then utter silence reigned again.

All three of us were in shock and bleeding heavily from our noses and ears. Other than that, however, we were remarkably unscathed. The bank had forced the blast up and completely over our heads, with the pensioners' houses farther behind us taking the full force. Had we not been in that location precisely, we would most certainly have died. My guardian angel had spread her wings over us: obviously, it was not time to go yet. Indeed, in a more general sense, there were no fatalities that night—only a few minor injuries were reported—and, apart from the widespread damage to the village, all was well. The incident would be recorded in a few brief lines in the Strabane Station Occurrence Book, under the simple heading, 'Bombing at Clady Checkpoint'.

And so life went on, for the community at large, as well as for those of us policing the Strabane area. Perhaps the only positive impact such terrifying experiences had on us police officers as individuals was to create an incredibly strong bond of comradeship between us, as colleagues who literally relied upon each other for survival. Only in my early thirties myself, I had men and women under my command who were even younger, and I found the responsibility for keeping them safe almost overwhelming at times. Each officer dealt with this heavy burden in his or her individual way. Some never went out at all, commanding only from the safety of a fortified station. The only way I could cope myself was to always be out there with those I was responsible for. At least that way, I wouldn't be constantly worrying from a distance whether they were alright. I think they appreciated it.

In July 1986, I was to return to the CID again, this time as Detective Inspector of CID Omagh. Whilst there, I dealt with a number of serious terrorist outrages and murders during this very active period of the Troubles, managing to make a number of successful arrests in relation to serious terrorist crimes, including murder. The vast majority of the people in Omagh were the salt of the earth, despite the town subsequently having gained undeserved notoriety because of the Omagh Bombing. One of my greatest friends, Harold Rainey, a part-time UDR Staff Sergeant, was typical of the majority of the people in the friendly town. A legend in his own time in the locality, Harold would always go out of his own way to help others: nothing was too much for him, and no distance too far. Sadly, he is no longer with us. I miss him greatly, as does his long-suffering wife, Kathleen, who would pick us up at the most unearthly hours from the most obscure places, often with very little warning, but without a single complaint.

During my time in Omagh, however, I was to witness at first hand the incompetence and bogus self-aggrandisement of the CID establishment at the time. Even more frustratingly, I was also to experience directly how my authority as Detective Inspector could be undermined by the black hand of Special Branch. As the Detective Inspector and sub-divisional head of the CID, one would have thought that I would have been privy to any intelligence obtained by Special Branch relating to the many terrorist and criminal incidents which occurred in the district. Sadly, this was not to be the case, and the Special Branch treated me and the rest of the department with their usual contempt. However, despite current allegations of a long-running campaign of collusion with loyalist paramilitaries, my own impression during my time in Omagh was that Special Branch were not interested in any shape or form in Loyalist paramilitaries. They seemed in fact to spend their whole time fixated with Republicans and their activities. Not that I got any help or intelligence in the fight against either group from Special Branch anyway.

It must be said that many Republicans in Tyrone were a breed unto themselves. There was an evil amongst them which Republicans in Belfast and elsewhere lacked. A black and cold-blooded hatred of Protestants and the security forces which they barely attempted to conceal, even in public. My experience of investigating the murder of David John Kyle in 1986 was to bring me face-to-face with this kind of bitter sectarian hatred in its ugliest form.

Kyle, a 40-year-old company director in a local quarry firm and a Protestant, entered a public house in Greencastle, Co. Tyrone, on Wednesday 30 July 1986. He bought a pint of beer and, before he had taken a sip from it, a lone gunman approached and shot him in the back of the head at point blank range with a former Police Ruger .357 Magnum revolver. As the unfortunate Mr Kyle lay on the floor, dead or dying by this stage, his assailant shot him deliberately and cold-bloodedly in the face. The gunman then walked calmly from the bar.

Sadly, nothing remarkable perhaps, in the annals of hatred and murder in Northern Ireland, but what was truly frightening and sickening in this instance was the reaction and behaviour of the good citizens of Greencastle. When I arrived at the murder scene, the witnesses—the few that is who bothered to wait until the arrival of the first response vehicle—were in the back bar area. The body of the victim was lying on the floor beside the main bar. I had known Mr Kyle to speak to in passing in the town. As I stood behind his now lifeless body, trying to imagine where the gunman had been, I realised that the shots must have hit the bar behind where the victim was standing—and yet, as my trained eye scanned the shelves, I noted that they all looked to be remarkably clean. Stepping behind the bar, I ran my finger along the shelves. There was not even the lightest dusting of powdered glass on their surfaces. I scanned the top of the counter, where the drinking glasses had been sitting. A member of the bar staff was able to confirm what I was having trouble taking in: even before I had arrived, the bar had been cleaned, glasses had been washed, and any broken glass on the shelves had been cleared away and replaced as if nothing had happened. I really believe that people would have carried the body outside if they had had enough time to do so.

It became obvious, from the very outset of the inquiry, that the majority of witnesses were lying through their teeth. Few of the people in the bar would even admit to being aware that the murder had actually taken place. One 'witness', who had clearly been sitting only a few feet away from a Magnum revolver being fired three times in a confined space, had the gall to look me in the eye and say, in response to my question as to why he hadn't heard the gunshots, 'Gunshots, what gunshots?' It was one of the few occasions, I swear, on which I felt like killing someone with my bare hands. I truly hope that that individual—or rather, that excuse for a human being—will be held to account at a Higher Court on his own day of reckoning. This experience led me to seriously question what I was doing with my life: it was one of the very few times I was to do so. It is my firm belief however that John Kyle's murderer finally got his comeuppance at Loughgall in 1987—as one of those killed during the SAS's successful ambush of IRA gunmen on their way to attack a local police station. And so justice has been served—after a fashion, anyway.

During the final year I served in Omagh—1987—I was to become personally involved in a series of events which would culminate in what is still to my mind one of the most bizarre episodes of the Troubles: the travesty of justice and truth by which Michael Stone would confess to and be convicted for the murder of Dermot Hackett. A married man with a young family, Hackett's only crime was that he was a Catholic and unlucky enough to be in the wrong place at the wrong time. The truth of the matter is that not only did Stone not commit the murder to which he so readily and spontaneously admitted, but that senior officers in the Belfast CID at the time, once they had knowledge of some of the true circumstances of the murder, colluded in Stone's charade by altering details in his 'confession' in order to corroborate his story! As a result, murderers have walked free, a gross miscarriage of justice has been allowed to happen, and the name of a good man has been falsely maligned.

The sequence of events in question began on 21 May 1987, with the brutal murder of a Captain Ivan Anderson of 6 UDR in the Carrickmore area. Ivan Anderson was ambushed by at least two gunmen on his journey home from his full-time job as headmaster at a local school. He died at the scene. I knew Anderson well and his death was a great loss to the area. His only crime was he was a Protestant and an officer in the Ulster Defence Regiment. Although no one has ever been made amenable for this crime, my men and I worked hard to piece together a picture of the murderers, and I believe I know who they were, and why they carried out such an atrocity. My only hope is that God will hold the final tribunal with those concerned and that some day they will get their just desserts.

Retaliation for Anderson's murder would come swiftly and without mercy, just two days later, in the form of an equally brutal attack on Dermot Hackett, a Roman Catholic bread server. Hackett was shot dead at the wheel of his bread van as he drove towards Omagh on the main Drumquin Road. I arrived at the scene shortly afterwards, and had to deal with the subsequent follow-up. Married with a young family, Hackett was an innocent, defenceless civilian who had done nothing to provoke his murderers. Tragically, there was in one sense nothing out of the ordinary about the circumstances of his murder in the catalogue of hundreds—or should I say, thousands—of similar deaths which occurred in Northern Ireland during the Troubles. What was different however about Dermot Hackett's death was the fact that the infamous Loyalist Michael Stone would, on the occasion of his arrest for the Milltown Cemetery murders, claim that he had been the perpetrator.

At the time, I had investigated the Hackett murder to the best of my ability, given the prevailing climate of hostility from Special Branch quarters. I have learned only relatively recently that Special Branch did in fact have relevant information at the time which would have helped my investigation considerably—but which they obviously made the conscious decision to withhold from me. I had an excellent team of experienced detectives at the Omagh CID office however and, by working tirelessly, we had been able to make important discoveries in relation to Hackett's murder. We had established, for example, that it had been organised by the local branch of the UDA, then under the leadership of a criminal family who had amassed a small fortune through organised crime, and extortion and burglary in particular. As a result of the ongoing investigation, the Omagh team were ultimately able to make amenable a youth who would subsequently plead guilty to involvement in the murder at Belfast Crown Court. This young man had supplied the vehicle used to carry out the murder, and he was able to give details about the planning of the atrocity and the subsequent disposal of the murder weapons. Specific information concerning the actual gunmen is currently *sub judice*: suffice to say however that Michael Stone was never mentioned in relation to the case. His name would only enter the equation some months later, after his arrest for the Milltown Cemetery murders. During the subsequent interview of Stone at Castlereagh police office, a certain Detective Superintendent made a call to the original investigating team, demanding that the file on Hackett's murder be sent to the police office. Stone, it appeared, was claiming that he had been the murderer. In such circumstances, it would be standard practice to allow the original investigating officer and his team to interview the prisoner, but in this case, this request was flatly refused without any further explanation.

Whenever the officers from the Omagh team did eventually get the chance to read the contents of the prisoner's so-called admission statement, they would find that Stone's account bore no relation to the actual circumstances of the murder as they had already established them to be. In fact, his outline of events was such as to prove that he could not have been involved. When this fact was pointed out however to the senior officers in Castlereagh who were orchestrating this travesty of justice, their immediate response was to threaten me with arrest for withholding information if I didn't give them details of all the discrepancies between Stone's statement and the actual events. Once they had this information, the same officers then had Stone's statement altered so that it would fit the facts of the case!

Stone would subsequently plead guilty to the murder of Dermot Hackett, along with a number of other crimes. During his incarceration, which was, tragically, to be all too short (he was released after serving only 12 years of his sentences), he went on to produce a plethora of fictional writings as well as a collection of nightmarish paintings, all of which—for those who can bear to look at them—betray something of the nature of his tortured mind. The episode in question was to take an even more bizarre turn however, in the autumn of 2005, when Stone would meet the Hackett family in a televised encounter presided over by Archbishop Tutu, as part of the BBC programme 'Facing the Truth', a series of 'televised reconciliations' between the families of victims of the Northern Ireland Troubles and their murderers. During this stunt, Stone persisted in his crazy allegations, although by this time, knowing the game was up, he had changed his story somewhat. He admitted that he hadn't been actively involved in the shooting, and now seemed intent on blackening the names of the security forces and of the victim himself, by claiming that he had been given access to top secret files allegedly showing Mr Hackett's involvement with the IRA. This was a complete lie and Stone knew it. The obvious question, in relation to this whole debacle, is this: who would have gained from such behaviour—apart, that is, from a madman whose ego might be bolstered by claiming to be responsible for a crime any normal person would shudder to even hear about? In my view, the answer is as simple as this: the guilty walk free, sanctioned by those who allowed it to happen...

I had the privilege to meet the Hackett family recently, at their request. I was able to tell them that Stone was a liar and to personally reassure Mrs Hackett that her husband's name has never appeared in any police files concerning membership of any illegal organisation. I was more than happy to do so, but saddened of course not to be able to do more for such a courageous family. Dermot's brother is without a doubt one of the most forgiving and genuine people I have ever had the privilege to meet. He may, like his late brother, be slight in physical stature, but morally and spiritually, he is a giant amongst men.

After my time in Omagh, I was posted back to the Belfast area. On 7 July 1988 I was appointed Detective Inspector at Donegall Pass RUC Station. During this period of my service, I was seconded to the Stevens Inquiry Team, whose brief was to investigate alleged police collusion in Northern Ireland. I was the arresting and charging officer in virtually all of the Stevens Team cases. During these years too, I received a number of commendations for leading successful murder and serious crime investigations. However, working in such a central Police station in what was the busiest Police sub-division in the Force did have some drawbacks. Being called out from home on at least four nights a week was the norm, and I found myself working virtually around the clock. As one of the most experienced Detective Inspectors in the city, I was often expected, in addition to my own duties, to assist with investigations into serious crime on somebody else's patch. As it transpired too, my position and duties were such that I would find myself under constant threats from terrorists. The seriousness of these threats would ultimately escalate to the degree that I was forced to move home with my family under the cloud of imminent terrorist attack.

It was a Friday and, due to a number of bomb scares and actual explosions, traffic in the city centre was at a complete standstill. I had been at the scene of one of these incidents and was trying to make my way to another when I was summoned by Control to the office of the Detective Superintendent in the centrally located station at Musgrave Street, which was also Divisional Headquarters. It was an urgent request: I was, if necessary, to drive on the pavements, but I was to get there immediately. We did just that, and managed to get there some ten minutes later.

I knew the Detective Superintendent at Musgrave Street well: Harry was one of the old breed of detectives. Ruthless and dedicated, he called a spade a spade, and didn't waste three words when two would have done. As I entered his office, and he told me to come and sit down, I knew by his voice that something was very wrong. Without missing a beat, Harry told me in a single sentence that I had to go home immediately and start packing: I was not to go back to my station. I was transferred: he didn't know where to, but I would be told in due course. That, he said, was the least of my problems. My desk would be cleared and my stuff delivered to me. I would have to move out of my current home there and then, and I would be contacted shortly by the Force's Emergency Housing Unit about alternative accommodation. I just sat in utter shock and bewilderment. My mind went blank. 'What's wrong?' I finally stuttered. 'The Provos are trying to kill you,' Harry replied. 'They know your house and your car, and they've been watching you.' 'My house?' I managed to respond, now thinking only of my wife and son, Patrick, who was just ten months old at the time. I was not to worry, Harry said, my house was under 24-hour police guard as we spoke, and would remain so until we left. 'Best get home now and get it sorted,' he concluded. I got up and drifted out of the room on autopilot, trying hard to get my head around what I had just been told.

I drove back to my semi-detached house on the outskirts of Belfast, to find my wife and son playing in the garden. Initially Eleanor didn't think there was anything unusual about my visit: I would often try to steal a few moments to nip home quickly to see the two of them during the eighteen-hour plus shifts I was working at the time. Eleanor was also oblivious to the overt but discreet police checkpoint on the road outside my house. I told her that we were under threat, that I was being transferred and that we also had to leave our home. There was, no doubt, a tear or two shed between us, as we sat holding our son for a short while, and then contacted our friends and family, trying to come to terms with our news.

I was later informed that I was transferred to Castlereagh Station, with immediate effect. This was a further bombshell. It was well known in police circles that the most exciting thing that ever happened at that time in Castlereagh was a door slamming! For a Detective Inspector, Castlereagh was Purgatory itself. Brooding over the matter that weekend, I decided that I was getting the rough end of the stick. No one had told me anything about an alleged threat before. Every cop in Northern Ireland could expect to be the target of one side or the other at some time in his or her career. In the CID, if you were doing your job in any way properly, you were bound to have made serious enemies. We didn't really give a fiddler's—that was the name of the game. I decided therefore that I would go and see the big boss at Headquarters, to have it out with him. When I got there, the conversation started amicably enough, but I soon told him bluntly that I wasn't amused about, 1) getting transferred to a station that I considered to be a watering hole for geriatrics, and 2) having to move my wife and child from the home we had done up to the best of our ability. In a grave tone, the boss told me that I would do as I was ordered: I was being shadowed by an ASU of the PIRA, who were hellbent on killing me. As recently as the last few weeks, they had tried to put a booby trap bomb under my car, which would have killed me but for the fact that I hadn't turned up when they were expecting me. The boss also intimated to me that they were believed to have actually carried out a *recce* on my house, posing as potential buyers when I wasn't in. He gave me enough details to convince me that it was the case. This was one which I really did owe to Special Branch: without their intelligence, I might not have escaped with my life. Such was the price you had to pay for hitting the terrorists hard. I was too high profile a figure in the fight against them at that particular time: it was better, the boss suggested, that I lie low and rest for a while and let others take the burden. For the next few months, I would sleep with my gun under the pillow.

On Monday 25 June 1990, I was officially transferred to Castlereagh CID Office by Force Order due to the threat. Although, as I have said, I was less than enthusiastic about the transfer, as it transpired I was about to embark upon the most interesting, challenging and rewarding chapter in my career. I was about to become one of the Bogeymen…

Chapter 4
The Bogeymen

My posting to Castlereagh was a deliberate move designed to keep me out of the limelight and out of harm's way, temporarily at least. The station there was known in CID circles as 'Sleepy Hollow', and in my initial time there, it certainly lived up to its name. Accustomed as I was to being at the centre of the action, at Castlereagh I felt like a caged animal, and would stalk the corridors looking for someone—anyone—to talk to about what was happening on the street. Very quickly, I was utterly bored, and I began to look round for something interesting and productive to do.

I soon became intrigued by an entity which was known simply as the CID Surveillance Unit, and which operated from the old station house in a corner of the large Castlereagh complex. I was amazed to discover that the sixteen or so officers who made up this unit habitually spent their days playing cards or working out in the gym. Covert operations at this time were the sole responsibility and domain of the all-powerful Special Branch, who only ever seemed to work to their own agenda. By starving this CID Surveillance wing of proper equipment and restricting access to them, Special Branch had been basically able to emasculate the unit, robbing it of the ability to operate independently or with any impact. Once I was able to determine for a fact that the men and women staffing the said unit did spend most of their days playing cards, I approached certain senior officers whom I knew to be no friends of the Special Branch ethos or agenda. I informed them of what was going on and lobbied tirelessly to get control of the unit. Perhaps to keep me quiet more than anything else, within a year I was given command of the CID

Surveillance Unit at Castlereagh, and from that moment I set about changing its role and standing as quickly and radically as possible.

Once I had completed some basic introductory training, I returned to my new position and the challenge of developing a more productive and positive crime-fighting role for the unit. Unfortunately, I was initially to receive very little support from the majority of senior command. Many of the senior officers in the Royal Ulster Constabulary at the time were of the old school. Some were vastly experienced in anti-terrorist strategies and in the fighting of insurrection within the State, but when it came to new and innovative policing methods, they were in the Dark Ages, and preferred to stay there—or so it seemed to me anyway. Others, despite their display of arrogance, were still living naïvely in the Dixon of Dock Green era, and in many senses were no more than dummies in suits. In certain quarters, in fact, strange as it may seem to the outside observer, there was open hostility towards anyone who dared promote a proactive agenda.

Fortunately, however, there were a few officers who did support me, including the then Head of Crime, Alfie Entwistle, who had known me from my 'B' Division days and appreciated the fact that I didn't shirk from hard work. I am also indebted in this regard to another officer, Joe Meeke. A former senior CID officer, Joe had been seconded to try to clean up Special Branch, some of whose officers had just managed around that time to make complete asses of themselves in court. When I privately complained to Joe over lunch one day about the complete lack of ancillary training available for the kind of operation I was trying to develop, he told me to simply go and organise it myself. He was adamant that the only way I was going to get the support I needed was to go out and find it, using back doors or telling a few white lies if need be! I decided to follow Joe's advice. Predictably enough, my determination to progress the unit despite any resistance was met with open hostility from many in the Special Branch hierarchy, who believed that any type of covert activity was their exclusive domain. I knew from bitter experience that the only way I could lead the unit in the right direction and be taken seriously was to get the necessary qualifications to be able to meet any critics on at least an equal footing. Using my sponsors at command level and personal friends who at that time had some influence over the CID training budget, I therefore embarked on a series of specialised courses.

First of all, I enrolled at the National Crime Squad training school in Ripley in England to learn the rudiments of surveillance training. These guys took their training very seriously. In a ruthless pass or fail course, I emerged with a Home Office approved Certificate of National Competence in Surveillance Training. I was the first RUC officer to do so. On this course I made many friends among students and instructors alike. I was then able to get myself on the Instructor's Course in Surveillance Training, and again became the first RUC officer to successfully complete the same. These achievements were treated with some derision by many among the surveillance fraternity within the RUC. They had of course their own Special Branch training wing and the arrogant delusion that they knew everything already in this important sphere of police work. As it transpired, this was the very mindset which would ultimately result in their—self-inflicted—alienation from what is classed as normal policing. But that is a story for another time.

In spite of all the resistance I encountered, I persevered. Friends I had made in the Metropolitan Police made me aware of a few specialised courses which were run at Scotland Yard. Through these contacts, I was able to become one of a select few officers to attend and pass the Home Office approved National Hostage Negotiators' Course, which was held at Hendon Police Training College. I am indebted in particular to Detective Inspector Brown from SO10 at the Met, who looked after me and guided me through the maze of red tape and bureaucracy which my enrolment entailed.

The National Hostage Negotiators' Course was one of the most professionally interesting and rewarding courses I have ever attended. The training was led by Commander Roy Ram of Scotland Yard's Special Operations Section. Larger than life in more ways than one, Ram was a charismatic individual who made most of the senior officers I had come across in my own force look like schoolboys. The course was attended by the elite from forces all over the world, and I made many friends who would later be able to assist me during my travels on the job. Some of the same contacts recommended strongly that I try for a place on Commander Ram's Undercover Course. Although places on this course were like hens' teeth, I was determined that I would be accepted, and, with assistance from my own sponsors and the personal permission of Roy Ram, I found myself embarking on one of the most interesting phases of my police career.

Held over many weeks at Hendon Police College, the Undercover Course was designed from the outset to test you to your limits—professionally, physically, intellectually and emotionally. The initial part of the training, which dealt with undercover techniques with the London Metropolitan Police's so12 Unit, was operationally led by Detective Sergeant Peter Holman. A legendary figure in the field and a mine of information, Pete knew everything there was to know about undercover work, and had led many successful large-scale operations against the top echelons of the criminal fraternity throughout the world. There would be little purpose, other than to educate criminals, in going into a great deal of detail regarding all of the various aspects of the training regime—but, as I have said, the main point was to take the participants to the very limit. Long hours of formal training would be followed on some occasions by debriefs which turned into late night drinking sessions. To the untrained eye or sceptical outsider, these debriefing sessions might have seemed to be nothing more than glorified piss-ups. The reality was that they were the complete opposite. While in some senses of course this after-hours socialising may have served as a form of stress relief as well, what it also represented in fact was a further opportunity for our instructors to take careful note of how various individuals reacted after consuming alcohol and in a social context. More than a few candidates would fail the course simply for talking out of school, or for displaying unusual or aggressive behaviour while drinking.

The training provided on the Undercover Course covered all spheres of Police operations. We were brought up-to-date with the latest technology available to the undercover operative by the various agencies involved at the cutting edge of researching and developing such equipment. Experienced veteran undercover officers from all over the world were flown in to share their experiences with us and teach us the rudiments of 'tradecraft': that is, the range of skills and knowledge which any undercover officer should have at his or her disposal to ensure the maximum chances of survival in a given situation. On the initial course at Hendon, and subsequent annual refreshers, we were lucky enough to get these lessons in covert policing and other grey arts from world experts in the field. Once learnt, these basic tradecraft skills stay with you for the rest of your life.

Contrary to popular perception, which is informed no doubt by the unreal glamour of Bond movies and the like, much of standard tradecraft is based on relatively simple practical principles and techniques grounded firmly in everyday common sense. This includes practical know-how, such as where to position oneself in a bar or restaurant so as to be able to watch who comes and goes, while still having easy access to an exit route. To this day, my friends will remark on the fact that I always stand in a public bar and avoid sitting unless I absolutely have to. To sit is to immediately put oneself at a disadvantage, both in terms of reaction time and being able to observe intently all those who enter and leave a room. Effective observation is a skill in itself: all manner of small but very telling details about a person may be enough, at the very least, to give you some kind of a marker as to whom you are dealing with. And at best, may actually save your life. You can guarantee that one of the first people to spot you will themselves be a fellow watcher!

Also crucial in the undercover officer's repertoire of skills is the ability to jump quickly and completely at a moment's notice into one or a number of aliases, or alternative identities. This takes some considerable training and practice, since the transformation must be complete and convincing: one small mistake, if noticed, could literally cost you your life. There is also the work of conceiving each alias, building up the various layers which go towards creating a convincing persona. Each detail must ring true, or else the safety of the undercover officer is likely to be compromised at any moment. Again, it was 'Big Pete' from Scotland Yard's Elite so12 Unit who taught us the rudiments in this field. Strange as it sounds, Pete's secret, his key recommendation, was to keep your personality, or personalities, in a briefcase. Literally! The first thing to do before going into character should be to empty the entire contents of your pockets into a briefcase reserved for that purpose. Once you are satisfied that you have absolutely nothing on your person relating to your old or real identity, you can simply don the elements of your new persona from a separate briefcase—i.e. wallet, credit cards, passport, driving licence, back-up papers (both work and personal), phone, and so on. Over and above the importance of having all of these practical indicators of an identity to hand, there is something about the very act of closing one briefcase and opening another which enables you to make the switch to the alias more completely. Over the years, I found this favourite technique of Pete's to be truly invaluable. In my own briefcases, I had 'Sean Murphy', the gangster with Republican connections, 'Billy Craig', the gangster with Loyalist connections, and a stand-by which I kept for times when things might get really tight.

Another simple, but very effective tool of the trade in terms of assuming an alternative identity was the use of private mail drops (i.e. not the official, PO Box type). It is amazing how many people make use of these for a whole range of reasons. Some just want to disappear below the horizon of life for their own private reasons, but others use private mail drops as a means of distancing themselves from the prying eyes of the law or other authorities. For the amateur spy, or the merely curious, there are multitudes of books which are readily available on the open market on the subject of creating and assuming a new identity.

Special driving skills, such as aggressive and combative driving, are another crucial part of the undercover officer's standard tradecraft. While I undertook some preliminary training in this area on the undercover course at Hendon, it was only much further down the line —once I had the CID Surveillance Unit at Castlereagh fully up and running—that it became apparent to me to what extent special driving skills would be indispensable to my team. Practical experience of live operations showed that undercover officers, suddenly isolated perhaps from back-up by circumstances beyond our control, or indeed operating alone of necessity in the first place, would all too often find themselves hemmed in by other vehicular traffic in a hostile environment and without the means to extricate themselves from the situation. Or—another scenario which would frequently arise—it would become imperative for an operative to ram a target's car, either to arrest him or to simply take him out of the game. Whatever the case, it soon became patently clear to me that we needed to add to our skill base in this particular field. Again, it was only through resourceful networking and research that I was able to find out that, while such training was not openly available, the West Midlands Police Traffic Branch were the recognised experts in such specialised courses. They were in fact, I was reliably informed, the preferred trainers of the Royal Protection Squad and the SAS in specialist driving skills. As usual, the West Midlands Police didn't let me down. At my request, their Head of Branch contacted me and we discussed my requirements. Costings were agreed and I then set about scrounging the money from the Crime Secretariat, where I was lucky enough to have a friend and colleague who was sometimes able to redirect funds from the Crime Branch budget to our unit when we really needed the financial help. I managed to take my whole team with me on a two-week specialist driving course held by the West Midlands guys at on old airdrome in Birmingham.

The Traffic boys were marvellous. Most of them were in the twilight years of their careers, but what they didn't know about high performance vehicles and driving skills wasn't worth knowing. The large Rover Automatic 7 Series were the preferred workhorses of the instructors in the unit. I was amazed in fact to find that large automatics were, apparently, the best type of vehicle for specialist driving. It's funny that one never thinks of a large automatic as that type of car: I could certainly never look on them again in the same light! Many of the high performance vehicles we were able to use on the course were virtually new and had been supplied by Vauxhall to the Police free of charge.

Soon, we could reverse at seventy miles an hour, pull the car through 180 degrees and head off in the other direction without losing a second—making escape from an ambush scenario a real possibility. We watched in awe as these guys showed us how to use a motor vehicle not only as a means of transport, but as a weapon too. The beauty of it was that these drivers were always in total control. While some of the tactics they taught us would hardly have done the engines and gearboxes of the vehicles in question any good, they were drastic measures for drastic situations, and the confidence boost our operatives experienced as they were put again and again through their paces was palpable. We were able to perfect manoeuvres such as 'Armagh gates', where the driver would reverse his or her vehicle through a gateway at sixty and seventy miles an hour, and then seconds later be able to propel themselves forward again at breakneck speed without touching the sides of the gate. As the course gathered momentum, the final stages involved performing the manoeuvres we had learned at higher and higher speeds, as well as tactical ramming and evasive driving skills. Soon we could take anyone out of the game just by knowing where to hit their car, while being able to avoid being put off the road ourselves. The only really hairy part of the training— albeit a bit of fun—was the course finale, which involved a showdown of sorts between all of the participants, with the last man standing, or in our case, still managing to move, being declared the winner. As the boss, I was aware that more than one of my operatives were taking the opportunity to put me in my place—but it was all good-natured enough, and we were each able to have a laugh at the other's expense.

As with a number of the other skills which formed the basis of the tradecraft we as undercover officers were equipped with during training, you always hoped that neither you nor anyone else on your team would ever have to use such special driving expertise. But the knowledge that, should the occasion arise, you had the wherewithall to extract yourself from a deadly situation, gave you an invaluable confidence boost. Such learned skills and aptitudes are filed away in the annexes of your brain like the array of weapons in a child's video game: ready to be deployed at a moment's notice, they are tools which could prove crucial for that one time when your life may depend on it.

Although most operatives come into the job with prior in-depth training in the use of virtually all modern weapons, the carrying of firearms by undercover officers is generally avoided like the plague wherever possible. (Again, this goes very much against the impression popular culture has created, in films, books and on TV, of the spy who has a vast armoury of state-of-the-art weapons at his disposal.) The reality is that if you are known to be carrying a weapon, the target will seek you out more aggressively than ever. On each deployment, a lot of background planning would be done, authorisations sought and assessments made regarding a number of important issues such as law, intrusion, human rights, etc. A large part of this preparation would involve 'Risk Assessments': the weighing up of the level of risk likely to be encountered not only by the operatives, but also by everyone else involved, including the targets. The risk of firearms was a threat we could all potentially face on a daily basis, but we would never deploy them ourselves as a first option. Our chief weapon, and one which would prove far more effective in terms of securing a result, was the concealed tape recorder, not the gun. The latter would not convict anyone. We did however receive specialist training in survival and assault techniques as part of our lessons in tradecraft. Again, for the reasons I've already mentioned, I'm reluctant to expand upon these here. Suffice to say, however, that you quickly realised that your hands and feet, supplemented by an ashtray or a sharpened pencil, were all you really needed in a tight corner. It wasn't so much the weapon you had—it was how you chose to use it.

One of the most interesting and entertaining of the veteran officers who lectured us on the Undercover Course, and who would later become such a good friend, was Joseph D. Pistone. Joe was a giant in his field, and author of the well-known book *My Undercover Life in the Mafia* (published under the pen name Donnie Brasco), which was later to be the inspiration for a film. On one of the occasions I met Joe, he gave me a signed copy of his book with the following inscription: 'Pleasure meeting you—take care and stay alert. Regards, Joe. p.s. This is the u/c bible.'

In his classes on the course, Joe shared a lot of tradecraft and experiences which were not covered in his book. One simple lesson he taught us has stayed with me ever since. This related to the mafia's tendency to judge someone by their clothes, and in particular, their shoes. It didn't matter who you were pretending to be, if you were a real operator you would wear hand-stitched shoes, and not turn up on the plot with rubber soles. A small thing, perhaps, but if you are a big hitter in a major gang and portraying yourself as such, you do not wear $20 slip-ons. 'Bling', be it earrings or flash watches, is for low-lives and drug dealers, and can easily be supplied or purchased anywhere...

Something which my personal experience has taught me is that you should never try to portray yourself as an ex-soldier or as having a military background as a means of intimidating others unless you have actually been there—otherwise, you'll be sure to come badly unstuck the moment you meet a person who really does have the credentials. I have been able to wrong-foot so many people—even in an innocent social context—who have bragged unguardedly about their military pasts. Once again, the tell-tale signs are so simple, but could be so deadly if you are in the wrong place with the wrong company...In the Forces, without your number, you don't go anywhere—even to the toilet. Particularly in the Army, you don't eat, drink, draw weapons or carry out any function without it. More importantly, for those very reasons, you never, ever forget your number. Those who are in-the-know will be able to tell, on the basis of your number, not only whether you are really who you say you are, but also what your length of service was, and even your age. I have never forgotten my number, even when very much under the influence of alcohol. If a simple question such as, 'So what was your number, mate?' is greeted with a bewildered look or a degree of hesitation, odds are the subject is not the genuine article, and warning lights should flash. In terms of assuming another identity, the real secret of success is to never travel too far from the truth. I have seen many wannabes in this business try with grand gestures and sweeping claims to pass themselves off as someone they are very obviously not, only to fail and fall spectacularly on their faces! At best, targets would walk away, smelling a rat; at worst, someone's life could suddenly be in the balance.

In the final event, no matter how many courses you took or exams you passed, your real training as an undercover officer would be completed in the field, and there was nothing to beat on-the-job experience. In that sense, the learning process was never over. You could know the law covering covert operations back to front, but you wouldn't get far on an actual job without common sense, an ability to listen to those who had been there before you, and the humility to do so. For this reason, I found it invaluable to be able to attend when possible the annual refresher course for undercover officers, which was held in a certain English town which has a large Police Training College attached to it (I will not identify the town in question as, to the best of my knowledge, it is still the site of such training). Strangely enough, the course would commence every year with a lecture from the Force's Chief Medical Officer, during which, as well as addressing a number of undercover issues, he would never fail to remind us that, according to their figures, the town had one of the highest rates of venereal disease in the country. I was never quite sure whether he threw this gem of information in merely as an interesting statistic, or whether or not he was warning us off! At these courses, which were a welcome respite from the run-of-the-mill on-the-job training, officers from all over the world could meet for two weeks in a concentrated learning environment. By sharing your own experiences and listening to accounts of other people's successes and disasters, you could learn invaluable lessons. These occasions were also opportunities to meet old friends again, and make new acquaintances. Some of the fellow officers I met while training would become lifelong friends and our families would spend many happy times together. (I am thinking here in particular of my friend Jeff from Belgium and his lovely partner, Ann.) The sense of being part of a network was uplifting. We were an elite drawn together from all corners of the world, with many highly gifted police officers in our number—although in all honesty I doubt if any of us would have fitted the conventional profile of an officer on the beat!

Of course, before you would get to meet the target in any operation, there would always have been a lot of people who would have assisted thus far, including other undercover officers who would have done the ground-breaking work, and informants too. The former will always be, in my view, the real heroes in any undercover operation, although more often than not their identities and the part they played will never be fully known or acknowledged. The informants were a mixed bag: some helped us for money, but many others, ordinary criminals with scruples (if there can be such a thing) would be willing to do what they could, simply because they, like me, had a particular disgust for people who traded in heroin and other 'hard' drugs. There were also the ordinary, decent men and women who had never been involved in any kind of criminal activity, and their contribution has often proved absolutely invaluable. Our unit at Castlereagh would prove to be particularly lucky in this respect: we were, in fact, the envy of the Undercover fraternity, as the only operation in the UK to have a full-time backstop at a functioning bar. We will be forever grateful to Pat, the owner of the bar in question. One of life's decent, honourable citizens, Pat was and is a family man who, I believe, hated drug dealers even more than I did, and was willing to do whatever he could to help, without ever expecting anything in recompense. Pat knew what I did for a living and never asked any questions. He and his senior barman knew about my aliases, would confirm my identity whenever required, and take any messages for me. This simple service was to save my life on more than one occasion. Pat was and is a personal and lifelong friend, and I literally trusted him with my life. I didn't abuse our friendship, but he was more than happy to do his bit in the war against the criminal mafia. If anyone deserves a medal, it is Pat.

Although I returned from my training with my enthusiasm fired and my resolve strengthened, setting up an undercover unit within my own Force would continue to be a one-man crusade, largely because of the resistance I was faced with from within the Criminal Investigation Department, as well as from the usual quarters within the Special Branch cabal. As it turned out, I had to set the unit up as a separate entity within the Special Operations Support Unit. Since it was regarded as a threat by the existing powers-that-be in covert operations, our unit was never to be given proper internal recognition or support. It was fated to remain a unit without a name, and those of us who worked within it, men without faces. Even internally, many didn't know what we did or why we existed. For this reason, we would become known as 'The Bogeymen of the CID'.

There were also particular difficulties for the newly revamped unit in the area of finance. Unlike London's Metropolitan Police, who were the recognised experts in the field and lived in the twentieth century with proper policing budgets, we were still operating in the nineteenth century, it seemed, and forced to beg for whatever resources hadn't gone towards funding the war machine. The reality was that during those years, the fight against direct terrorism always got top priority in terms of government budgets: 'ordinary' crime was way down the list—even though in Northern Ireland of course, paramilitary activity and drug trafficking were always inextricably linked. I found myself therefore with no unit resources of my own, having to fund the building of legends and back-up for the unit from my own pocket, or with help from friends both within and outside the job. I managed to set up covert bank accounts using my own money, and with the help of well-disposed bank managers and the assistance of SO12 at the Met. I was able to obtain passports and official driving documents in the names of my aliases by pulling similar strings. Eventually I managed to squeeze a little funding from our Crime Department for legend building, which meant that we were able to spend some time with contacts we had made during the training courses, looking at their set-ups and seeing how we could mutually assist each other in operations.

The undercover unit which I pioneered was subsequently to not only operate throughout the United Kingdom, but was also able to backstop for and provide logistical support to other Police forces and government agencies in the Republic of Ireland and the rest of Europe. Little did I know it at the outset, but I would work in this unit for some nine years, during which time I was the recipient of many commendations for good Police duty as a result of leading countless successful operations in the fight against what is undoubtedly one of the biggest scourges of modern society: the criminal drugs trade.

Chapter 5

Operation Boom and The House of the Rising Sun

One of my first major deployments as an undercover officer was to prove to be one of the most dangerous, embroiling us in the murky world of international terrorism and the heroin trail from Turkey to Europe. It was late 1993 and we were aware that the price of heroin on our home turf was dropping dramatically, due to rapidly increasing supplies of the drug coming into Ireland mainly from the UK. Our colleagues on the mainland were able to confirm that the price of heroin there was falling fast too—by as much as £5,000 a kilo within less than six months, and for the same reason: because all at once there were large quantities flooding onto the market from an outside source.

The scale of these importations and the sophistication of the subsequent operation to distribute the drugs had led the operational team in the UK to the conclusion that there were more than just a few isolated criminals behind it all: this was obviously the work of a large organisation. SO12 at Scotland Yard had been able thus far to identify the architects of the operation as agents of the PKK (Partiya Karkerên Kurdistan), the large and particularly violent terrorist organisation which was and still is fighting for independence for ethnic Kurdish populations across Turkey, Iraq and Iran, and other areas. In order to finance their terrorist activities and buy weapons and munitions, the PKK were selling their most readily available resource—namely, heroin.

In a highly organised operation, they were able to collect, refine and distribute the drug throughout Europe by using their numerous cells and contacts in various ethnic communities, and in particular, the Turkish population in Britain. The Special Ops team at Scotland Yard were determined to break this vicious cartel once and for all.

When the operation, and our proposed involvement in it, was first mooted by so12, I was eager to assist, both for professional and personal reasons. Professionally speaking of course, this would be a challenging and valuable opportunity to cut our teeth, so to speak, with the big boys. In terms of personal motivation, I have what can only be described as an absolute hatred for anyone involved in the distribution of heroin, an utterly filthy drug which corrupts all it comes in contact with. I had all too often had to witness how this scourge of society can immediately rob people, young and old, of every shred of personal dignity. I had watched it lead children to steal from their parents and parents from their children, often bringing murder and depravity in its wake. And therefore I have never had any qualms of conscience whatsoever in bringing those who deal in heroin to account under the law, regardless of what misery may have ensued for them personally.

So it came to pass that I and another undercover officer I shall refer to as 'John' were summoned to attend a larger than normal briefing in London, in order to learn more about what our roles were to be in the Scotland Yard operation, which was already up and running. I was to use the alias Billy Craig, which gave me Loyalist credentials and meant that the PKK would be unable to check us out reliably with the strong Republican contacts they were known to have. John and I were to act as the money couriers for the criminal mob we supposedly represented: it would be up to us to carry out the final face-to-face negotiations about cash with the Turkish gang, who were based in London, and in and around a certain public house on the Holloway Road in particular. Also involved in the operation and present at the briefing were the two undercover officers who made up the other half of our team: Roy, a burly North Yorkshire guy we had worked with before, who was the spit of Billy Connolly, and Jock, a Glaswegian with a shaven head, who was on his first job. They would be collecting the drugs from the targets (the handover would take place some distance from the money) and checking out the quality of the heroin. If successful, this operation would represent a very important strike, and at the briefing we were pointedly told that this would be the first time ever that a UK police force had authorisation to let £22,000 run as a confidence buy. The whole undertaking was under the control of Paul Condon, who was later to become the Chief Constable of the Met. As a Commander, Condon was already demonstrating the kind of leadership which would take him to the top.

Our first encounter with the Turks was in late October 1993. We had arranged to meet them at Garfunkel's restaurant in Heathrow Airport's Terminal One. John and I had travelled over the night before and were fully briefed and wired with our Nagra tape recorders by the technical people. The meet was arranged for teatime, and we settled in the restaurant and waited for the phone to ring. The call came, and as soon as we gave details of where we were, we were approached by a small fat Turkish guy, who introduced himself as George. George was in his forties, with a shiny, bald head, and not unlike Danny DeVito in height and build. Wearing the Turkish male 'uniform' of black leather bomber jacket, black trousers and highly polished shoes, he was carrying a small mobile telephone in his left hand. His fingers were adorned with heavy gold rings. George's English was good, but heavily accented. All three of us sat down at the table and ordered a drink. I could see that George was eyeing us up from head to toe, as he launched into an introductory rant about the need for mutual trust and confidence in each other. Every now and again, he would stop and, either purposely or for mere effect, look all around him as if expecting to be stormed at any moment.

John and I explained to George that we had been brought in to look after the money side of things and close the deal. As briefed, we told him that the money was on its way to London as we spoke, and that we wanted to do the proposed deal for the fourteen kilos of heroin the next day. We said too that our instructions were to first of all do a deal for one kilo for £22,000, and, if our bosses were happy with the way that went, we would then go ahead with the deal for the remaining thirteen kilos immediately afterwards. George agreed to this, but again stressed the importance of caution, as they hadn't done any business with us before.

We then had a general conversation with George about the drugs scene in Ireland. He seemed to have a good grasp on prices and the heroin trade in particular over here, and it soon became apparent that the Turks had been involved in getting heroin into Ireland before, albeit through third parties. Anyway, now that our introductions had been made and the ground rules for the exchange agreed, we all shook hands and arranged to meet the following morning.

The first thing John and I did the next morning was to attend a briefing with the operational and surveillance teams, as was standard practice on jobs like these. We were not expecting to encounter any major problems during the 'test' deal for the initial kilo of heroin: the crucial time would be during the main exchange of drugs and cash. I made contact with George, and it seemed that everything was still okay. The next meet would be at a small hotel near King's Cross. To say that the place was down-at-heel would have been an understatement. Our feet stuck to the carpet as we hurried along corridors reeking of drink, urine and God knows what else. Our room had already been wired by the operational team and we settled in as best we could, although I tried not to sit on the beds, which seemed, oddly, to have a life of their own.

At approximately 2.30 pm, there was a knock at the door and John opened it. George was accompanied this time by another Turkish-looking guy who appeared to be in his late twenties or early thirties. He was taller than George, about 5'10", and had long dark hair with a short cropped beard. His face bore the signs of an earlier serious acne problem. He was carrying his mobile telephone in his hand and he too had a large number of rings on his fingers. Both walked into the room and George came over, with a small packet about the size of a sachet of Beechams powder in his hand. I could see that it contained a brown substance which looked like heroin. He went to hand it to me, referring to it as a 'photograph'. I refused it, telling George I didn't need any photographs if I was buying the real thing.

I showed the Turks the two holdall bags we had with us. One had the £22,000 in cash in it for the first kilo, and the other had £286,000 in cash, which was the remainder for the thirteen kilos which were to follow. George and his friend sat on the bed and started to count the £22,000, note by £20 note. They were talking in Turkish, and then the friend started dialling a number on his mobile. I took it from him, telling him there would be no phone calls in the room. George asked what was wrong: did we not trust him? I told him that when it came to us and the £308,000 we had with us, we didn't trust anyone. The discussion was abruptly cut short, as the friend tried to tell us that the £22,000 was £1,000 short. This was quickly resolved however as being down to their bad counting. George confirmed that we could now do business: the one kilo now, and the remaining thirteen the next day.

The operational team had been prepared for this, since they had been able to establish in advance through other covert means what the Turks' likely game plan would be. I confirmed the arrangements with the team anyway. George said the kilo would be delivered to our other two associates, Roy and his pal, at another location. George's companion, accompanied by John, then left with the £22,000 to arrange the delivery of the kilo. When George returned with John, we had a very frank discussion about how the handover for the next day would be done. George was insisting that we should give him the remaining £286,000 the next day, and that he would then go away and deliver the drugs to us later. John and I both told him he must be on drugs if he thought we were going to let this happen! I told him the only way it was going to be done would be if he remained with us the whole time—we didn't care where, even on his territory if necessary—and we would stay with the money until the drugs were handed over.

John mentioned to me that when they had met earlier, George had been talking about wanting our help in settling some personal business for him. Apparently, some private businessman in Manchester owed him twenty three grand. George said he would split the money with us if we managed to recover it. He didn't seem to baulk at the idea of us finishing this guy off. He said the business-man's name was Tony, and when I looked a little sceptical, George said with a snide laugh, 'Well, my name is George but it is not George, if you know what I mean. And I think your name is not your own, either, is it?' In his heavily accented English, he continued, 'I come from a political organisation. You know, that's why we're used to illegal life of course. Do you understand? Have you heard of the PKK, by any chance?' 'The *who*?' I queried. 'We are working for the PKK,' came the reply.

George then went on to boast that he had restaurants in Turkey and England, and told us all about life in Turkey. At one stage, he asked me how much money I had ever seen on a table. He said that he had once done a job for 200 kilos of heroin and had seen £4,000,000 in cash—which he had had to change into guilders in Holland before moving it on. The money belonged to the organisation, of course. He went on to talk about other loads he had moved through Holland,

and the fact that the previous year, his organisation had lost about 17 tons in the Mediterranean when the customs had taken out a major consignment. It quickly became clear to us that George and his accomplices were probably responsible for about two-thirds of the heroin coming into Europe. After a further lecture about the fight the Kurds were making for independence, George said he had to go, and we arranged to meet the next day to do the rest of the trade.

There was a slight hitch, however, when I rang George the next day as arranged. He said they couldn't do the trade that day, as his cousin had been arrested the night before, doing a drugs trade in possession of a gun. It was obvious to us that the Turks were stalling for time, and waiting to see if we would make a move to recover the money and arrest their courier. If we were police, they would be expecting us to do so, because they knew, or thought that they knew that the police wouldn't let an amount such as £22,000 run. This assumption was to prove to be their Achilles' heel. We decided, crucially, to withdraw at that point—to return to Belfast and keep up contact from there. That weekend, I rang George from the pub we used as a backstop. He said that his people were now happy to proceed with the main transaction of the thirteen kilos, and we arranged to do the handover in London on the following Tuesday.

We travelled to London the night before the handover, and attended a full briefing at a nearby Police station on the morning of the job. Judging by the number of surveillance teams and other specialist units assembled for the briefing meeting, it was obvious that the Metropolitan Police were sparing no effort on this one, and making sure that they would have more than enough men on the plot. Once all were ready and deployed, John and I made a number of calls and arranged to meet George outside the Odeon Cinema on Holloway Road at 12 noon. About ten minutes after we got there, we were joined by George, this time accompanied by a different companion, who was introduced to us as 'Eddie'. He was obviously Turkish too, appeared to be in his twenties, and was clean-shaven, well-groomed and wearing glasses. Eddie, George was quick to inform us, was a University graduate with a degree in psychology. He certainly spoke excellent English, with only a slight accent. These introductions over, all four of us crossed the road and went into a nearby bar, The Red Monkey. Once we ordered a drink and sat down, things began to take a bit of a bizarre turn, to say the least. George started by informing us that Eddie had special powers, and that he would be able to tell if we were undercover cops by simply looking into our eyes…At this level of operation, and given that we were supposedly dealing with a highly sophisticated organisation, the whole thing struck me as more than a little ridiculous. Especially when it became clear that George and, more disturbingly, Eddie himself, actually seemed to believe that he had such abilities! For a moment, I wondered if Eddie had been sampling the powder they were selling us, but in fact I think he actually believed that he was gifted with special powers of insight. He kept staring at us, thinking perhaps in his own ridiculous way that he could unnerve us by doing so. He was sadly deluded. During this 'psyching out' session, I looked around the bar. There were very few people there, except for one or two locals playing the fruit machines, and they certainly didn't look as if they were part of the Turkish gang. After some time, we were relieved to be told that Eddie had given us the all-clear with his mind reading, and George confirmed that the deal was on and that Eddie would be doing most of the talking from now on.

Eddie said we were to take the money to George's house, and that the drugs would then be handed over to our testers, Roy and his mate, in a nearby pub in Palmers Green. George was insisting that we go with him to his house in his car, but for security reasons we tried to resist this suggestion, knowing that it would not go down well with the operational team and Mr Condon himself in the Control room, or indeed the vast army of surveillance personnel outside. This was the era when mobiles were just taking off and we had a phone with us which had a one-way mike concealed in it. We were keeping everyone briefed as we went along by speaking through Roy—i.e. by constantly updating him over the phone, on the premise that he was our drugs man and needed to be kept informed. We eventually had no choice but to agree to go to George's house for the handover of the money after all. We arranged to meet George and Eddie back at the pub at 3.00 pm, when we would have the money with us.

Before the 3.00 pm meet, we returned to the operational team. They were going ballistic about us agreeing to travel in George's car— we had to turn that around, they told me. I got the sneaky suspicion they were more worried about losing the £286,000 than about our welfare—but perhaps I'm wrong! In any case, it was their job, and we had to try and comply with all of their wishes as best we could. Yet another briefing followed, and then we redeployed and returned to the area of the pub for 3.00 pm. John and I parked our car opposite The Red Monkey, and I left John in the car looking after the money, which was in a holdall in the boot.

I went into the pub and ordered a gin and tonic. I was joined a few minutes later by George. As instructed, I told him I was having second thoughts about going in his car. We didn't know them and we were carrying too much money: they easily could whack us and take the money. If the tables were turned, I said, it would certainly be something which would occur to me! George wasn't at all happy and we began to argue quite seriously. At one point, he said he was calling the job off. Then he accused us of being undercover cops. At this, I burst out laughing, and asked him how many cops he knew who would buy drugs in the way we just had done. George thought for a moment, then had to agree with me. He finally said that we didn't have to go in his car after all, and it seemed that the operation was back on track again.

In hindsight, I have often wondered exactly why George and his gang were so insistent that we travel in his car: what difference would it really have made to them if we travelled in our own vehicle? The more I have thought about it, the more convinced I have become that the Turks had most likely been harbouring the wicked thought of simply taking us out and ripping off the money…They were certainly more than capable of doing such a thing: according to our briefing and indeed our own impression of George, he wouldn't think twice about murdering someone.

Having agreed to our request to travel in our own transport, George sat thinking for a while, and then made a number of calls. Would we be happy to go to a hotel of his choice with the money, he asked, and then the drugs could be handed over nearby? He then got another call on his mobile phone and spoke to someone in Turkish: I heard the words 'Edgware Road' being mentioned. In the meantime, I made a call to Roy and, through him, alerted the control room that we were going to move to a hotel of George's choice. Predictably, they went completely ape at this further unexpected development. It was alright however for someone to sit on his arse in a control room and come up with a perfect plan, but I was at the coal face and I knew if we messed about any more and moved the goal posts too often, the Turks themselves would smell a rat. In any event, what they were suggesting was workable and the only people at risk would be John and I. I knew John was happy enough to carry it through to the end scenario whatever that might be, and so was I. I told the operational team that that was it, or we wouldn't be dealing. I hadn't time to discuss it on the phone, so they would have to cut their cloth accordingly and go with the flow.

I went out and joined John in the car, and took the opportunity of telling Roy (and therefore Operations) that I thought we would be heading in the direction of Edgware Road. I'm sure the Operations team and commanders were having kittens, but it was a 'Catch 22' situation. I suppose they were worried about their money, and if we ended up dead, that would mean double the paperwork. We just had to go with the Turks; it was a judgement call and I reckoned we could depend on the support teams to stay close enough to us to at least make an intervention if things got out of hand.

We followed George, who was driving a large white Datsun Sports car, in the general direction of Edgware Road and the Turkish quarter of London, until we pulled into the gates of a dingy looking hotel. As we entered, I could see some Turkish guys closing the gates behind us. A clever enough touch, I thought: that should get the Ops team shifting on their seats! We drove after George through an underground passageway, and came out on the other side of the hotel. Other Turkish guys appeared seemingly out of nowhere to open the rear gates and then closed them behind us. Nice one, I thought again. They had obviously done this before and it was a pretty effective measure that would have tested most surveillance teams. I knew however that we were still technically under the Ops umbrella and that they would know our location to within a few metres by global positioning.

George stopped briefly to pick up a tall Turkish-looking guy with a red bomber jacket on, then beckoned to us to follow again. As we did so, we were able to get in a short call to the Ops team, to let them know our rough location just in case there was any doubt. Eventually, we parked behind George outside another hotel, part of a Victorian terrace. It was a tall building, and like so many others in that block, more of a seedy bedsit type place than a hotel. This was known as the Turkish quarter and the hotels were used for everything from prostitution to cheap temporary accommodation for the many migrant workers, stateless and nameless people who frequented the area. If you weren't part of the Turkish community in this neighbourhood, you would have felt distinctly uncomfortable, particularly at night. George went into the hotel using his own key. I followed him up to Room 201, on the fourth floor of the seedy, rundown building. Badly furnished and in poor repair, the room was painted in garish colours. On opening the door of the room, I could see a small bed, a chair, a wardrobe and a cabinet. This rickety furniture almost filled the room, leaving very little space to move around in. George disappeared and came back with another chair which made the room seem even smaller. A small window looked down onto the street below. Looking out, I couldn't see any sign of surveillance activity: our back-up were doing their job well—I hoped so, anyway! The other, more frightening alternative was they hadn't a clue where we where!

Now that I'd checked out the hotel, I went down to get John, who had been waiting in the car with the money. He said he had been speaking to the team and the reassuring news was that they were all around us. As he lifted the money from the boot of our car, and we began to climb the hotel stairs to our room, we were both acutely aware of being watched by the Turks the whole time: there were at least two of them on the landing of each floor. Once in the room, John unzipped the holdall and emptied the contents out into the bed. George sat among the bundles of £20 and £50 notes which covered the bed and started to count out all of the £286,000, note by note. Meanwhile, John and I hovered near him, nervously watching the door and taking the odd look out onto the street, trying not to appear too obvious.

My concern was that even if the strike team had located the hotel, it was certain that they wouldn't know which room we were in. They would know that we were on one of the upper floors, but no more than that. As we watched George counting the cash, we spoke briefly to Roy and his pal on the mobile phone, but we couldn't take the risk of talking about the room or hotel in case the Turks would overhear us and become suspicious. We were very vulnerable at this point. The strike would be called by the Operational team as soon as the handover of drugs was complete. We would know roughly when this might be, but not the exact moment. It was vital that we attempt to tell the strike team where exactly we were located, not only so that they could safeguard us, but to also enable them to arrest the principals.

I asked to go the toilet at this point, and took our rather large Motorola mobile with the open mike with me. If the Ops team were close enough, there was, I hoped, a chance that I could make contact with them. The toilet was on the next floor down, and I passed two of the self-appointed guards on my way there. I locked the door behind me, but was aware that my two Turkish friends weren't too far away. I couldn't start talking to anyone, or they would be sure to hear. Instead, I starting to sing to myself, one of the only pop songs I knew, *The House of the Rising Sun*. I'm sure it sounded as bad then as it does now. It's not likely that anyone would have recognised my rendition of it—and especially not the third verse I sang on that occasion, which went something like: 'We're on the fourth floor in the blue room—la la, la la, la la…' To this day, I still laugh when I think of this ridiculous situation and how bizarre my tuneless droning must have sounded at the time! However, it worked and that was all that really mattered. My singing was picked up by a receiver in the backpack of a hippy type character—actually one of our technical team—who was hanging out near the hotel.

I returned to our room to find that George was still busy counting the money and had distributed it in little piles all over the surface of the bed. Then Eddie came into the room. He and George exchanged a few words in rapid Turkish, and George handed Eddie a key and a £50 note. Eddie left again, and George told us there wasn't long to wait now: the handover of the drugs would be taking place very shortly. John and I did our best to make further small talk with him, but we couldn't help exchanging nervous glances every now and again. The strike was imminent, that was certain. As the sun started to set and late afternoon turned into evening, George took a call on his mobile, then turned to me and asked me to instruct our testers to go to the exit of Edgware Road tube station with the Marks and Spencer store nearby.

I rang Roy and passed on the message to him. For John and myself, the sense of anticipation was now becoming unbearable, as we knew the operation was just about to go down. The tension in the room was such that every sound seemed to be magnified. I had positioned myself right behind the door, so that I could attempt to block it should we hear the Turks outside raising the alarm and trying to capture us. John was standing close to the window, looking anxiously out on to the street four floors below, so that he'd be able to see any unusual movement down there which would give us that crucial few seconds' warning. Suddenly I heard a dog bark. Although the animal barked just once, I knew it was an Alsatian or some other attack size dog. I saw John's eyes widen slightly as he looked even more intently onto the street below, and I scanned his face for some clue as to what was happening.

The moments which followed took on the sort of surreal quality that you later recall with some humour. John was jerking his head to one side as if he had some kind of nervous twitch. As he rolled his eyes toward the ceiling, I thought for a brief second that he had completely flipped, or might be in the early stages of a fit…What he was actually doing was trying to tell me to get the hell away from the door I was standing against. The bark had come from a Police attack dog, which John had observed debussing from a large builders' van which had just pulled up in the middle of the street outside the hotel. A full team of the Metropolitan Police's famous Blue Berets assault squad had alighted from the vehicle. All I can recall is George lifting his head in alarm, as he, like me, heard a slight rumble which lasted no more than a few seconds. The next thing we knew, the bedroom door had been blown off its hinges and I was flung to the ground, with the door on my back. A few members of the assault team padded over the top of it with the agility of big cats, and within a twinkling of an eye, before the cloud of money which had flown up into the air had even had a chance to settle, George was pinned to the ground and utterly helpless.

The guys of the assault team had entered the hotel and run up four flights of stairs, downing all opposition and blowing the door off our room, all within what seemed like literally a moment in time. They surely were the elite and I still take my hat off to them. As John and I ran from the room, we got the odd slap on the back from members of the rest of the attack team lining the stairs. On each side of the door of the room we had been in, lay an attack dog flat on the stairs. Like their handlers, they were like coiled springs ready to attack when and only when the moment was right. As we passed them, they ignored us, not moving a muscle: even the dogs are the elite, I thought! Every other person in the hotel was smelling the carpet, trussed up like turkeys. John and I ran to our car, and in a moment of pure adrenalin and emotion, we hugged each other in triumph.

Jumping into the car, we followed a motorcycle outrider, who seemed to have appeared out of nowhere and had motioned for us to tag along behind him. We went straight to the debrief and gave our full report. Later we joined the operational team to celebrate being part of the biggest successful heroin undercover operation ever carried out in the UK, a record haul of drugs with a street value of nearly £20 million.

George and his accomplice Eddie, who had handed over the drugs to our undercover colleagues, appeared at Southwark Crown Court on Friday, 23 September 1994. George got twelve years' imprisonment with a recommendation that he be deported at the completion of his sentence. Eddie got six years. It would appear that his psychic abilities weren't all they were cracked up to be—otherwise he would surely have seen it coming...

There were two interesting postscripts to this particular operation. One of them was an unconfirmed report that our friend George had somehow managed to make it back to his beloved Turkey. Unfortunately for him, however, the security services there were waiting for him and he was never seen or heard of again. The other item of interest was more purely personal to me. Almost a year later, around Christmas time, I was in London with two other undercover officers: John, who had been with me on Operation Boom, and another colleague. We were there on our way to Scotland Yard to attend a Christmas party. As we walked along in the direction of Regent Street, a guy coming the other way stopped dead in his tracks and seemed to be frozen to the spot. He just stared at me, not moving an inch as we walked past him. He followed me with his eyes, but still didn't move, except to turn his head in our direction. It was only then that it hit me who he was. A little fatter and with slightly more facial hair, but there was no doubt that it was George's friend, the one who had delivered the first kilo of heroin. I walked on with a smile. I suppose he couldn't believe he wasn't being arrested—again. There were genuine reasons for some decisions. There were in fact reasons behind everything we did in the murky world we inhabited, the world of undercover work. As I turned into Regent Street, I looked back: the same guy was still rooted to the spot. We greatly enjoyed the party that evening.

Chapter 6
The Met and the Mob

After Operation Boom and the significant coup in the war against international drug trafficking which it represented, we went on to assist the London Metropolitan Police on a number of more minor operations, some of which were equally successful in their own terms. In many senses, the best types of undercover operations were always those which enabled major criminal conspiracies to be nipped in the bud *before* they could be realised as actual, fully accomplished crimes. This was by far the most desirable scenario, not only for the obvious reason that the negative consequences of criminal activity would be avoided, but also because, as undercover officers, we always had to be conscious that we were operating within the limits of a strictly defined code of conduct. If we went beyond these limits, not only would any actions we had taken against criminals be inadmissible in a court of law (and any case against such criminals might subsequently be thrown out), but we were also running the risk of suffering legal consequences ourselves because of involvement in the criminal activity in question. Showing an active interest in a crime which was already underway was arguably within our legal remit; playing a major part in facilitating such a crime was most certainly not. Perhaps to encourage us to always keep in mind the difficult line we were obliged to tread, we were required to sign a declaration of compliance, 'Instructions to Undercover Officers', at the outset of each and every operation in which we were involved (see Appendix B). Real life being what it is however, the truth is that there were some occasions when it took considerable powers of discernment, not to mention dedication to one's duty, in order to be able to abide by this code of conduct in its strictest sense.

One job, in which early undercover intervention provided a casebook result, came to us as a request from the London Crime Squad to assist them in infiltrating a London gang who, according to reliable sources, were planning a major bank heist. Apparently, the gang were looking via the usual underground networks for someone with specific expertise in a certain make and type of computer. The gang were keeping the name of the intended target bank very close to their chests, but were putting it about that they would be able to get such a person in and out of the bank in question without being noticed, while also ensuring them unrestricted access to the main computer. Initially, being sceptical about such seemingly unrealistic claims, the Crime Squad had had their doubts about whether the intended heist was a genuine runner. However, the calibre and reputation of the gang in question were such that the rumour couldn't be ignored, and it was decided that the only way of testing the veracity of their claims was to have a crack at them and see what happened.

The boys from the Met reckoned we could provide some valuable help on the job. Their agents and undercover officers proceeded to make it known to the gang that there was a person with the IT expertise they were looking for in an Irish gang, based in Belfast. The London mob were accordingly fed our contact numbers and they took the bait almost straight away, getting in touch to set up a meeting. On our first trip over, we met with their front man, who identified the bank by name (for legal reasons, I cannot give details here), and told us the plan was to enter the bank building late on a Friday night, access the main computer there and then, and transfer millions of pounds to a number of foreign accounts. Within a few days the money could be moved on through a network the crooks had set up. In any event, this latter part of the plan was not our concern— but, our mobster friends insisted, we would be well paid for the part we were being asked to play.

Like us, the Crime Squad were intrigued as to how the London mob intended to bypass some of the most sophisticated security systems in the City. The front man we were meeting was a typical East End crook, with all the swagger and confidence which only the London mob can have. Everything was, 'Okay, me old cock,' 'Lovely Jubbley,' this, that and the other. We had been briefed however that these people were not half as entertaining in real life as their jocular image might have suggested. They were serious villains, experienced armed robbers who in the past hadn't baulked at shooting anyone who got in their way. They were a ruthless and highly professional outfit. This would be borne out by the fact that nothing had been left to chance in relation to this job: everything was meticulously planned down to the very last detail.

Although the gang had given us the name of the bank, they hadn't told us which branch they were targeting, nor how they intended us to get into the building undetected. They did however give us the exact specifications of the computer, down to the serial number, and so on. They also assured us that they could get the necessary codes to enable us to access the system: our expertise, however, was required to take the heist forward by gaining access to the main frame. Armed with this information, Crime Squad were able to approach the Head of Security of the bank in question, and, much to the latter's dismay, inform him that there was police intelligence to the effect that their elaborate security systems had been compromised. This of course went down like a lead balloon, with the gentleman concerned having visions of himself being made speedily redundant! Self-preservation being the all-powerful motivator that is it, he readily agreed to assist us with whatever we needed—which in this instance was for one of us to be given a crash course in the bank's computer systems, so that we could demonstrate enough knowledge to be able to convince the London mob that we knew what we were talking about. Time was of the essence however, and the pressure was on. The Crime Squad had to ensure an early intervention for reasons of damage control and the preservation of public confidence. The name of the game was as always to make sure the villains didn't get away with the loot. Arresting someone after the horse had bolted, so to speak, wouldn't have been much consolation if the gang had managed to clear the bank of millions of pounds of customers' money in the meantime. And of course, the legal limits of any undercover operation had to be carefully observed too.

Within a few weeks, one of our team was sufficiently trained in the necessary computer systems and procedures to be able to bluff our criminal friends. We still didn't know which branch of the bank was to be targeted, and the operational team were obviously under some considerable pressure to find out. So we concocted a ruse, and decided to tell the London crooks that it was vital for us to be able to inspect the computer itself prior to the job, so as to make sure that there weren't any extra security systems or measures we hadn't anticipated, and which might otherwise prevent us from successfully hacking into the computer mainframe when the time came. Luckily, they fell for it, and shortly afterwards their contact got in touch to set up another meeting. We travelled to Heathrow early on the morning of the job, and met up first of all with the operational team from the Met. We then got in touch with our contact in the London gang: they weren't keen on meeting us at Heathrow, and suggested we make our way to a tube station in the East End.

These guys knew what they were doing, anyway: their refusal to come to Heathrow was no doubt a cautionary measure to ensure they wouldn't be captured on the myriad of CCTV cameras which cover the airport complex. It took us an hour and a half to get to the designated tube station. When we got there, we were directed to a nearby side street, where our contact from the gang was waiting. Ever the professionals, these guys were playing one card at a time, like a slow game of poker. Tonight, we were told, they would show us the intended target. They knew perfectly well however that any subsequent police investigation would immediately zero in not only on the bank's CCTV cameras, but those of the buildings in the surrounding streets, days if not weeks prior to the job actually going down. Therefore, yet again, they were proceeding very carefully. We drove around for a while in the dark saloon car Dave, our contact, was driving. As we did so, I scanned the vehicle for any clues as to its origin. It seemed remarkably devoid of anything of the kind in fact, and, I reckoned, must have been either a plated-up, stolen vehicle, or one bought specifically for this job. If either of these was the case, it was another sign that we were dealing with a very professional outfit.

After a while, we parked in a darkened street close to a taxi depot and all-night café. To passers-by we would have just looked like some taxi drivers sitting having a chat. Each time our friend Dave's mobile rang, he would get out of the car in order to carry on his conversation —yet another security measure. Each time he left us, I carried out a quick rummage of the vehicle, but I wasn't able to find anything of an evidential nature at all in the glove compartments or side pockets: this confirmed my earlier theories about the car. After about twenty minutes or so, it came to my attention that a blue Ford Mondeo had cruised past us at least twice. I was about to mention it to Dave, when he pre-empted me, telling me not to worry: it was just their people checking out the area. This guy was as sharp as a needle, there was no doubt about that. He must have been watching us very intently to have picked up so quickly on the fact that I had clocked the blue car. After another call taken some distance from the car, Dave returned to tell us that in a few minutes, the other vehicle would be picking up my companion, whom I shall simply refer to as 'X' (for ongoing security reasons)—the colleague with the computer expertise. Dave then briefed 'X' about how he should proceed from here. As soon as he was driven to the street corner with the bank, he was to get out of the car immediately and go straight into the bank entrance. The door would be opened for him, and then he would only have a very short time to get inside: the CCTV cameras would be elsewhere for one moment and one moment only.

Within a few minutes, the Mondeo drew up beside us again, 'X' changed cars as quickly as he could, and he was then driven off into the darkness. Meanwhile, my mobster companion Dave and I made small talk, mostly about the crime scene in Ireland, which he seemed to be fairly curious about. After what seemed like an hour, but was in reality a much shorter time, 'X' returned, getting back into the car as quickly as he had left. 'X' then pronounced that he was happy with his inspection of the bank's computer: he reckoned that all was in order, and that there would be no problem. The only thing we would need would be details of the security codes being used that week.

Dave seemed satisfied enough that the evening had gone without a hitch, and he dropped us back to the hotel we were staying at, arranging to meet in the morning before our flight home, so that we could discuss the way forward. Once we were sure that he had gone, 'X' and I left the hotel again and went to our debrief with the Operational team. We had now identified the premises of the bank to be targeted—a major result in itself. What was however alarming for the bank in question, and the Crime Squad team, was how the undercover officer had been able to get into the building. The answer was surprisingly and shockingly simple: both of the security guards in the bank were working for the London Mob! 'X' recounted how one of these guards had fixed the cameras so that they didn't pick up anything unusual and were focused elsewhere during the few seconds it had taken for him to dart into the doorway of the bank and gain access. He went on to relate that, using one of the guard's electronic pass cards and keys, they had been able to pass through the building within minutes and get up to the fourth floor where the target computer was situated. As the debrief went on, there was further cause for concern. The guard who had taken 'X' into the bank had obviously thought he had been more thoroughly briefed by the gang than had actually been the case, since he let it slip that there was a third person in the bank who was part of the proposed heist. He had only referred to this third person with a nickname, which sounded Asian to 'X'. More worryingly still, it seemed that this third person was at management or junior management level in the bank.

After the debrief, 'X' and I left with some of the team to unwind over a beer in a nearby pub, whilst the Command staff and members of the bank's senior management had an urgent meeting to discuss the way forward. We were informed later that we should try to meet our friends from the gang the next morning, should the opportunity arise—otherwise we should arrange to contact them soon and leave it at that for the time being. In the meantime, the investigation would continue at both physical and electronic surveillance levels.

As it turned out, we got a call from our contact, Dave, the following morning at breakfast. He said he had had a bad night on the juice, but would contact us as soon as the job was on and they had all the data that we required. In fact, this was to be the last undercover involvement in that particular job. This was not unusual and would happen on many occasions. We had, after all, succeeded in our deployment's operational objectives, i.e. to determine the particular bank and the branch being targeted, and where the weak point in terms of the bank's security lay. Subsequent surveillance of the targets, including the two security men, would ultimately establish the identity of the third member of the bank's staff who was in on the job. This turned out to be a junior manager who happened to be on his way out of his job there anyway. It was decided, quite rightly, that London Crime Squad would nip the whole thing in the bud, as they had more than sufficient evidence to both search and arrest the culprits. There was no point to be made or nothing to be gained by allowing the principals to proceed any further. There was also the integrity of both the bank and its systems to be considered.

In the weeks that followed, all the principals were rounded up and, faced with the overwhelming evidence against them, had little option but to negotiate a deal for themselves with the prosecution counsel. For our part, my team and I had been very happy to assist our London colleagues. The success of this particular operation was yet another illustration of how undercover infiltration can produce many of the answers in an operational deployment at a fraction of the cost and far more quickly than a traditional police deployment.

Chapter 7

Operation Chameleon and the Rasta Conspiracy

A s the revamped Surveillance Unit at Castlereagh began to find its feet, we quickly gained the confidence to be able to mount our own undercover operations in our own territory. One of our first 'homegrown' operations as the reformed unit was in early 1994 and involved a strike against a group of money counterfeiters in Belfast.

We had been aware for some time that the local market was being flooded with counterfeits of varying quality. Our intelligence on the ground had identified a group based in the Short Strand area of Belfast, a particularly hard-line Republican area, as a very prolific counterfeiting outfit. They were producing high quality copies of banknotes of various denominations, as well as convincing forgeries of other official documents, such as MOT certificates and car tax discs. Not content with passing the notes and other documents off within their own locality, they were extending their greedy hands further afield and openly selling them to any criminal who approached them. As was in my experience so often the case with criminals of all shapes and sizes, it was this sheer greed which was to lead to the downfall of these particular crooks, creating the opportunity for us to infiltrate the group and ultimately take them out.

We had been keeping the chief targets under surveillance for some considerable time and had, we believed, managed to identify the commercial premises which were being used by the printer in the nearby Ormeau Road area. It was important however that we not only take out the printer, but all those behind the operation, otherwise they would simply move location and start all over again somewhere else. Surveillance and intelligence gathering was a risky business in this extremist PIRA stronghold, but we were slowly able to build up a picture of how the group were working at street level. The gang's principals would visit the printer frequently. Would-be buyers would call at the main house from which the dealings were done, and would either be asked in to wait or told to come back at an agreed time. Runners would then leave by the back door of the main house, and go to houses nearby in which the stash appeared to be kept. We were again very much aware that intervention at this stage would be premature and only enable us at best to catch one of the minor players in possession of a small quantity of false documents. In order to catch the principals, we would need to try to infiltrate the gang but, again, a lot of caution would be needed. We knew however that the gang, in their greed, were very eager to do business, and so we decided to send in an undercover officer cold to see if they would deal with a complete stranger. It was a risky strategy but our intelligence indicated that they would sell to literally anyone. We planned to put a heavy surveillance cordon around the target house with solid uniform back-up: we would stay outside until the goods were brought to the undercover officer, who would pay up front and arrange to call back at an agreed time.

The undercover officer in question had referenced himself in by mentioning an association with a criminal we knew had been buying counterfeit currency from the gang. They had seemed to accept this without any hesitation and the undercover officer had been asked into the target house to wait. He used this time to inquire about the extent of their capabilities and the range of products they were offering.

The gang's portfolio of forgeries now covered the complete spectrum and included MOT Certificates, Road Fund Licences, Goods Vehicle Certificates and banknotes, from £100 denominations and below. In terms of counterfeit notes, the forgers were also branching out now to other currencies, including Irish Punts, and they were keen to talk to our undercover officer about future purchases of much larger quantities of notes. We knew however that if our man was to offer to buy a very large parcel of currency from them, they would begin to ask questions as to whom he was representing in the Belfast area. We were very conscious too that we were as yet novices at this game, and needed to move with extreme caution to avoid the whole thing blowing up in our faces.

After some thought, we decided that the best strategy would be to introduce an outside party into the situation—someone about whom the counterfeiters might not ask so many questions. To this end, we contacted our friends in Scotland Yard and they were happy to oblige. Granted, this particular job was relatively small beer for an elite and vastly experienced outfit like the Met's so10 group, but they were eager to help us get on our feet in the undercover business, and so were only too glad to come over.

I hope the reader won't mind if I allow myself a short aside here on what I have observed about the nature of greed during the course of my career and in particular during my time as an undercover operative. It—greed, or avarice—is the single, most powerful driving force behind all criminal activity, and frequently the one factor which will lead criminals to overreach themselves and thereby contribute to their own downfall. Time after time, I have witnessed how the criminally-minded have been quite simply unable to resist the opportunity of adding to what they have already got, even if it means taking risks they would not normally take. In fact, as undercover officers, we were as a rule able to rely on this basic truth—that almost always, greed conquers all. People who know me well have often remarked on what a jaded view of human nature I seem to have at times, but in this instance, I make no apology for stating what I have found to be almost unfailingly the case. Each time I witness this principle at work, I am reminded of *The Canterbury Tales* by Chaucer, which we studied at school, and the figure of the Pardoner whose tale focuses so much on the power of greed, or Avarice, which was regarded as one of the Seven Deadly Sins. The joke is that the Pardoner, a truly objectionable man who observes and exploits people's weaknesses, is driven by the very thing which he condemns in others…(Indeed, if the truth be told, there was a fair bit of avarice in evidence too in our own undercover unit, where certain members of the team were so greedy for overtime that they would have quite happily, to use the Belfast vernacular, 'worked [during] the two minutes' silence'!)

To get back to our Belfast counterfeiters, they proved to be no

exception to the rule. On his next buy, our man told them that he had
several contacts in the London mobs who were very interested in
buying large amounts of the high value notes they were offering.
When they heard this, the Belfast gang were only too happy to oblige,
and were eager to meet the London crooks. As it turned out, they were
to be honoured with the presence of the master himself, Big Peter—
perhaps the most experienced undercover officer in not only the UK
but Europe, and the same who had tutored us on the undercover
course.

Undercovers from our unit had been meeting and calling with the
counterfeiters over the preceding days, and they had been eager to
show them various Bank of England notes which had a variety of
random serial numbers. (Although commonplace these days, the
ability to produce notes with different numbers was relatively rare at
the time—these guys were ahead of the crowd in that respect.) The
production quality of the notes was very good too, by the standards of
the time anyway, and they would definitely have fooled most people.

On the day of the first meet between Peter and the gang, we
decided to suggest a place outside the crooks' usual territory. This
would have a number of advantages for us, including the fact that it
would be a far safer environment for us to work in. We chose a well-
known local beauty spot, Shaw's Bridge, which was on the outskirts of
the city but still only a couple of miles from the bad guys' lair. It was
a sunny June morning and I had earlier briefed the surveillance squad
and given the QRF their line-up positions for the strike whenever it was
called. When the covert umbrella was in place, I gave the signal for the
undercover officers to proceed with the meeting with the head of the
counterfeiting gang, whose name was Black. A short time later, they
arrived on the plot with Black. Big Peter from the Met was in position
in a covert vehicle of his own, which had been wired for recording.

Black got out of the car and the undercover officers introduced him
to Peter, who invited him to get into the front seat of his car. One of
the undercover officers (we'll call him 'Jim') got into the rear. Peter
went to the boot and brought back £18,000 in flash money, which he
had previously broken down into £1,000 bundles of £100 notes for
easy counting. Black examined the money and—this has to be the
best bit—had the audacity to carefully check the notes for
authenticity. Peter started to talk about what notes they had available
for sale, and after they had discussed this, Black said he would be

happy to go ahead with the deal, but wanted one of his guys to check Peter's money before taking things to the next stage. Peter agreed to this, and Black left with Jim, our undercover officer, to get the agreed number of counterfeit notes.

In the meantime, Peter put the flash money back into the boot of his car and settled down to wait for Black's return. We retrieved the tape from Peter's car, installed a new tape and took the first one back to base to be copied. It took Black and his associates some time to get their parcel together, for it was only that evening that he finally contacted us again. He was now, he said, in a position to do the final trade, and would meet us at the same place at Shaw's Bridge for the handover.

It was about 6.55 pm, when a large blue Ford Granada car came into the car park and circled Peter's car. Black was in the front passenger seat. The car passed behind Peter's car to park at the bottom of the car park, overlooking the beauty spot. Peter got out of his car and began to walk towards them. As he did so, Black dismounted and shook hands with him, inviting Peter to get into the rear of his car. Black introduced the driver of the car as 'Michael the Printer', and they shook hands. Peter inquired as to the delay, saying he hadn't anticipated having to wait so long. Muttering something about them having to be very careful, as they didn't know him, Black then gestured at a folder lying on the seat beside Peter: this was £20,000 in good faith. Peter took out the money, putting on plastic gloves before doing so. According to Black, they had done their best to spread the notes over as many different denominations as possible. Peter had obviously impressed Michael, particularly with the precautions he had taken with the gloves and in his careful examination of the notes, for Michael went on to say that he hoped this would be a regular thing. Peter reminded them abruptly though that the deal wasn't finished as yet, since he had negotiated for £200,000 but only had £20,000 in his hands. Again citing reasons of security, Black said that the remainder would be delivered to him at 10.00 am the following morning. Peter agreed to this, and then Black produced a variety of other forged merchandise: MOT Certificates, Road Fund Licences and some examples of £100 notes: would Peter's mob be interested in buying any of these? Peter said he hadn't much of a market for the motor documents, as they all related to Northern Ireland only; the £100 notes would however be of great interest. Michael the Printer said they would happily oblige: all Peter had to do was order the notes on a Monday, and they would be ready for collection by the Wednesday of the same week.

They all agreed that they would be able to deal much more easily in the future, and Black said he now felt much happier. They arranged to meet again the next morning for the handover of the rest of the parcel. Peter left, carrying the counterfeit notes he had been given wrapped up in his coat. The moment he got into his car, I called the strike and on my signal, the uniform QRF, who had been quietly closing in on the plot all the while, careered into the car park to arrest Black and Michael. Based on our existing intelligence, we then carried out a number of other arrests and searches in the Short Strand and Ormeau areas. We uncovered the master presses at the printer's premises, and in the process recovered forged currency and other documents with a collective value running into millions of pounds. This included large quantities of foreign currency notes, which were still on the presses! It proved to be the biggest haul of such items ever recovered in Ireland at that time: we had for a fact disrupted a major criminal enterprise. The confidence boost to our team was palpable. We had all undoubtedly learned a great deal from being able to watch experts such as Peter and his team in action.

A case which resembled this one in many ways was to arise several years later, in 1997, and centred on the distinguished world of top-level banking circles in the City of London. We had a very good friend and colleague in London, with whom we had worked on a number of missions and who was originally from our part of the world. Jack was a Level One undercover officer within the Met, who would often find himself involved in undercover infiltrations into the murky world of the City's financial institutions and related businesses—since of course the City was part of the Met's patch.

In this instance, Jack had rung us, asking for our help in terms of providing support and 'backstopping' on a job which was already underway, and involved the attempted theft of over four million pounds by means of forged bank securities and money drafts. This was Jack's field of expertise and a highly specialised area which few undercover officers would ever get involved in, for the same reason. Amongst other things, Jack was a trained accountant. For the hard work involved, his job undoubtedly had its perks, and he would often make us envious with tales of his globetrotting exploits through the financial honey spots of the world, including of course the Far East. A high-flying lifestyle, yes, but still fraught with many of the same dangers as any area of undercover work.

In relation to the job he was approaching us about on this occasion, Jack explained that he would be taking care of the whole financial aspect: all he wanted us to do was play the all-too-familiar part of the Irish paramilitaries who were backing him up. For better or worse, this role was one in which we had by then some considerable expertise, and we readily agreed to assist. In my ignorance of such matters, I had imagined that the targets would be part of some relatively sophisticated English mob, possibly with bowler hats and pinstripe suits and all the rest. I was therefore more than a little bewildered and taken aback to find out at our briefing that the criminals in question were in fact of Afro-Caribbean extraction, and members of some kind of Rasta gang.

As myself and the Belfast contingent of undercover officers travelled over to London, I was admittedly feeling, for perhaps one of the few times in my life, slightly out of my depth. In any case, once we got into Heathrow, we proceeded to travel to a large block of flats in a predominantly black neighbourhood. Our arrival was the subject of some considerable amusement and I was aware that we were under discreet surveillance from a number of quarters. We got out of Jack's top-of-the-range saloon car, which was only surpassed by his debonair Savile Row suit. No doubt, my companion and I looked like a 'tick man's' minders, as we shuffled sheepishly behind Jack until we all reached a second floor flat, where we were greeted by a massive coloured guy with Rasta curls and teeth as white as I have ever seen.

I would like to assure the reader that in relating this account, the very last thing I intend is for there to be any racist implications in any of my remarks or descriptions. I am merely trying to create as vivid an impression as possible of what was for me a very surreal episode. It should be remembered too that, coming from Northern Ireland, I had never before encountered anyone from the Rasta culture, or even indeed from an Afro-Caribbean background. Perhaps the extent to which I experienced the whole incident as bizarre was more than anything else a reflection of my own lack of experience at the time!

As we entered the flat, it quickly became clear that, despite the fact that it was only about 11.30 am or so, there was a party in full swing. The place was packed with a number of men, women, and indeed children. We were ushered in, and my other undercover chum and I sat in bewilderment as Jack introduced us to the 'main men', and began to talk about the bonds and other material which these people apparently had for sale.

Apart from what Jack said, I could barely understand one word of the conversation. I was aware that Jack was wearing a Nagra tape recorder, and I couldn't help secretly thinking that it was just as well, because otherwise I would probably end up making a complete idiot of myself in the witness box later in court! All my colleague and I could do was nod and smile at everyone, and keep repeating, 'Pleased to meet you,' to anyone we were introduced to. They must no doubt have thought us to be a bit simple, to say the least: God only knows what we were nodding to! Once or twice, when Jack was insisting that we wouldn't stand for any rip-offs or messing about, I did my best to look very serious and menacing, but I think this only made us seem all the more ridiculous, because my hosts just grinned wider than ever. It seemed however that Jack was satisfied with the meeting, because after a while he motioned for us to leave, and we escorted him back to his car, which was being guarded by some of our host's friends, who were also doing their best to ensure that the mob of kids clambering all over it didn't completely dismantle it.

As we drove off, I couldn't contain myself any longer, and with tears of laughter and perhaps relief too, I confessed to Jack that I hadn't understood a word during the whole meeting. Again, there is no racist intent in any of this: the fact that I couldn't decipher anything the Rastas said was exactly comparable to the difficulty a Londoner might have on hearing a Belfast man or woman in full flow, or *vice versa*. At any rate, Jack, it seemed, was more than pleased with how everything had gone: everything was on track, he said, and our hosts had been very impressed with us! Perhaps the fact that we had been obviously completely bewildered by what was going on around us in the flat had convinced our Rasta friends that we really were the Irish terrorists we said we were.

Whatever the explanation was, the meeting had been a success for Jack, and there was no need for a repeat visit on our parts: the gang were quite willing to produce their bonds and certificates for him just before they were all arrested. As is often the case in these types of scenarios, where large sums of the public's money is at stake, police intervention could not wait until the case against the targets had come to full fruition or had developed any further. The usual rules of engagement didn't apply, as even a 24-hour delay could result in millions of pounds disappearing off the radar.

To us, this case had seemed like a walk in the park, compared to others we had been involved in, and without the same ring of deadly seriousness. The reality however was that the counterfeit operation had been a major criminal conspiracy, the work of a highly organised gang with Yardie connections, who wouldn't have thought twice about causing us serious harm. At the time of our intervention, the crime and the operation against it had been relatively far advanced. And so it stands to reason that my colleague and I were slightly bewildered and a little embarrassed, when a short time later, we were called over to London to be presented with Certificates of Commendation from the Detective Chief Superintendent of the City of London Police Force, who praised us for our part in the top-level operation which had successfully averted a four million pound fraud.

Chapter 8
Operation Gurnos and the Adams Family Fraudsters

In July 1994, when the Metropolitan Police's Flying Squad (the elite unit within the London CID specialising in the detection and prevention of armed robbery and similar crimes) asked for our assistance in infiltrating one of London's top criminal gangs, I knew we were again about to plunge into the seedier side of life and a sordid underworld fraught with danger. When you dealt with the counterfeit and drug dealing gangs in London in particular, you were always guaranteed to find yourself up close and personal with the real dregs of society: people who had few morals and would cut your throat for a penny. I was not to be disappointed on this score on Operation Gurnos, for the criminals in question were 'The Adams Family', a well-known London gang notorious for their viciousness and utter lack of scruples.

The Flying Squad had obtained intelligence that the Adams gang, who specialised in armed robberies and major counterfeiting scams, were hoping to form alliances with criminal gangs in Ireland as a means of broadening their scope of operations. This was the perfect opportunity to get us involved and exploit the fact that, among the mainland criminal fraternity, we were a completely unknown quantity as an undercover operations unit.

Through the Squad's underworld contacts, a meeting had been set up for us with the gang in London, and on Saturday, 23 July 1994, we found ourselves in the King's Cross area of London. Even in daylight hours, King's Cross can be a dangerous place for the uninitiated. Tourists travelling through seldom notice the drug dealers and pimps on virtually every corner, and the vagrants from all over the world, looking for any opportunity to take advantage of the careless or naïve. Of course not all the people in this neighbourhood were hostile or bad, and there were many in this cesspit of humanity who struggled to make a decent living. In subsequent years, we were to make particular friends with one couple who ran a restaurant in the area. (I won't name the restaurant, even though the couple are now retired and back safely in their homeland.) We were introduced to these people by other undercover teams from the Met. The couple were aware that we were undercover officers, but they knew us only by our aliases and did not have any idea who we really were or what exactly we did. They accepted these circumstances without comment or complaint and, at great personal risk to themselves, often provided invaluable backstopping for us. The only way we could repay them was to make sure we spent as much money as we possibly could in their establishment whenever we passed through. We lived on the best of their country's wines, and their T-bone steaks were out of this world. Our festivities at their restaurant would invariably go on into the early hours, and we were often joined by their family members. Without such good people as these, we would not have achieved a fraction of the successes which we did in the war against organised crime—that much is clear.

On the morning of the meeting with the Adams Family gang, my undercover colleague and I went to a well-known public house and favourite underworld haunt near King's Cross station. In many circumstances, undercover officers from our team would go to meets with criminals alone, but in dealings with counterfeiting gangs, and the Adams family in particular, I made it policy that we should work with at least one other colleague at all times. My reasons for insisting on this were simple: the members of these gangs, as I have already suggested, were generally ruthless, highly unpredictable criminals who would have no qualms whatsoever about knifing you if you happened to look at them the wrong way, or killing you in a sudden fit of temper. And the Adams family were notoriously the most volatile and violent of the lot.

I made a few phone calls to our contact in the gang, to let him know we had arrived. A short time later, I was approached by the contact, who appeared out of nowhere and introduced himself as 'Pat'. An East Ender and a veteran criminal, Pat had, it seemed, spent his life in crime and specialised in armed robbery. As we walked, he told me how he had made Irish connections during his time on the run after a prison escape, when he had been holed up in Newry, Co. Down, for some months. He referred also to the big Irish immigrant population in this area of London. For someone who was claiming to have all sorts of links to Ireland, however, Pat wasn't exactly very savvy about the basic politics of the place or people. Although I was going under the alias of Billy (the Loyalist paramilitary), Pat would manage, as we shall see, to make one *faux pas* after another from a political standpoint during the time we spent with him. In fact, if I had really been a Billy, I would probably have ended up decking him—or worse —for some of the things he came out with…Pat was about fifty years of age and wore a duncer, Andy Capp style cap that, fortunately enough, partially hid his battle-scarred face and piercing blue eyes which glinted from hollow sockets.

We walked a short distance to Pat's car and then drove to nearby Inglebert Street. As we alighted from the vehicle, Pat suggested we go for a pint of Guinness. It is wonderful how anyone who meets an Irish guy automatically assumes that the black stuff is all we drink. I swear to God, some seem to think we are weaned on it!

The pub Pat took me into was well known in undercover circles in the area, but no undercover officer would ever have risked going there without being 'referenced in'—i.e. brought there by a regular. The chances of getting out in one piece would otherwise have been slim, to say the least. The establishment in question was in the Borough of Islington. Immediately we went in, I was acutely aware that every eye was on us. The glares of hatred, contempt and suspicion directed at us as newcomers quickly changed to disinterest, once our chaperone Paddy was recognised. His general greeting to the floor was met with grunts from individuals in various quarters of the room, all of whom seemed to be engrossed in their own secretive dealings and confabs. When I say 'individuals', the word 'creatures' seems more appropriate. I was momentarily reminded of that scene in the first Star Wars film, where Luke Skywalker enters a bar on some forbidden planet and finds it filled with every zombie, freak and alien weirdo in the universe. By the look of some of these guys, even the Men in Black with all their expertise in alien life forms would have struggled to work out which planet they were from!

Two particularly ugly-looking specimens, one of whom had long greasy hair which hung over his pockmarked face, were busily examining some cigarette papers through a large magnifying glass. This was a familiar enough scene to me, and one which I had witnessed many times in clubs and pubs in Ireland. The scrunched up cigarette papers in fact bore messages, and had been smuggled out of prisons. Lying on the table top over which these two creatures were hunched were other such messages, cigarette papers still pill-sized, scrunched into tiny balls and wrapped in cling film. These are passed from mouth to mouth in that parting kiss between inmates and lovers or wives or other couriers in the many prison visiting rooms around the country every day.

Pat led me and my colleague to the back recess of the bar, where we sat on wooden bench-type seating. Pat took great pride in pointing out the holes in the dark tobacco-stained ceiling which, he claimed, had been blasted out by shotgun fire. Once he had got our pints for us, we were to find it very difficult to get a word in edgeways with our host, who seemed very eager to impress us. Pat explained that his gang were particularly anxious to get their hands on the methods and formulae we Irish were using to launder diesel fuel. He was obviously aware that the IRA were developing quite sophisticated equipment in order to perfect the laundering process and seemed well informed about the latest developments in this regard. He didn't however seem to twig that as Billy Craig, I might not have been privy to all of the IRA's secrets! By way of a return for such information about the fuel operation, Pat was able, he said, to sell us a complete range of 'dodgy' goods, including drugs and high quality forgeries of £50 notes, and every kind of official document a criminal might need, from driving licences, to birth and MOT certificates, as well as, believe it or not, Marks & Spencer luncheon vouchers!

The luncheon vouchers, I must admit, were a first for me. I made a show of examining some of them: they were indeed high quality forgeries, I pronounced, but, I informed him in no uncertain terms, I would take some convincing of their actual fiscal value. Pat assured me that his gang had made a small fortune from luncheon vouchers. They produced them in bulk, in denominations of £1.50, and supplied them in bundles to various companies who would distribute them to their employees. The restaurants would collect them and cash them in in decent quantities about every six weeks or so. Although I took Pat's word for the brilliance of the scam, I hadn't really the heart to tell him that as far as I knew, there weren't any Marks & Spencer outlets with restaurant facilities in Northern Ireland at the time! In any case, it would be up to the Flying Squad to make the call: this was their job, after all.

Next on the agenda were Pat's counterfeit £50 notes. These were really high quality forgeries, and came in five different serial numbers. I had a fair idea of who might be producing them, as I had seen the workmanship before, in previous encounters with the London mob. The notes were very close to the real thing—down to the metallic strip and watermarks: in fact, to the naked eye, there was no difference at all. When I expressed an eager interest in taking a large quantity of these notes, Pat was curious as to how I would be able to shift such an amount, especially in £50s, but I spun him a yarn about moving them through Bureau de Changes on the border, and he seemed satisfied with this explanation. He was very keen for us to take some of the drugs he had on offer, suggesting that ecstasy tablets would be the easiest for him to supply. The price per tablet, he informed us, was £6.50. This was absolutely outrageous: at nearly twice the going rate in the street at the time, Pat was obviously adding a huge mark-up for himself! I wasn't there however to get a good rate for the Met, and I was quite happy to let Pat think he was stroking us. I knew very well that we would be having the last laugh.

As a first transaction with Pat and his gang, I arranged to buy £200,000 of £50 notes and luncheon vouchers, as well as a consignment of 1,000 'E's. Pat promised that other drug samples would be supplied to us with this first order on the day of the transfer. We discussed where we would do the trade and I asked that we do the deal on the North side of London, so that I wouldn't have to go right into the city, and could travel home directly towards Scotland and the ferry afterwards. I suggested that we meet at one of the nearby service stations, and Pat said we could meet there initially, but that we'd have to move on somewhere else nearby. He didn't like service stations as a rule, he explained: they were full of surveillance cameras, and one of his mates had been nicked at one the previous year with a £3 million heroin haul.

Pat really was full of helpful tips and advice, such as how it was a good trick to always carry a false set of plates with double-sided tape, since they were so easy to put on and take off again. I thanked him for this gem of wisdom, secretly amused at his apparent assumption that because we were Irish, we were obviously brain dead. After some consultation, we eventually agreed that Toddington or Scratchwood service stations would fit the bill.

Pat and I concluded the discussion about this first deal by agreeing a price of £25,000 for the currency. I said that we would be carrying up to around £34,000 with us altogether, in order to cover what drugs he could bring on the day.

Once this was all settled, Pat continued with his own particular line in criminal small talk. He was a real mine of information, and there were no limits, it seemed, to his ingenuity when it came to ripping other people off. He had recently, he told us with some pride, taken about five of the local banks for £10,000 at a time. All you had to do, he bragged, was to open a current account with a bank, and then after a while apply for a small loan from them. As long as you ensured that you paid off this first amount on time, you could then hit the branch in question for a bigger loan, something more in the region of their £10,000 limit. As long as you made a few payments and then moved location, the bank would not treat non-payment of the whole as fraud: it would merely be put down to bad debt and written off. Pat was delighted with his own inventiveness! He was also completely typical of the type of criminal involved in the London counterfeiting and drug dealing gangs. Petty crooks and conmen, they had little if any moral code, even by criminal standards. They had their sticky fingers in virtually any area where there was a quick buck to be made by ripping someone off, and, as I have said, they would have had no qualms whatsoever about resorting to violence, given the least opportunity or excuse.

Now that our business for the day was done, Pat decided that we should seal the deal over some real drinking in a real Irish pub. He knew a place, he said, where we would fit right in. This turned out to be Pat's most glaring *faux pas* of the day. As it transpired, we arrived at Flaherty's Irish pub just in time to be taken aside by some spotty kids with serious-looking faces, who waved collection tins in our faces and asked us to contribute to the fight for Irish Freedom. These kids, and the pub itself, were about as Irish as green beer and Leprechauns. Moreover, it was hardly likely that Billy the loyalist gangster would

have been tripping over himself to make a donation to the said Irish
Freedom Fighters. But such was Pat's ignorance. I managed to resist
the temptation to tell him a few home truths, however…

It wasn't until some hours later that my colleague and I were finally
able to take our leave of Pat, our new-found alliance cemented with
the aid of about a gallon of Guinness. When I debriefed the Flying
Squad, they seemed elated by our progress. I then returned to Belfast
and kept in touch with Pat by telephone over the next few days,
making sure to record all our conversations for evidence as usual. The
following Monday, I rang him from a public phone box in Belfast and
he said they were ready for the handover. The next morning, I
travelled with another undercover colleague to Scotland Yard on the
redeye shuttle flight from Belfast, and we were in London early for a
briefing with the Detective Inspector in charge.

By 2.30 pm that afternoon, I was sitting in Toddington Services on
the M1 in a hire car, ready to put a call in to Pat. He told me that it
would take him about an hour to get to me, and we agreed that I
would wait in the nearby burger bar until he got there: my companion
was close by with the car and the cash. About an hour later, Pat joined
me in the burger bar. He was full of the joys of spring and I bought
him a coffee. As usual, I was sitting in a place where I could watch the
door. I was also observing Pat closely, looking for signs of his making
contact with anyone else in the diner, but he seemed to be alone and
obviously at ease. Yet again, he brought up the subject of the diesel
laundering. It was becoming increasingly obvious that the gang's
main purpose in engaging us in this particular deal was to ultimately
secure our help in setting up their own fuel laundering operation. I
told Pat however that we needed to concentrate on the business at
hand first of all.

I explained to Pat that my companion was waiting with the money
in our car in a nearby garden centre at the last turnoff on the
motorway, just five minutes' drive away. We set off in Pat's car, a new
Peugeot 405. I noticed that despite all his street-wise advice, he still
had his own registration number on the vehicle. We drove on the
A5120 toward Flitwick, and within a few minutes reached the Spruce
Garden Centre.

The large car park at the garden centre was to be the site of the
strike by the Ops team. I was to call the strike by simply scratching the
back of my head with my right hand. Pat seemed completely at ease

and I directed him to our car with my waiting colleague. He pulled up beside the car and we got out and went first of all to the boot of this car. I noticed that the time was 3.50 pm precisely. Pat was momentarily spooked by a guy unconnected to our operation, who pulled in and parked close by. Satisfied however that the guy wasn't a threat, Pat pulled a small bag from his pocket and told me it contained sample Es, which I could try: if I wanted more, he would do them at 500 at a time, he said. He also showed me samples of the luncheon vouchers he was carrying, which had twelve different serial numbers. By this time my companion had got out of the car and was watching my back. I could see a number of boxes and bags in the boot of Pat's car, including one of which was full of £50 notes, and four boxes of the luncheon vouchers. Satisfied that the goods were on the plot, I went over to our car, lifted our money bag from the boot and gave the strike signal.

In true Sweeney style, four large Granada cars packed with Flying Squad officers, wearing the traditional baseball caps, wielding baseball bats and God knows what else, swept into the car park at speed, and spilt their human contents onto the tarmac. Pat hadn't a clue as to what was happening, but my companion and I were already on our toes and sprinting across the car park, pursued by the Flying Squad's finest, who were screaming at us at the top of their voices. I was oblivious to everything, until I heard a phrase which made the hair on the back of my neck stand on end in terror: 'Stop or I shoot! I am an armed police officer—halt, or I shoot!' I couldn't recall anyone telling us at the briefing that they would have guns on the plot, I found myself thinking frantically.

Aware as I was that only the senior ranks of the team would know that this was an undercover operation, I looked over my shoulder and saw to my horror that the author of the threats was a very serious young Flying Squad cop with a large mop of red hair, who was now aiming his revolver very earnestly and shakily at my back.

I skidded to a halt and was almost simultaneously battered to the ground by the ensuing throng of baton-wielding cops. With my hands cuffed behind my back, I was dragged over to one of the Granada vehicles. Out of the corner of my eye, I could see my companion and the unfortunate Pat getting the same treatment. I was slammed up against the car, with my face held against the bonnet so I couldn't see what was happening. I don't think the Flying Squad realised it at the time, but their car engine had obviously been running for hours and you could have fried an egg on the surface of the bonnet: my face felt as if someone was holding a blow torch to it. I had visions of being called 'Scarface' for the rest of my life, and fought like a maniac, using my head and feet to down the two officers nearest to me. I was brought down again, and this time found myself pinned against the car boot, which at least was slightly colder. At this particular instant, and in one of those surreal moments which only seem to happen in such circumstances, a very well-dressed woman hurried past with her young son, who was clad in a uniform of black and white stripes, most likely from one of the big public schools. 'Look,' she scolded the boy in the *plummy* tones of an upper class English accent, as she pointed at the scene of the arrests, 'Look, that's the way you'll end up, if you don't mend your ways!' I would later ponder as to what this public school boy could have been up to himself, to warrant such a dire warning. A short time later, sanity reigned again, and I found myself escorted by the team leader to his car and taken from the scene. So ended the Adams family's first and last attempt to break into the Irish market…

On 14 April 2003, I was presented, on behalf of His Honour, Judge Stokes QC, with a written Court Commendation for my 'professionalism demonstrated at all times during (my) involvement in an investigation concerning conspiracy to supply Class 'A' drugs'. My own authorities never even acknowledged my contribution, or that of anyone else on the team in relation to the success of this case. In sharp contrast, some months after I had retired, I was summoned with the rest of the team by the Chief Constable of the Nottingham Police to attend a special function given in our honour. At this occasion, we were all personally thanked by the Chief Constable for our work in the case and handed our court awards. I was amazed to find that every Chief Officer in the force was present in uniform as a tribute to us. Later that evening, over a glass of wine, I pointed this out to the Chief Constable. He seemed a bit taken aback at my sense of surprise: 'Listen,' he said, 'you have risked your lives and assisted our Force in a very important inquiry, which has resulted in convictions and long sentences for those involved. It is surely the least my officers and I can do, to express our thanks.' This to me was better than any commendation or medal: the man genuinely meant it.

Chapter 9
A Bent Solicitor is Brought to Book

I was intrigued, to say the least, when in 1996 I was contacted by the Manchester Crime Squad to assist them in bringing a particularly bent solicitor to book. As a police officer of some experience, I had had dealings with various solicitors over the years, of course. Some of these had become personal friends; others I respected as professionals doing a difficult job. A small minority I wouldn't have broken bread with, as I knew they were in some cases worse than the clients they were defending. In Northern Ireland, as elsewhere in the UK, to openly criticise a solicitor or even to cast doubt on his or her reputation would leave you open to sniping from all quarters, from the judiciary down. So it was with some trepidation that we were to embark on Operation Annex.

From the outset it was clear that this would be no walk in the park. Considerable police and legal resources had been brought together to make sure that the case against the target would be watertight. To ensnare anyone in an undercover operation, you had to make sure there were no legal loopholes through which they could escape. As I have explained, our code of conduct as undercover officers was strictly defined, and could be enforced to the letter in a legal context. Imagine then how much more sound and irrefutable a case built through undercover activity would have to be to entrap a solicitor in his own web of deceit and criminality! For this reason, I myself and another two of the most experienced undercover officers in the United Kingdom had been brought together to work on this operation. We would be directed by a large and experienced Crime Squad staff which included legal officers from the Prosecutor's Office who would be able to advise us on every step of the way, if necessary.

The target in question was Tony Darnell, a high-flying criminal lawyer with a thriving practice, who had built a reputation on his willingness to take the Police on—and, it has to be said, with a fair measure of success in doing so. Darnell was, it seemed, an extremely wealthy man in his own right and had amassed an extensive property portfolio both in the UK and abroad. His confidence in his own abilities knew no bounds, and his arrogance was such that he seemed to enjoy taunting the police and legal authorities: half-jokingly, he would refer to himself as 'Rumpole of the Bailey', and boast openly within the criminal fraternity about being an expert in police surveillance techniques. He was certainly prepared to go to extraordinarily complex lengths to make sure he 'cleaned' himself after being involved in any shady dealings. And the dealings he was involved in were certainly shady: the Manchester authorities had very strong evidence to suggest that Darnell was involved in all kinds of serious criminal activity, including the supply of large quantities of drugs.

The legal department were insisting, quite rightly, that not only would Darnell have to instigate the criminal behaviour but that the evidence against him would have to be of the highest possible standard. The corresponding operation would therefore be complex and long-running: one incriminating meeting with Darnell would not be enough. Special care would have to be taken that we did not instigate any criminal conduct: the crimes would have to be 'laid on', as the jargon went, and instigated by Darnell. This was going to be a highly challenging case, both operationally and at the subsequent trial; of that there was no doubt.

Over and above all of this, there was a further consideration still. At our first briefing, we were told that there was more than a slight possibility that a number of local police officers and even detectives in the Crime Squad itself might be in the pay, or at the very least, under the influence, of Darnell. Subsequently, it had been decided at command level that, although we would have the remote support of a full Operational team, we would be acting in the field almost entirely on our own, in the sense that only a few of the senior investigating team would know our exact movements and our real identities. As it turned out, this was to prove a vital factor in the operation's eventual success.

———

It all began on a clear night in mid-April 1996, as several unsuspecting uniform patrol officers from Manchester's traffic division found themselves giving chase to a Northern Ireland registered car in the city's ring road area. After a protracted motorway chase, the vehicle in question was abandoned, with the undercover occupants making good their escape. The pursuing officers found 1,000 ecstasy tablets in the glove compartment of the abandoned car. Subsequent inquiries led to the arrest, in a nearby hotel, of the person renting the vehicle: a middle-aged woman who went under the name of Maggie Devlin, but was in reality a senior undercover officer. Maggie Devlin soon found herself awaiting interview in the cells of Stockport police station.

There was nothing random about the timing of the arrest of Maggie Devlin. This particular night, the duty solicitor was none other than Tony Darnell himself. The subsequent interview between Devlin and Darnell would be covertly taped by virtue of a High Court warrant. Yet again, that particularly unappealing trait of human nature—sheer greed—would win the day: for all his cunning and intelligence, Darnell would prove in this regard to be no different from any other common criminal.

During their first meeting, Maggie was able to intimate to our learned friend Darnell that she had a key to a safety deposit box, which she did not want to fall into police hands. Darnell actually offered to take the key, and made it his business to smuggle it out of the police station, take it to his own office premises and hide it in a flowerpot there! Thus began a series of meetings between Maggie and the bent solicitor, which started with the recovery of the key and soon led to a situation where Darnell was offering our undercover officer large quantities of drugs. On some occasions, Maggie would be accompanied by another undercover officer, in order to make her cover more credible. On every occasion on which they met, the conversations between Darnell and Maggie were recorded by means of covert tape recorders. Additional corroborative evidence was supplied by the army of surveillance operatives deployed whenever the meetings would take place.

The whole operation was backed up by a formidable professional covert umbrella, which included safe houses in Belfast, where Darnell would communicate with what he thought were Irish criminals. Ironically enough, Darnell himself would frequently warn these 'criminals', in reality of course undercover officers, about the particulars of police surveillance techniques, the dangers of bugging devices, and so on! He was evidently practised at covering his tracks and those of his accomplices, and even suggested, among other measures, to the undercover officers that, if they were ever stopped by police *en route* to his office with large amounts of cash for the drug shipments, they should say that the money was in fact the legitimate deposit for a house. More than once, Darnell actually gave these officers brochures on various properties in the Manchester area, which they could use as cover, should they ever be stopped and questioned! This guy was a pro, there was no doubt about that.

My role in the operation was to act as a courier, organising the collection of the drugs Darnell was supplying to Maggie from Brian Farrell, otherwise known as 'Benny the Mule'. Farrell was a well-known criminal associate of Darnell and his right-hand man in relation to his drug-dealing activities.

On 17 May 1996, I arrived in Manchester. I was met by a senior member of the Operational team, who briefed me and handed over a sports bag containing a covert listening device. Since the targets were expecting me to arrive by train at Manchester's Piccadilly station, I travelled to a location some distance from Manchester and boarded a city-bound train. I didn't know if I was being watched by the targets and their associates, so I was careful to arrive with plenty of time to spare, at around 4.00 pm, and made my way straight to the pre-arranged meeting place, a nearby café called Pepe's. Knowing that the area was under surveillance by the Operational team from at least one fixed observation point, I sat near the window, so that the team would be able to keep an eye on me. As was almost second nature to me by this stage, I immediately began to check out the other people in the room. Soon I was reasonably happy that all the other customers in the café were innocent enough—just ordinary people going about their everyday business.

Just before 4.45 pm, a man came into the café. He was of medium build and approximately 6'0" in height, with dark short hair and a moustache. Dressed in a dark checked sports jacket and black trousers and shoes, he had the smart, well-groomed appearance of an ex-Army officer, and was obviously someone who looked after himself. He had a rather distinguished air about him, and certainly didn't look like a common criminal, by any stretch of the imagination. This was obviously 'Benny the Mule'. He approached my table and asked me if I was alright. Before I had time to reply, he put his finger to his lips, gesturing me to keep quiet and said, 'Let's go.'

I followed my new friend outside and we turned right. Benny said that he was sorry for keeping me waiting, but they had been watching me for a while: they needed to be very careful, as this was the first trade we had done, and they had to be on the lookout for undercover cops. Whenever I heard criminals say this sort of thing—and they often did—I always wondered what they meant by it. How would they recognise an undercover cop, if they were to see one? Thankfully, these guys obviously hadn't a clue. I told Benny that I was hoping to get the 5.00 pm train back to Glasgow. He said it wasn't going to happen, as he had to leave now and wouldn't be back until 6.00 pm. He explained that, as it was the first time we had done business, things would take longer than usual. When he realised I didn't have a car with me, Benny suggested that I wait for him near the phone boxes close by at 6.00 pm, motioning to a nearby pub where I could pass the time until then.

Even with the best-laid plans, there is always the chance that something unexpected will happen and threaten to blow your cover. This turned out to be one of those occasions. I went into the bar Benny had pointed out, and surveyed the scene. The fact that he had suggested I wait there meant that there was a real possibility that some of his people were already planted there. I ordered myself a pint and stood at the bar, surveying the scene. Other than myself, there were a few punters playing the fruit machines, and a couple of drunks. There were also two female members of staff behind the bar, busy washing glasses. I had taken no more than a few sips of my pint, when I suddenly became aware of a presence to my right. Dressed in a long scruffy overcoat and with a rucksack over his shoulder, this guy was standing staring at me defiantly, like a dog squaring up for a fight. He had all the appearance of being completely deranged.

'What the fuck are you looking at?' the same individual slurred in a thick Glasgow accent that would have made Rab. C. Nesbitt proud. I noticed that he had his right hand hidden under his coat and was obviously holding something there. I glared at him with my best Belfast stare. 'Fuck off,' I spat. He glowered at me for a few seconds, rapidly weighing me up, and then, with a half-crazed laugh of recognition, he acknowledged me as a kindred Gaelic spirit: 'Irish, eh? We'll show these English bastards!' I was both horrified and bemused when he suddenly pulled out and began to brandish what was underneath his coat. It wasn't a gun, or a dirk, but it was obviously the new Gaelic weapon on the block: a huge, carved wooden…owl! What its significance was, I do not know—but this mad Glaswegian proceeded to systematically demolish every beer pump and glass he could find at the bar, much to the amusement of the rest of the punters in the place! It seemed that his rage had been piqued by the bar staff's earlier refusal to serve him anything to drink.

At the sight of this madman and his frenzied attack on the bar, the staff retreated into the back of the premises in hysterics. Locking themselves into a type of protective wire cage, they were screaming for help, shouting that they going to call the police. At this, I knew I had to get out, and fast. Any cops who came in response to the call would be sure to look on me as a witness—and if one of them was particularly zealous, and asked me for ID, they would doubtless want to know what Sean Murphy, a known Irish terrorist and gangster, was doing in their fair city. Especially since some of my deluded fellow countrymen had rearranged the centre of Manchester just a few months previously…

And so I had to abandon Rob Roy to his fate and beat a hasty retreat from the bar. I was able to watch from a distance as Manchester's finest arrived some time later, and after a battle royal, finally succeeded in carrying off my belligerent brother-in-arms.

I didn't have much time to recover my composure after such a close shave…At 6.00 pm sharp, I returned to the vicinity of the phone boxes to wait as arranged. A short time later, Benny appeared in a 7 series Rover car and I got in. We headed out of Manchester, and I could see from the road signs that we were travelling towards Stockport. During the drive, I received a number of calls on my covert mobile phone: it was the other undercover officer I was working with, asking what was happening. Benny was a bit unnerved by these calls, but of course I didn't give him any indication of who the caller was. I simply told him that it was my people, who were getting a bit nervous because I was taking so long. This wasn't too far from the truth, of course. Benny again apologised for the delays, assuring me that it wouldn't take so long the next time: they had had to run checks to make sure I was okay. Again, I wondered what exactly he meant by this, and my mind began to race ahead, imagining all sorts of possible scenarios.

We eventually arrived in Stockport and stopped at a pub in Mottram Street. Benny reversed the car into the rear of the car park out of sight from the doors of the pub, and went inside. I used the time he was away to search the car, and found a Commando knife in the glove compartment, along with papers with a Manchester address identifying Benny as Michael B. Farrell, and some other documents. Clearly these people weren't as switched on as they would have me believe.

After about fifteen minutes, Benny came back to the car, carrying a coloured plastic bag which he stowed in the boot. As we set off again, he gave me a small plastic bag which contained eight little paper packets. These, he said, were the speedballs we had been promised: we should try them out. Benny then drove us into the car park of another public house, just off the Scarcroft Road. This was a larger establishment than the last and sat well back from the road, surrounded by a very large car park. There were also quite a few punters' cars parked there. As we drove in, I saw a large skinhead guy sitting in a Mercedes car. I could see Benny making eye contact with this guy as we passed, but he gave no other outward sign of recognition. We drove around the car park once and then came back to park alongside the Mercedes. The skinhead stared straight ahead and, again, Benny made no movement towards him. Benny said I should go inside and order us both a pint: he had a quick errand to do. I went into the bar and chose a spot from which I could see the car park. I watched as Benny approached the skinhead in the car and engaged him in conversation. I got two pints of beer and took a seat in the bar.

A short time later, Benny appeared, with the skinhead in tow. As he lifted his pint, I could see that he was carrying the coloured plastic bag I had seen him with earlier. Walking over to a window seat, he threw the bag on the seat. He told me that there were 1,200 in each bag, and that I should take it and put it away. The skinhead, who bore a remarkably close resemblance to a gorilla, had yet to utter a word. Benny said that he was a friend, and, glancing over at the guy's bulk and sheer size, I remarked that I was very glad of that—which finally forced a smile from the skinhead. Benny then informed me that they had ordered me a taxi for 7.20 pm. The taxi arrived on the dot, and I took my leave of Benny and the Gorilla, shaking their hands. And that was that.

Later that evening, I gave the contents of the bag and the speedballs to the operational team as exhibits. We had secured a haul of almost 5,000 ecstasy tablets, which we were very happy with for a first operation. In order however to build a rock-solid case against Darnell and his cronies, we had to bring in more evidence. On 30 May 1996, I again found myself at Pepe's café in Manchester for a pre-arranged meet with the Darnell gang. This time I was wearing a Nagra tape recorder strapped to my back, and had a Vauxhall Astra car in a nearby car park, also fitted with a covert tape recorder.

I went into Pepe's at about 3.25 pm, and had just sat down when Benny came in at my heels. As before, he didn't speak, but beckoned me outside. I followed him across the road and stood there as he got into his car. He spoke to me through the car window, and beckoned towards the footwell of the car, where I could see a small bag of tablets in a plastic bag. He told me to take this, and that meanwhile he had to go and get the rest of the drugs. Benny still seemed very nervous generally, and was obviously waiting to see if he was going to be suddenly ambushed. He collected me later again, as arranged, at 4.45 pm near the telephone boxes in Ducie Street.

As soon as Benny picked me up, he drove off at speed, and immediately cut right across the traffic in a blatant anti-surveillance move. As with any target behaving in this fashion, Benny was making me feel very uneasy, to say the least. With this type of scenario, you never really knew where you stood: when targets were as paranoid as this, they could suddenly insist on searching you. All you could do was hope that the surveillance umbrella wasn't too far away. Yet even if they were close by, that knowledge in itself wouldn't always be enough to stop the hairs on the back of your neck from standing on end in fearful anticipation. The bulky Nagra tape recorder strapped to your back would always be a dead giveaway if your criminal friends did decide to search you after all.

On the way to our destination, and as I had been briefed earlier to do, I pulled Benny up on the large number of apparent breakages in the last consignment. He muttered something about the fact that the drugs came across from the Continent in sealed plastic packages, and that as such they had little control over breakages, etc. However, he said that they had included some extra gear in this consignment as compensation for the breakages.

This time, Benny left me to wait in a bookmakers on the Hyde Road, telling me that he would be back soon. As the time passed, I became aware that the tape running in my car wouldn't last, so I walked out of the bookies to check it. I turned it off. I'd had it with me as a precautionary measure, really—in case Benny had decided that we would be travelling in my car rather than his. In these situations, you never really knew how things were going to unfold: all you could do was go with the flow of what the targets suggested and hope that you would have the wherewithal to get the covert recordings you needed.

This time, standing beside my car just outside the bookies, I had, yet again, another very close call. Just at that moment, Benny pulled up, sitting in the passenger side of a black xr3i which was driven by my friend the Gorilla. I just about had time to flick on the recorder again without being seen. The Gorilla seemed very agitated. Benny asked why I was now outside the bookmakers, instead of waiting inside as per his instructions, and I improvised quickly, telling him that the staff had been getting suspicious of me hanging about for so long and that I was afraid of them calling the police. This seemed to keep him happy for the time being. Benny got out of the car and started to walk up the road and, following him, I could see he had a bag under his arm. He went into a kebab shop, ordered a kebab and then threw me the plastic bag he had been carrying. A few minutes later, the Gorilla pulled up in his car again, still highly agitated. Benny jumped in beside him and they both roared off. I got a kebab and started to dander towards the City with my bag of drugs. I walked to a taxi rank and got a taxi to my Astra car.

The subsequent two-hour debrief with the Operational team revealed another haul of almost 5,000 'E's in the bag which Benny had handed me. My third and last meeting with him was on 19 June 1996. Things proceeded very much according to the pattern established during our first two encounters, and yet again, yielded an excellent result: another lot of around 5,000 'E's. The only slightly uneasy moment was at the end of the meet, when Benny warned me off using the black taxis in the area, denouncing them as 'grassing bastards'. I was left wondering what exactly had given rise to this outburst.

On 27 June 1996, all the principal players in Darnell's set-up, and most of their hangers-on, were arrested in a major swoop by the Manchester Crime Squad. The principals were remanded in custody and the case was conducted at Chester Crown Court between 28 May and 5 June the following year. Darnell was sentenced to eleven years' imprisonment, and his two main associates, of whom one was Benny (i.e. Brian Farrell), got eight years and five years respectively. The Manchester police were also able to apply for a number of asset recovery orders against Darnell.

In December 1997 I was commended by the Chief Constable of the Greater Manchester Police and awarded a written citation for displaying '…skill, professionalism and courage during Operation Annex'. By this stage, our new team in Belfast were beginning to establish a bit of a reputation as the golden boys of the undercover world—the new secret weapon in the undercover war against organised crime. We were suddenly in constant demand, although we were usually brought in as a last resort when standard tactics and procedures had failed. It certainly wasn't always plain sailing, and when the wheel did come off our plans, there were times when we found ourselves in very tricky situations indeed. Yet the adrenalin rush at times like these was undeniable, and some of the most dangerous operations could also be the most exciting.

Chapter 10
More Successes and Muddy Pools

One of the Detective Sergeants I worked with in Castlereagh in the late nineties used to remark cynically to me every once in a while, albeit in a light-hearted way, 'Boss, you're the only cop I know who checks his car *inside* the barracks!' I didn't start out in life with a naturally dim view of my fellow human beings, however. The truth is that I had learned through bitter experience that, when push comes to shove, there are very few people who can truly be trusted, even among those you should in theory be able to trust.

Just as very early on in my career in the police force, I was forced to revise my innocent assumption that telling the truth to one's colleagues and superiors always pays, later experiences would make me painfully aware that it was just as naïve to assume that every police officer always acted with the most honourable of motives and the most honest intentions. As if our fight as undercover officers against organised crime wasn't difficult enough, there was also the sickening phenomenon of inside corruption to contend with: those unscrupulous colleagues who would be actively collaborating with the very criminals we were trying to defeat. After one particularly unpleasant encounter with such 'dirty cops', which I shall now relate, I was determined to play my cards very close to my chest in the future. The problem was however that even when the bad guys had been weeded out, you could never be quite sure that the corruption wasn't more widespread than you had originally thought.

In 1997, the drugs trade in Northern Ireland was flourishing to such an extent that the street price of specific drugs was falling considerably, and it was clear that there was more than one organised gang involved in their importation. We knew that Loyalist criminal gangs and terrorists had for some time been cashing in on the lucrative drug trade, but now it was obvious, from both the quality and quantity of the drugs that were readily available on the local market, that there was a degree of organisation and sophistication behind the whole operation which we knew to be beyond the capabilities of such Loyalist groups. We were actively on the trail of a number of the 'godfathers' behind it all, and had identified a strong connection between certain so-called businessmen in Northern Ireland, most of whom were masquerading as car dealers, an activity which of course provided the perfect cover for moving illicit goods, the exchange of large sums of cash, and the laundering of such income. Painstaking conventional detective work, backed up with good intelligence and very effective agents, had enabled us to achieve a number of significant successes. Increasingly, we were finding ourselves able to intercept incoming shipments of drugs, disrupting supply routes and obstructing couriers. With each success, our understanding of the criminal infrastructure behind the whole operation was growing, and we had been able to identify a distinct triangle of activity going on between criminal gangs on the UK mainland (in Liverpool and London), in Northern Ireland and in Dublin.

We were particularly interested in one individual in Northern Ireland who appeared to be at the centre of everything here. He had a relatively sophisticated set-up and would only speak in code in telephone conversations and on pagers. However, as a result of a good deal of meticulous detective work, we not only had been able to map out his supply routes and identify his associates, but more importantly, had managed to break his code. He was money-laundering through a number of businesses which he had set up for his relatives: these businesses included a City centre public house, a clothes shop and a large confectionary concern. He himself was masquerading as a car dealer—which, as I have said, was the ideal front for his drug trading activities. He would habitually trawl various auctions near Liverpool, purchasing a few cars at a time. He would then arrange for caches of drugs to be concealed in these vehicles, which would be left at the original car dealers' premises for perhaps a

Clady border checkpoint—'The Last Frontier'. (*Pacemaker*)

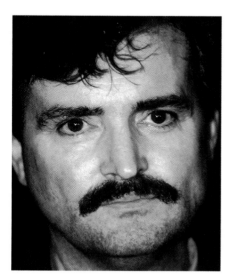

Michael Stone; the face of a
psychotic killer and fantasist.
(*PA Photos*)

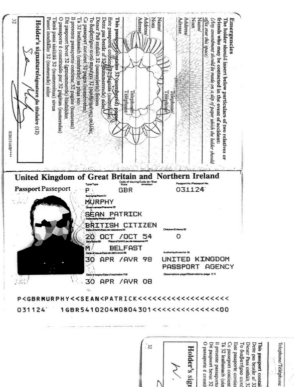

United Kingdom of Great Britain and Northern Ireland

Passport Passeport

Type/Type: P
Code of Issuing/Code de l'État amateur: GBR
Passport No./Passeport No.: 031124

Surname/Nom (1): MURPHY
Given names/Prénoms (2): SEAN PATRICK
Nationality/Nationalité (3): BRITISH CITIZEN
Date of birth/Date de naissance (4): 20 OCT /OCT 54
Sex/Sexe (5): M
Place of birth/Lieu de naissance (6): BELFAST
Date of issue/Date de délivrance (7): 30 APR /AVR 98
Children/Enfants (9): 0
Authority/Autorité (8): UNITED KINGDOM PASSPORT AGENCY
Date of expiry/Date d'expiration (10): 30 APR /AVR 08
Observations-page/Observations-page (11):

```
P<GBRMURPHY<<SEAN<PATRICK<<<<<<<<<<<<<<<<<<<<
031124    1GBR5410204M0804301<<<<<<<<<<<<<00
```

United Kingdom of Great Britain and Northern Ireland

Passport Passeport

Type/Type: P
Code of Issuing/Code de l'État amateur: GBR
Passport No./Passeport No.: 0200222

Surname/Nom (1): CRAIG
Given names/Prénoms (2): WILLIAM
Nationality/Nationalité (3): BRITISH CITIZEN
Date of birth/Date de naissance (4): 20 OCT /OCT 54
Sex/Sexe (5): M
Place of birth/Lieu de naissance (6): BELFAST
Date of issue/Date de délivrance (7): 27 SEP /SEPT 95
Children/Enfants (9): 0
Authority/Autorité (8): UNITED KINGDOM PASSPORT AGENCY
Date of expiry/Date d'expiration (10): 27 SEP /SEPT 05
Observations-page/Observations-page (11):

```
P<GBRCRAIG<<WILLIAM<<<<<<<<<<<<<<<<<<<<<<<<<
0200222   6GBR5410204M0509271<<<<<<<<<<<<<06
```

Commendation in 'Operation Boom'.

CITY OF LONDON POLICE

This Merit Certificate has been awarded by
Detective Chief Superintendent Patrick P. Crossan

to

Detective Inspector

for

his professionalism with which he conducted himself
in an investigation that led to the charging of four
persons who were engaged in a series of attempts
to obtain funds in excess of £4 Million by
fraudulent bank transfers.

November 1997

P.P Crossan
Specialist Crime Department

Certificate of Commendation in the Rasta conspiracy, City of London.

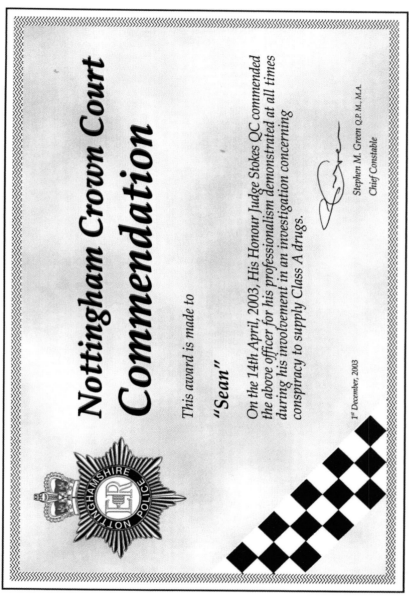

Nottingham Crown Court
Commendation

This award is made to

"Sean"

On the 14th April, 2003, His Honour Judge Stokes QC commended the above officer for his professionalism demonstrated at all times during his involvement in an investigation concerning conspiracy to supply Class A drugs.

1st December, 2003

Stephen M. Green Q.P.M., M.A.
Chief Constable

Certificate of Commendation, Nottingham Operations.

Tony Darnell, Mr Untouchable.
(*Manchester Evening News*)

Nine bars of cannabis
en route to a
handover under
armed guard.

Brendan 'Speedy' Fegan (left), enjoying the highlife but destined to die in a hail of bullets by DAAD.

Vacuum-sealed bags of ecstasy, 1,000 tablets in each, Dutch style.

Detective Superintendent Eddie Rock of the Garda Drugs Squad with some of the five million pounds worth of drugs seized in Cork. (*Photocall Ireland*)

Robert Briggs-Price, the Don of Nottingham. (*PA Photos*)

Photo of 18,000 ecstasy tablets in a hold-all originally destined for Cork, seized in Belfast city centre.

week or so, and would then be collected by one of the legitimate car transporters operating regularly between the UK mainland and Ireland. The cars would be delivered to various well-disposed local car dealers, where our friend would keep the vehicles under observation for a while, before eventually sending some of his minions to pick them up, take them to a secluded spot and remove the drugs. The whole process was more or less risk-free for the individual in question, especially since he kept his own involvement very much 'hands off'. The hub of the drugs operations, from which the drugs would be supplied to Ireland both north and south, was Liverpool. The revenue which this trading activity was generating was mind-boggling. We knew that payments for the drugs were being made to a particular individual at an upmarket, private address in Liverpool on a weekly basis by a courier from Belfast, who was delivering bin bags stuffed full of cash.

As part of our routine investigatory procedures, I had put in a request, through our ACC Crime to the Detective Chief Inspector of Liverpool Drugs Squad, that the house to which the payments were being delivered was to be kept under surveillance. I had sent a full intelligence briefing with the request, which should have made the whole thing plain sailing for them. Some months further down the line, however, I still hadn't had any feedback from the Liverpool team. Telephone calls to their Drugs Squad failed to elicit any meaningful replies, and follow-up reports and requests went unanswered, which was strange, to say the least.

During our investigations, we had zeroed in on a woman who was working in tandem with the main gang in Liverpool, and who, we had been able to determine, was responsible for supplying most of the heroin coming into the Ballymena area. In relation to this, we had identified an opportunity to make an undercover intervention, and it was decided that I would travel to the Liverpool area to talk the matter over with the Detective Inspector in charge of their Undercover Unit, which was undoubtedly one of the most advanced in the UK, second only perhaps to that of the Met. The Liverpool unit was a covert outfit in the true sense of the word: their very existence was known of only by a few senior officers in the Force, and their operatives, who never went anywhere near a conventional police station, were based in an off-site location which fronted as a normal business operation. I had been told that the unit had had some security problems: just how bad these were would soon become evident...

While I was in Liverpool meeting with their Detective Inspector, I took the opportunity to mention to him the problems I was having with their Drugs Squad, namely their failure to comply with any of our requests or provide any follow-up regarding the surveillance of the drug dealers' main house. The Detective Inspector seemed more than usually intrigued by my story, and when I said that I smelled a rat, and wanted to have the matter out directly with their Drugs Squad, he willingly agreed to take me across Liverpool to their Drugs Headquarters.

On our arrival there, we were shown up to the Drugs Squad main offices, where we were greeted by a fat Inspector in a very brash pin-striped suit which would have done an upscale barrister proud. The man's mouth was as loud as his suit, and I found I could hardly get a word in edgeways, as this buffoon proceeded to tell me all about his career to date, his glowing prospects for promotion and God knows what else. He would gladly talk about anything, it seemed, except the surveillance request about which I was there to inquire. Each time I broached the issue, he just blanked me completely.

After a short time, we were joined by the Detective Chief Inspector of the Unit, who struck me as a dodgy character the moment I set eyes on him. He looked like a nonce, and dressed like one too, with long, crimped hair hanging in ringlets on his shoulders. Like his subordinate, he simply ignored every attempt I made to ask about our request for surveillance on the house. The Detective Inspector who had accompanied me just sat there beside me, obviously deeply embarrassed about the whole situation. I, however, was having none of it, and had decided that these were bent coppers, no doubt about it. I brought the proceedings to a rapid conclusion by demanding answers: had they or had they not done anything at all in relation to our request? They just stared at me blankly again. I couldn't hold my feelings back any longer, and began telling these excuses for police officers in plain Belfast speak—no holds barred—exactly what I thought of them, that they were bent as a nine bob note and could go f*** themselves as far as I was concerned. They obviously weren't used to anyone being quite so blunt with them, and began to protest loudly that they were deeply shocked and offended by my behaviour. Ignoring their protests, I stormed out of their office with my companion in tow. He was chortling to himself: he couldn't believe that I had just said what I did, but promised to raise the matter directly with his ACC.

I returned to Belfast to follow another line of inquiry in the investigation. What I didn't know at the time was that my intuition had been spot on. It subsequently emerged that the Detective Chief Inspector in question was indeed bent, and had in fact been under constant surveillance by a special internal investigation squad, even during the time we had spoken. No doubt the surveillance guys had had something to keep themselves amused that particular evening, as they listened to the tapes from that day! The reason that the Detective Chief Inspector had consistently ignored my requests was that he himself was a drug dealer, in cahoots with most of the criminal mafia in the city of Liverpool. Shortly thereafter he would be arrested on charges of corruption and would later be given a long-term prison sentence.

As I have already said, the problem with corruption within the force was that you never knew just how far—or how high up—the rot had spread. Unfortunately for me as regards the case in question, the corruption would not end there. Not long after my encounter with the said Detective Chief Inspector, our main drug dealing target in Northern Ireland was to receive the following message on his pager: 'All pager and phones compromised: close down immediately.' The language itself was highly suspect: this was hardly the sort of terminology that would have been used by the ordinary criminal on the street—it was more consistent with someone who moved in military or police circles. I would be dogged for a long time by the conviction that there was a mole very highly placed within our own ranks—but that is another story. Suffice to say that from this point on, I would tread very carefully in terms of whom I kept in the loop regarding our covert activities.

In spite of the bent Detective Chief Inspector and his cohorts, the Liverpool undercover operation went ahead as planned. Our undercover officer travelled to Liverpool and, with the back-up of one of the specialist Liverpool team, arranged a meet with a target called Linda, who was operating from a council housing estate in the city. Linda offered to supply us with heroin and ecstasy tablets, to be delivered to Belfast by one of her couriers. A few weeks later, after a high speed chase in the Malone Road area of Belfast, we were able to intercept the courier with the consignment in question, while the Liverpool Crime Squad moved in and made important arrests at the Liverpool end. This wouldn't unfortunately stop the heroin trail between the mainland and Northern Ireland, but it did close down this particular avenue—a significant one—for some time.

Chapter 11

Fighting the System: Operation Thresher

Insider dirty dealings were one thing, but sometimes during my career as an undercover officer, it was truly difficult not to believe that the workings of the legal system within which we were operating had been put in place to actually make our lives more difficult, rather than facilitating our job.

A good example of how an overly bureaucratic system could only get in our way was the legislation whereby numerous authorisations and permits would have to be sought each and every time we had to operate across force boundaries and national borders—something which, in the fight against international drug trafficking, was self-evidently part and parcel of our *raison d'être*. And it was of course all doubly frustrating, given the fact that the criminals we were up against were able to operate entirely unrestricted by national borders or any of the many political or legal problems which the police and security agents of both the UK and Éire would have to deal with. In simplistic and hypothetical terms, a criminal from Dublin could, within the space of a single day, travel to London to arrange a drug deal, collect the drugs and return home via Holyhead in Wales or Stranraer in Scotland with the consignment on his or her person, all without the slightest notice being taken. If, on the other hand, an on-duty police officer actively pursuing a criminal in the process of committing a crime needs to pass through the three jurisdictions of Ireland, England and Scotland or Wales, the regulations and agreed protocols are such that he or she will have to notify each of the forces in question, with all the paperwork and written authorisations which this involves. In theory, this could take weeks. In the case of an undercover operation involving, say, the movement of drugs through different force areas, the written permission of an officer of at least ACC level would be required for each of the regions in question. Again, this would generally entail a mountain of paperwork and perhaps hundreds of hours of administrative work. Police officers could therefore spend days if not weeks in seeking bureaucratic nonsense, while drug pushers and the like could continue with their sleazy dealings unhindered.

One operation which was to prove how self-defeating it could be to have to jump through such bureaucratic hoops when moving across force boundaries was Operation Thresher. This had been in many senses a routine undercover anti-drugs operation which had started off in the Rotterdam area, as was often the case. We had infiltrated the gang at the Dutch end and had been able to monitor the handover of a large consignment of some 250 kilos of cannabis to one of their lorry drivers bound for Ireland. We had been involved in an early stage in the chain and had been able to extract ourselves from the equation at the first opportunity. As I have suggested previously, in terms of any undercover operation, this was of course the perfect position to be in: all we had to do now was sit back and take the parcel out at a time of our choosing, without the bad guys ever being able to work out where exactly their weak link had been.

Although we weren't in direct control of the goods, we knew they were in the criminals' lorry, which, as a HGV (Heavy Goods Vehicle), was relatively easy to keep under normal surveillance. We were expecting the vehicle to travel overnight from Rotterdam and then make its way directly to Ireland, most likely via Liverpool. Our intention was to intercept the drugs whenever those who were to pick it up showed themselves. Although our said actions no longer required authorisation as a full-blown undercover operation (since we had extracted our undercover officers by this stage), we still had the necessary cover in place and paperwork cleared, and had made the required arrangements with Customs, with whom we were working closely to provide a minimum of surveillance, in case of any emergency which could occur en route to Ireland.

What we couldn't have anticipated was that, either by accident or design, their driver, having arrived in Liverpool where we expected him to board the ferry, suddenly took off in the direction of London. I and some of my team had been tailing the HGV from a very discreet distance, in a covert vehicle. By the time we had got as far as Liverpool, we were all shattered and looking forward to a warm bath at home. The gang's lorry driver had even got as far as the booking office and had returned to his vehicle, as we thought, to await the boarding of the ferry. Suddenly however he had taken the lorry out of line and headed back onto the motorway southwards towards London. If the surveillance team onsite hadn't been keeping a tight watch on the vehicle, we would have missed him completely.

Had we judged the situation wrongly, and were the drugs actually destined for the English market instead of for Ireland? We had to go with the flow now, however, and we were thankfully able to enlist the further assistance of the National Crime Squad, with whom we decided to simply keep watching, to see as far as we could what was going to happen next.

As it transpired, the vehicle had obviously been rerouted to make some more routine pickups en route to Ireland and at one site, we were convinced, had even taken a further consignment of drugs onboard. Now our real problems began. Although the tasking had been under the protective umbrella of the National Crime Squad up until this point, it was now becoming increasingly clear that we had a journey ahead which would take us right through England and Scotland, and some twelve different Force areas. It didn't help our general level of comfort either that the vehicle we were travelling in had by this time all the outward and inward appearance of a refuse cart—and I'm pretty sure that we ourselves smelt accordingly! In terms of clothing and washing plans, we certainly hadn't anticipated this delay and we had been living on a diet of burgers, crisps and coke.

As our original authorisation no longer applied, we had to frantically attempt to contact an officer of at least ACC rank in each Force area to get permission to pass through their jurisdictions, which some of them seemed to regard as their actual fiefdoms! Part of the reason that the National Crime Squad had been brought into being in the first place was to circumvent a lot of this bureaucratic nonsense, but the master plan behind it all was still in its infancy, and Chief Constables and their underlings were reluctant to have outsiders crossing their boundaries. And the mention of the Irish police would send them into a further spin. Therefore, during any downtime, when the lorry was loading, or the driver was having a meal break or enforced rest, we would career into the nearest police station and start frantically telephoning and faxing for permissions. Some officers couldn't do enough for us, and willingly gave us verbal permission there and then. Some from other areas however came close to deliberate obstruction, demanding reports in triplicate from senior officers in the National Crime Squad and from our own Force at home. There were times when it was very difficult not to believe that there were some who didn't want us to succeed at all! Eventually, however, we managed to reach Stranraer and catch up with the driver. We were both mentally and physically exhausted, it is true, but in the end it proved to be worth all the hassle. When the lorry landed in Belfast and some well-known faces turned up for the slaughter of the drugs, we were able to make a number of significant arrests and recover some 200 kilos of cannabis in nine bars. This was one of the biggest seizures to date in Ireland at that time.

Chapter 12
Operation Plover and a Very Close Call

Shortly after our return from our travels on Operation Thresher, we got an opportunity to pay back our London friends in kind for their assistance and hospitality in this and earlier operations. The job we were subsequently to become involved in was to take me as close to death at the hands of criminals as I had ever been before, or would wish to be again. The circumstances of Operation Plover are etched indelibly in my memory, along with those other moments in my career when it seemed that for me anyway, the game was finally up.

London Regional Crime Squad had asked for our help in relation to a target who for some time had eluded all their attempts to bring him to book as one of the biggest counterfeiters in the south of England. Philpot was the son of a wealthy businessman and headed up a crime syndicate which not only specialised in high-calibre counterfeit operations, but also masterminded armed security heists and indeed virtually every other type of criminal undertaking under the sun. As always, the gang were eager to expand their activities and influence by working with other criminal groups. They were also keen to get a foothold into the Irish market, which they felt was in many ways more secure than their own. This is where our undercover unit in Belfast came in. Through months of good conventional detective work, along with expert intervention by other undercover officers, the London Regional Crime Squad had managed to engineer a set of circumstances in which Philpot, the 'Don' of this particular mob, wanted to meet my alias Billy Craig, who had been referenced to him as a leading Irish gangster and criminal with Loyalist paramilitary connections. More specifically, the rumour had been put about that Billy Craig and his gang were looking for printing plates for counterfeit £20 and £50 notes of the highest possible quality—which, according to our intelligence, Philpot had in his possession and was looking to sell on.

At our initial briefing on Plover, the Crime Squad Commanders placed great emphasis on the fact that Philpot and his people were highly dangerous criminals who generally carried arms, and had been known in the past to simply wipe out those who represented a threat to them or their plans. A lot of groundwork had already been done in previous months by other undercover operatives, in terms of gathering intelligence on the gang. One officer in particular had spent a considerable time with these thugs in their East London drinking dens. He had been able to testify to the fact that, under the influence of a mixture of coke and alcohol and God knows what else, members of the gang had shown themselves, with very little provocation, to be highly volatile and capable of the most vicious acts of violence. On one occasion during a lunchtime meeting in a well-known drinking den, the proceedings had been interrupted when one of Philpot's lieutenants learned that a female traffic warden had just put a ticket on his sports car, parked on the pavement outside. Without a word, this thug nonchalantly left the bar and sauntered out onto the street, to the general amusement of his cronies. The laughter soon turned to silence however at the sound of approaching police sirens, and as the word went round to rapidly split the scene.

Outside on the pavement, the poor traffic warden lay in a pool of blood with serious facial wounds. It would later take some 100 stitches to tack her slashed features together. It was a terrifying demonstration of the violent unpredictability of this gang, who had no respect whatsoever for the normal laws of civilised society...

The risk assessment on the operation was such that it was decided to take the unusual step of sending a total of three undercover officers to the plot together: this reinforced for us the extent to which the threat which these people represented was perceived by the Crime Squad as very real indeed. As Billy Craig, I was to be accompanied by two other Irish colleagues, who would act as my associates and bodyguards. The idea was that, if rumbled, the three of us could at least hold our corner until the cavalry arrived. Well, that was the master plan, anyway. It was also decided that only I would carry a covert recorder: our hope was that, as the boss of the Irish mob, Philpot's lot wouldn't dare to search me. In addition, we had a full, dedicated surveillance team with armed back-up.

And so it was that at approximately 11.00 am one weekday morning, we three Irish Musketeers found ourselves standing at a pre-arranged meeting place on the country-bound lane of a dual carriageway near Vauxhall on the outskirts of London. We had no idea about who was going to meet us, but suddenly a white two-door Ford XR2i, driven by one of the hugest creatures I have ever seen, pulled up abruptly in front of us. The driver had hair in proportion to his bulk, and these tresses hung over his shoulders like a lion's mane. He grunted a greeting, pulled the passenger seat forward, and motioned for me to get into the back of the car. As soon as I had done so, he banged the seat down again, and, with another grunt, beckoned for one of my companions to get into the front.

My colleague had barely sat down when the car roared off again, leaving one of our threesome standing there, frantically telephoning the back-up team to break the news: that the wheel was off the master plan, big time! Our number now reduced to two, we were at the mercy of our maniacal driver, who sped off down the dual carriageway and then, without any warning, mounted the central reservation, spun the car into a 180 degree turn, and headed off in the other direction. I caught the eye of the other undercover officer in the driver's mirror, and saw the expression of alarm on his face: I knew what he, like me, was thinking—'That'll certainly f*** up surveillance for a while anyway.' Our mad chauffeur then proceeded to take us on an urban safari, hurtling at breakneck speeds through housing estates and back roads, thereby ensuring that there wasn't a hope in hell that the surveillance team could keep track of the car.

Sometime later, we careered to a halt at a roundabout. At this point, our driver leant over, flicked open the passenger door, and with one push propelled my unfortunate colleague in the front seat out of the car and onto the ground on his butt. 'Sorry, mate, I was told only to bring you—you know how it is,' he muttered, without even looking at me. 'Oh no, why me?' I thought, and as I leant back into my seat, the Nagra recorder reminded me of its presence at the base of my spine.

Off we roared again into the countryside at suicidal speed. This time I knew I was completely on my own, and with the realisation, I had a sinking feeling in my stomach. In hindsight, it was clear that the crooks' plan, although simple in its execution thus far, had been carefully thought out. There had been nothing sophisticated about any of it—the choice of car, the driver, the urban safari and everything else—but the whole strategy had been highly effective and basically foolproof. The Crime Squad's surveillance umbrella had been completely thrown off the scent, within a matter of minutes.

As we sped through the countryside, I was frantically trying to spot a landmark or some other sign as to where we may have been, but to no avail. My hairy friend didn't speak during our journey at all, and any attempts I made to engage him in conversation were either ignored or greeted with a non-committal grunt. After a while however he slowed down and I caught sight of a sign for a health farm on our left. We careered into the car park, where, despite the hot weather, a middle-aged gentleman with a shaved head was standing, wearing, of all things, a heavy duffle coat. On catching sight of him, my chauffeur at last spoke unprompted, volunteering the information that this guy's name was 'Mick', and he had just done a ten-stretch for a security job. Perhaps this was an attempt to impress me, but in the situation I found myself, it wasn't the sort of detail I was keen to learn! The giant then parked near the steps of the main building, which had all the appearance of an old country house.

My hairy friend walked with me into the foyer of the house, where we were greeted by a rather slick-looking young guy of about twenty five, who was dressed in a smart suit and grinning from ear to ear. He intimated that I should go over with him to the young lady behind the reception desk; then he mumbled something to her and threw her a £20 note. To my horror, the receptionist proceeded to hand me a towel and a pair of flip-flops. My blood ran cold in my veins: 'Christ,' I thought, 'I have a bloody Nagra taped onto my spine, it's hardly micro-sized!' My stomach was in a complete knot. All I could think about was a film I had once seen, a Bond movie, I think, in which the hero arranges to meet one of his enemies in a sauna—a ruse to ensure that no-one can tape the conversation. Real life isn't like the movies, however. They never tell you about times like these in training. Moments of sheer, cold terror which, thankfully, you only experience once or twice in your life. My mind was racing with panic-stricken thoughts, whilst as if on automatic pilot I followed my criminal pals to the large staircase beyond the reception desk. Every step was bringing me closer to my personal Armageddon.

It is part of the human psyche, however, that when you are confronted with such situations, the huge adrenalin rush which is delivered to your brain takes over and you see things with absolute clarity. In front of me, on the bend of the stairs, was a large bay window. Perhaps I could go through it? It looked substantial, however: I would probably just bounce off it, knowing my luck. 'My God, nobody even knows where I am,' my thoughts were chattering.

At this point, I was convinced I was in serious trouble: it was one of those few moments in my life in which I really thought I could die. I kept my nerve, however—maybe it was my training kicking in, somehow. I knew that if I panicked, there was very little chance of my walking away from this unscathed. 'Right,' I thought, 'as soon as we start to strip off, I'll pretend I have the runs and try in some way to stuff this Nagra on my back down the loo.' The Nagra was by this stage feeling as obtrusive as a camel's hump.

To my very great relief however it turned out that life isn't always like the movies after all—and in this instance, thank Christ. Instead of leading me into a sauna, my slick friend in the suit suddenly grabbed my towel and threw it onto a chair. 'In here,' he motioned, opening a door which led to a large bar area, where approximately ten hangers-on were playing pool and drinking. A cloud of cigarette smoke hung below the ceiling. Some health spa!

I didn't know whether to cry or laugh. These cretins however obviously thought I was beaming from ear to ear in greeting instead of from heartfelt relief, and a few of the pool players waved. I was taken through a gap in a divider in the room, and there sat my target, like some Mafia don, behind a farcically large director's desk. He rose to greet me. He was a lot younger than I had expected, but was obviously in command of the situation. The next hour was spent talking about how much the counterfeit master plates would cost us. Every so often, the Don would start bragging about how tightly run his organisation was, and how many times in the past they had blown Crime Squad operations and rumbled undercover cops. 'They'll never get me on tape,' he boasted. Words he would shortly have all the time in the world to regret, as it turned out!

Nevertheless, it was to a greatly relieved Operational team that I was able to report my whereabouts an hour or later, once I had been dropped off at a garage on a roundabout in the middle of a nearby housing estate. Needless to say, it was Billy Craig himself who was most relieved of all. I was, thankfully, unharmed after my ordeal—and definitely a few pounds lighter too...

Chapter 13
Walking Away

Just as there would be many times when our work would result in the successful seizure of drugs or illicit goods and the arrest of felons, there would occasionally be times too when we would have to abort an operation, and let the bad guys walk. This was never easy for us to do, or for the public to understand, but our reasons would always be compelling ones—if, for example, our operation was cutting across a more serious or important initiative by another agency, or if there were compelling security reasons to be considered. There were also the rare occasions on which the baddies couldn't actually deliver the goods or commodities they had promised, and when for operational reasons we would be forced to withdraw from the job in order to preserve our own integrity or that of the sources who had 'referenced us in'. Thankfully, these times were rare, and I would only experience them a few times in my career.

One such operation came about in late 1996, as the result of a request for assistance from by the Undercover Unit of the Met's Regional Crime Squad. Some of their men had, it seemed, come across two individuals of particular interest during the course of another large-scale operation. One of the suspect individuals was a Palestinian guy, who allegedly had associates with links to the PLO (Palestine Liberation Organisation). The other was a Londoner of mixed Turkish origin. Both of these men were putting it about in criminal circles that they were able to supply large quantities of counterfeit currency, and in particular very good quality, high denomination Bank of England notes. They also alleged that they were involved in the illicit movement of top-of-the-range sports cars and land cruisers to the Far East via Europe. The Crime Squad were asking if we could infiltrate the group these men was involved in, in order to ascertain the veracity of their claims. Perhaps because of their own origins and possible terrorist connections, it seemed that these two men were particularly interested in making contacts within, and supplying to, the Irish market, and this would be our 'in'. We were introduced to them as Irish criminals with paramilitary connections.

Our first meeting with the two suspects took place in London's Heathrow Airport, through an intermediary. The Londoner introduced himself as 'Farqu', and was a second or third generation Turkish guy, approximately thirty years old and with jet black hair and moustache. Apart from a slight foreign accent, his English was perfect. He introduced his associate to us as 'Ahmed'. Ahmed was in his mid-thirties, and dressed in a good quality, three-quarter length tan leather jacket, designer jeans and expensive shoes. He also spoke English, but not as well as Farqu, and with a heavy accent. It seemed that he preferred to communicate with Farqu in French, in which he was fluent.

From the outset, our briefing had been somewhat vague, as the Crime Squad seemed to be as yet unsure of the real capabilities of our two friends. During the first meeting, Ahmed told us that he dealt in high-end private vehicles, which he sold to his friends in the Middle East: top-of-the-range jeeps and Mercedes, which he would steal to order. He had many connections in the PLO, he said, and was able to move these stolen vehicles across Europe to his friends in Palestine. The Crime Squad were later able to confirm this as a distinct possibility: they had intelligence that millions of pounds' worth of such vehicles were arriving in the Middle East via this route every year. The problem was such, in fact, that a special unit had been set up within the Crime Squad to deal specifically with this issue. I had been reliably informed that one in three vehicles in the West Bank and Beirut were believed to have had a dodgy past. Once the vehicles in question reached their destination, it was of course highly unlikely that they would ever be seen again, and the Crime Squad special unit was not about to take off to the Middle East and start checking out stolen vehicles on site.

It quickly became clear to us that Ahmed was prepared to deal in anything from which money could be made, be it stolen cars, guns or drugs. As per usual, we had been reminded at our briefing of the carefully defined limits within which we could operate and that, as undercover officers, we could never cross the line between showing an interest in a crime already in progress and actually inciting criminal activity. In this instance too, as the conversation with Ahmed progressed, I was becoming increasingly aware that his criminal connections and activities were very much bound up with terrorism of the PLO variety. He mentioned that he had contacts in Ireland, and alluded to a couple of addresses, one of which I knew was suspected of being a contact address for the PLO in Belfast. Even more reason for us to tread extra carefully with this one: we had enough problems of our own, without importing those of the Middle East, and I certainly had no wish to start delving into that murky field of operations, which was completely outside our remit anyway.

Farqu, on the other hand, was exclusively involved in the shady world of London's criminal East End, and was anxious to offload forged £20 and £50 Bank of England notes. He had some samples with him, and they were of the very highest quality. I had seen counterfeit currency of this calibre before, and knew it was the particular specialty of the London Mob. The problem was however that the market was awash with such forged notes at the time, and that half of the country's precious undercover policing resources could have easily been tied up in conducting operations against the various counterfeiting outfits…

Although forgery is of course a crime, all the government really gets back for its outlay in policing resources, when it comes down to it, is a room full of printed waste paper, whose only real value is in recycling terms. For this reason, any operations we undertook against counterfeiting gangs really had to be targeted against the principals, those in control of large amounts of the forged cash, and not the foot soldiers, so to speak. They could be dealt with by other policing units further down the chain at street level. It did seem however that Farqu had access to sizeable amounts of the forged money, so I suggested to him that we would be interested in very substantial amounts only. I explained that we preferred to do one sizeable transaction as opposed to numerous smaller transactions, as these would be more likely to leave us open to compromise and detection by the police.

I needed above all to establish whether Farqu had easy access to a large consignment of cash. He did seem to have some savvy anyway, since he raised the point that we would surely have difficulties moving large quantities of English notes within the Irish market. I told him that he was right, but that we had control of a money exchange on the border which we were able to use to launder such items if necessary. Farqu seemed to think that this was a marvellous opportunity, and said he could be able to provide up to £1,000,000 at a time. I said that I needed to run everything past our Boss, and agreed that Farqu and I should meet again.

In the following weeks, I made sure to keep in touch with the shady duo. They were keen to keep up the contact, but they were treading warily and suggested that they come over to see us before committing to any kind of deal. They obviously wanted to see if we were for real. The Crime Squad were anxious for us to proceed, and it was decided that we should bring Ahmed and Farqu over to Belfast and call their bluff.

A friend in the local estate agency trade helped us to arrange the short-term rental of a furnished farm house in a secluded area only a few miles from the city of Belfast. We decided in advance that we would covertly wire the complete house for camera and audio surveillance, and planned to engineer a situation in which our criminal friends would be left alone on the premises. We would then monitor any conversation they had, not only to check out the veracity of their various claims, but also to see whether they would contact anyone in Northern Ireland. In order to create a lived-in effect, we filled the house with all sorts of documentation and other props, including such finer points as children's toys, and so on.

A few weeks later, we met Farqu and Ahmed off their flight from London and took them on a sightseeing tour of the city centre. Comically enough, they even made life easy for us, by insisting at one stage that we take their pictures in front of Belfast City Hall. We were only too willing to oblige and took the opportunity of using our own camera to capture the moment also! That afternoon, we told them we would be driving them to my house—the farmhouse—where they would be staying the night.

On the way to the house, I told our guests that my wife would be taking our children to her mother's for the night, and so one of our girls even had a walk-on part later that afternoon, as she called in to collect some toys for the children she had supposedly forgotten. Ahmed and Farqu fell for it, hook, line and sinker. As planned, I told them I had to go and speak to someone regarding some urgent business: would they mind if I left them alone for a short time? Whenever we reviewed the footage we had taken later that evening, it seemed that, while the pair did take the precaution—or liberty—of having a good rummage around the house, they were very content with us and obviously believed we were for real...A 'little bit of theatre' can work wonders!

When I returned from my supposed business meeting, we were joined by my undercover colleague, John, and the four of us discussed how we could proceed with a deal on their forged currency. John and I told the pair that we would not be taking the risk for less than one million pounds' worth of £20 and £50 notes, and we settled on a fee of £50,000, on condition that all the forgeries had mixed numbers and were as good as the sample we had been shown originally. This seemed acceptable enough to Ahmed and Farqu, but they were very reluctant to stray very far from their home turf, and so we offered to go over and collect the counterfeit cash from them. Our PLO friend Ahmed was interested in the possibility of us supplying him with stolen vehicles, but he said he would only take particular makes and models, and promised to get back to us with full specifications. The counterfeit money, they assured us, would be ready within about two weeks, and we agreed to meet them in a hotel of our choice in the vicinity of Heathrow: we knew that the Crime Squad had a lock-up nearby.

And so two weeks later, we flew to Heathrow. We met the Operational team for the usual briefing, then deployed in a hotel near the airport. The hotel in question had a large car park and could be easily covered by the surveillance teams. We had arranged to meet our criminal chums that afternoon, but they were late and didn't arrive until nearly 5.00 pm, when they made their way up to our hotel room. The Operational team had been dubious as to whether the targets would be able to produce the size of parcel they had promised us, and suspected that they were middling for the main men. As it transpired, their fears were well-founded.

When doing that type of deal with the London mobs, one of the biggest dangers was that they would try a rip-off, and attempt to grab the flash money. On this occasion, we had covered this possibility by arranging adjoining rooms. When our friends came up to the room I was in to inspect our money, I locked the door behind them. John then joined us from the next room, let them see the money was real and went back into the room next door, where armed officers from the Met's firearms team were waiting in case we needed them. The inspection of the flash money went without a hitch however, and I suggested I go downstairs with Ahmed and Farqu to check their parcel. It was clear that they were uneasy at this suggestion. They then blurted out that there was a slight problem: they had in fact only been allowed to bring £250,000 on the first trip. Farqu went on to assure us however that as soon as this first handover went down, they would return within two hours with the rest of the consignment of forged notes. They were really just taking precautions, he insisted.

At this development, I needed to stall for time: I would have to await instructions from the Operational team—although I thought anyway that it was highly unlikely that they would want to play this hand. I suggested however to the pair that I go down to inspect the money they had, and that we would see. Once we were in the car park and they had opened the boot of their Mercedes car, I could see, judging by the size of the two holdalls inside, that the £250,000 in Bank of England £20 and £50 notes did appear to be there at any rate. I told the pair to wait in the vicinity, and that I would contact them after taking instructions—which was the truth in any event.

As soon as we made contact, the instruction came loud and clear: we were to abort the operation immediately. The Crime Squad bosses were not prepared to risk the flash money or, more importantly, compromise our unit's undercover operatives for what, it was rapidly becoming clear, was merely a 'level two' buy. By keeping our integrity in place this time, the opportunity might well arrive in the future to move against Ahmed and Farqu more effectively. Ahmed's connections merited further and more careful analysis in any case, and the surveillance umbrella would be able to track the parcel they were carrying in the meantime, so that it could be taken out at a later point.

As soon as I had been given this decision, I contacted the two crooks as I had promised. We weren't prepared to take the risk for the £250,000, I explained. Careful not to burn any bridges however, I assured them that we could remain friends, and that if we could ever help them or they had anything worth the risk for us, they should not hesitate to contact us. We allowed them to leave, although as it happened they stayed close by for some hours, trying their best to get us to change our mind about the £250,000. We weren't biting, however. We would live to fight another day.

From a short-term perspective of course, hundreds of man hours had been wasted. But such was the nature of the undercover game. In the words of Kenny Rogers,

> *You have to know when to hold 'em, know when to fold 'em,*
> *Know when to walk away and know when to run.*
> *You never count your money when you're sitting at the table—*
> *There'll be time enough for counting when the dealing's done.*

(*The Gambler*, 1978)

Chapter 14
Helping out on the Streets

As I have mentioned earlier, to many of our other colleagues within the force, even those in the CID, we undercover guys were known as 'The Bogeymen' since, for various reasons, of which office politics was probably the most important, we were destined to remain a nameless and faceless entity about which very little was known, even internally. I have no doubt that some of our CID colleagues must have been puzzled on occasions as to what exactly our purpose was and how precisely we spent our time. I am sure that some believed that we were more interested in living the high life, in leading what they might have imagined as some sort of glamorous existence in the shadowy world of undercover operations, than actually helping them in a practical way in the everyday fight against crime on the streets.

I know that some experienced detectives, finding that their requests for our assistance on surveillance matters were frequently turned down, might have felt some understandable sense of grievance, a feeling of being left at the coal face to fight a lonely battle against the mounting tide of ordinary crime, without our support. The truth however was that, just as we were forced to operate within strict limits once we were engaged in an actual operation, there were criteria relating to the nature and scale of the crime in question which had to be fulfilled before an undercover operation could be mounted in the first place.

While therefore our hands were often tied in terms of the extent to which we could intervene to assist our other CID colleagues, we were always eager to help when it was possible—and there were occasions when both units were able to work together very effectively. One of these joint operations which worked well concerned an individual called Crockett, a prolific burglar who was operating right across the Province as well as border areas.

Burglary has always been one of those everyday crimes which are the bane of any local police operation's existence. Around this time, in 1996, the burglary rate across the Province was sky-rocketing, and it was clear that there were some highly organised and sophisticated criminals operating in this area. Crockett was one of these, and in covert operations we were getting an increasing number of requests for surveillance on him from divisional CID offices. All our intelligence was suggesting that Crockett was indeed extremely active and possibly responsible for as much as sixty percent of major house burglaries at that time. He had a substantial criminal record and, with a number of suspended sentences in the offing, he was being extra-vigilant, operating alone, and proving very difficult to catch up with. It appeared that normal policing methods were just not producing the results. The whole issue was given added impetus by reports that Crockett was under constant death threats from vigilante paramilitary groups because of his burglary activities, and that he was now reputed to be selling stolen firearms to some of these groups as insurance for his own safety. It was decided that our covert unit should now be brought in to put an end to Crockett's criminal career as quickly as possible.

Our first step was to spend some time assessing all the available intelligence from our various sources, including the CID and their informants and agents. One reason, it soon became clear, that Crockett was so hard to keep tabs on was that although he had an address in the Lisburn area, he rarely stayed in the same place for more than one night, such was his anxiety over the threats from paramilitaries. We were however quickly able to identify a possible opportunity to infiltrate Crockett's peer group, and we decided to give it a go.

Bill, the undercover officer we selected for the job, was introduced into Crockett's circles as a fence for stolen jewellery and valuable paintings—commodities we knew he currently had in his possession but that he was having trouble moving on because of the death threats. It wasn't very long before Crockett took the bait, contacting Bill and asking him if he would be able to sell on some high quality pieces of fine jewellery he had recently obtained.

Bill arranged to meet Crockett at a public house on the Lisburn Road and our criminal friend turned up with a holdall in which he had quite a cache of high quality loot. Bill inspected the items, memorising the most notable pieces. He then told Crockett that the merchandise was better than he had been expecting (which was in fact the case), and that he would therefore have to bring in another fence who specialised in such items. This was of course the classic undercover tactic of introducing another link in the chain into the scene, to further muddy the waters. By checking Bill's descriptions of some of the more valuable items against our burglary records, we were able to surmise that they had been part of the spoils from a number of high-end burglaries which had been carried out within the last few months. Further analysis of the crime data revealed the extent to which Crockett was a pro. The premises which had been burgled in each case were nearly all large houses, with quite sophisticated burglar alarms. Yet the burglaries had been carried out without the alarms being activated or the culprits discovered. Later examination by forensic teams had revealed no real evidence as to the culprit's identity, and certainly no fingerprints or anything of the kind.

This is where I came in. A few days later Bill was contacted by Crockett, asking to be introduced to me, preferably at Crockett's house near Lisburn. We weren't overly keen to meet him there, as we reckoned the paramilitaries would be very likely to have a go at him if they knew he was back at the house, and we had no wish to get involved in any kind of a clash with them in these circumstances. It appeared however that Crockett's stash was close to his house, and this was why he was prepared to risk going back. Agreeing to meet him there after all, we drove up to the front of the house, where Crockett appeared from an alleyway to direct us into the driveway. The house was a small bungalow-type dwelling in a poor state of repair. Rather like Crockett himself, in fact: a grotesque individual with appalling skin which wasn't helped by his mass of straggly, greasy hair. His teeth were stained black from the numerous roll-ups he chain-smoked. His filthy clothes stank of smoke and stale sweat, and obviously like himself had not seen soap for some considerable time. All of his fingers, including his thumbs, were adorned with gold rings, most likely spoils from his robberies which he had decided to keep for himself.

Once we were all in the house, Crockett disappeared into the kitchen area and brought out two bags. One of these contained the jewellery Bill had seen the last time, along with the proceeds of a number of other burglaries. The other bag contained an oil painting and two watercolours. I happen to know quite a lot about certain art and local artists (this has always been a hobby of mine), and I was able to use this knowledge as part of my cover as a high value fence in jobs such as these. I recognised the oil painting as a Frank McKelvey. The two watercolours were by another well-known local artist, Rowland Hill. Both artists had been members of the Royal Ulster Academy in their lifetimes, and the paintings were quite valuable.

I had been given some funds to use to purchase 'confidence buys' from Crockett, in order to corroborate my cover. There was no way however that I had enough to purchase the items he had for sale here, even on the stolen market. I did though give him £400 for the jewellery, with a promise of more if I was able to move some of the pieces on. I also said I could probably move the paintings on through another fence, a contact of mine in an art gallery, but that he would have to wait for the money. Crockett however was impressed by my knowledge of the paintings, and seemed pleased enough with our meeting. He knew in any case that he would never have been able to walk into any shop with the paintings under his arm, as they, like him, would smell to high heaven! He assured us that he was casing a number of other good jobs, and so would have more paintings for us soon. Not wishing to prolong the encounter any longer, we made the excuse that we were keen to hide the gear we had got from him, and we left Crockett at this point, promising however to keep in touch.

Back at base, our support team was quickly able to tie the stolen goods down to specific burglaries, and we had a meeting with the tasking Detective Inspector and his team to decide how we should proceed. At this point, we had to be very careful that we did not actively encourage Crockett to steal to order for us, thereby inciting new crimes: particularly now that we had cast ourselves in the role of fences for him, this was a real possibility. I decided therefore that we would have to take him out at the first opportunity and somehow distance ourselves from him by the time the strike went in. Bill kept in contact with Crockett subsequently, in an attempt to elicit from

him details of where his next burglaries would be, but beyond
confirming that the next targets would be in the north of the city,
Crockett didn't reveal anything further. There was nothing else for it
—we would have to draw him out with the gear.

About a week later, Bill got a call from Crockett, who proudly
announced that he had a lot of good loot, including a valuable
painting he knew would be of interest to me. Having a pretty good
idea of the sort of houses Crockett would have zeroed in on, we
contacted each station in north Belfast. We discovered a number of
crimes which had taken place in the previous few days in the more
affluent area of Fortwilliam and which looked like our pal's
handiwork.

We arranged to meet Crockett in a public house on the Upper
Lisburn Road the next day. That morning I had briefed the rest of our
surveillance team and our Uniform QRF, and our plan was to get the
crook out on the move with the gear on him. Once Bill got to the bar
for the meeting, Crockett told him the loot was in his car outside. In
the boot of what turned out to be a stolen Vauxhall car were bags
containing jewellery, silver and paintings. Bill then told Crockett that
I was away to fetch the money for the goods, and that we would ring
him soon to arrange to meet somewhere nearby, like the Boucher
Road: there were too many people about at the bar at present. Once
Bill left the scene, we briefed the surveillance teams and the QRF with
details of the target's vehicle, etc. We then put the call in for Crockett
to meet us. A short time later he came out of the bar and drove off in
the direction of Boucher. As the net closed on him, I thought for one
horrible moment that he might escape.

Crockett was certainly not going to be taken easily and, seeing the
QRF close in on his car in the line of traffic, he rammed two of their
cars and an innocent passer-by, before he was forced to a stop. Even
then, he got out of his car and tried to bolt for freedom. Thankfully,
he was no match for the athletic young uniform officers, who brought
him to the ground before he got too far. Caught red-handed, he had
no choice other than to throw his hands up. He ultimately struck a
deal with the investigating detectives, and admitted to a complete
catalogue of crimes throughout the Province in the course of recent
months. Crockett received a lengthy prison sentence, albeit with some
time deducted in return for his co-operation. His short but prolific
career as a burglar had been brought to an abrupt halt.

Chapter 15
An Unusual Identity Parade

In 1996, colleagues from the Birmingham Crime Squad asked for our assistance in infiltrating an Asian gang who were suspected to be amassing a huge fortune from their drug dealing activities. These guys were serious players: intelligence confirmed that heroin was the main product they were pushing and that they were dealing in sizeable quantities. They were also proving to be very elusive indeed. Evidently well-versed in anti-surveillance tactics and the *modus operandi* of anti-drugs Crime Squad initiatives, they had even managed to resist several attempts at infiltration by specialist agencies, including undercover operations. A new angle was needed— and this is where our team in Belfast came in. It was to be another highly challenging operation for us, and one which was to graphically highlight the importance of good intelligence and record keeping, and a reliable back-up team. For those of us on the plot, one missed connection on the part of the Operational team could mean the difference between life and death.

The team in Belfast had worked against Asian gangs in the Manchester and Birmingham areas before this particular operation, but our operational back-up guys were as certain as they could be that there had been no crossover between any of these groups. It is true however that on these types of operations you would often only see the actual targets for a few minutes at a time, and then in high-pressure circumstances, where it wasn't always easy to remember their faces or those of their associates. It was also a possibility that some of

the more minor players or their associates might be allowed to run or
might simply escape the arrest net.

We knew, as I have said, that infiltrating this particular group was
not going to be easy. The principal offender and main target of the
operation, Waseem Malik, was a slick customer. Arrogant,
opinionated and highly astute, he had a lavish lifestyle and dressed
accordingly. From his permed designer hairdo, to his expensive
clothes and diamond-encrusted watches, he obviously wasn't one bit
afraid of flaunting his ill-gotten gains. Motivated as always by the lust
for more, Malik's gang were eager to find new avenues in which to
trade and expand their empire.

Our first move was to engineer an introduction for me to Ali, one
of the gang who was dealing in his own right in sizeable quantities of
heroin in the Manchester area. In order to secure the introduction, I
was to call upon the services of a professional informant. This was the
first and last time I was ever to work with such an individual, and it
proved to be an unforgettable experience in more ways than one. An
important difference between this 'professional informant' and most
ordinary informants is that the latter are fairly anxious in general to
protect their identities and remain anonymous. The guy I was dealing
with in this case didn't care who knew he was an informant or, as he
preferred to call himself, 'a police agent'. He told me that he saw
himself as doing the public a service and, as the people he was acting
against were dealing in drugs, they were fair game. It was, however, a
public service with a difference, in that he expected to be highly paid
for his work. In fact, he had in the past actually publicly sued the
Manchester police because he felt he hadn't received proper
remuneration for some of the assistance he had provided! I asked him
once if he was not afraid of people knowing who he was and seeking
retribution. He replied disdainfully that he was not indeed, that he
regarded himself as being in effect merely another branch of the
police. It was all quite novel, in a way, I suppose.

Anyway, I had flown over to Manchester to meet this self-styled
bounty hunter, who lived in one of the large, sprawling housing
estates which surround the city centre. All credit to the source, he had
in fact managed to successfully infiltrate the local drug scene, and had
for some time been making small, controlled purchases of heroin in
order to gain the gang's confidence. He took me to a bar in the
Sparkhill area, where he introduced me to the clientèle as his 'Irish

friend'. I had good references from a number of criminal sources, as the leader of an Irish criminal gang who was interested in moving a lot of heroin.

Among the regulars I was introduced to that day was Ali: as I have said, one of Malik's chief associates. Of Indian or Pakistani origin, Ali looked to be in his late forties and was dressed in an open-necked shirt, jacket and trousers. He certainly didn't look like a dealer in heroin, apart from anything else because of his age—I hadn't dealt with anyone as old as this before at street level in the heroin game. Ali said he was a family man and that he had already done time for possession of heroin. He kept insisting that he couldn't afford for anything to go wrong, as he knew another stretch inside would kill him. In fact, he repeated this so many times that, knowing I was going to help lock him up, I almost began to feel sorry for him—almost.

We discussed the drug scene in Manchester and Ali confirmed that the gang he was involved with was responsible for distributing most of the brown powder in the Manchester and Birmingham areas. He was eager to do business, saying he was aware that there was a big heroin scene in Dublin, and that they could supply us regular consignments at the right price. The price he was quoting was £25,000 per kilo, which was easily £3,000 over the market price for moderate strength heroin, but I figured he was adding on a good cut for himself. He said he could do any amount up to a kilo in one go, but that he would need to see what was available at that time, and then let me know when we could do business. We gave Ali a covert mobile telephone number which had been assigned for this operation. I also gave him the number of Pat's bar, our Belfast backstop.

Pat and his bar manager Gerry had been warned that an Asian guy might be calling the bar, looking to speak to Billy Craig. And sure enough, about two days after I got back from Manchester, I heard from Pat that there had been a number of calls for me. Ali had in fact been ringing so often, in his eagerness, that even some of the punters in the bar were able to tell me he'd been looking for me. Finally, on the evening of 31 August 1996, Ali phoned me on the covert mobile number, wondering whether I knew he had been trying to contact me at the bar. I told him that I had been given the message, but that I was lying low at present, as the police had apparently been in the bar looking for me. I explained that for security reasons I couldn't talk to him now, but would be in touch again soon. The real reason I was stalling was that I had to seek permission to go live on the operation, as well as notify the Operational team, so that they could set the necessary wheels in motion: there were many legal and operational steps to be taken. There was also the fact that whenever Ali rang, I hadn't been in a position to record the conversation on a covert recorder.

The object of the game now was to get close enough to the principal players in the gang, and to Malik himself, to set up a face-to-face meeting about the purchase of a number of kilos of heroin. Over the next few weeks, and in the course of numerous phone calls with Ali, all of which I was recording, I discussed with him how the trade could be done and gained his confidence to the extent that he gave me his home phone number. Ali was now offering to sell us regular consignments, but said that he wanted to do a test deal of one kilo at £25,000 first of all. At the end of every call with Ali, I would make copies of the tapes and rush them to the Detective Inspector running the covert side of the operation at West Midlands Crime Squad. Only he, a few of his most trusted staff and the overall commander would ever know my identity.

The calls between Ali and myself continued, as we discussed the finer details of the proposed handover. For operational safety reasons and for evidence purposes, we needed the drugs brought onto the plot. This did not however suit Ali very well, as his masters were insisting that we should hand over our money first of all, and then wait for the drugs to be delivered to us. This wasn't going to happen, and not just for the legal and operational reasons I have already mentioned. The fact was that we would be using £25,000 of taxpayers' money for the test buy, and all hell would break loose if it went for a walk! Sometimes it really seemed that the primary concern of most of the operational bosses in these types of jobs was the safety of the bloody money. Our welfare was secondary—or so it felt sometimes anyway. Still, we knew the form and never really queried it: that was, quite simply, the way it was.

Had the amount of heroin on offer been greater—say, a number of kilos—the operational team might have considered taking a risk with the flash money, as in Operation Boom. This particular team however were dealing with much smaller quantities as a rule, albeit on a frequent and consistent basis. There was also the very real danger of us getting ripped off no matter what, anyway. My feeling was that to achieve anything worthwhile, I needed to speak to the organ grinder and not the monkey—i.e. to Malik himself.

On Tuesday 17 September, Ali contacted me to say that he had a kilo of heroin ready for sale, and I confirmed that I would be in Birmingham the next day. The next morning the Operational team supplied me with a covert recorder and a car and, accompanied by another undercover officer, I went as arranged to meet with Ali at a Trust House Forte Hotel near the old Birmingham airport. After breakfast, I contacted Ali and he said that he was nearby and would come to meet us and take us to his home. He arrived at around 11.00 am in a dark Nissan Sunny car, and made a great show of hugging both me and my companion by way of greeting. He must really have taken us for fools: the hugging was in reality a body search so thorough that any airport security guard would have been proud of it! It was just as well that we had anticipated this precaution on Ali's part, and that my miniature covert recorder was nestling safely in my pants with my most prized possessions…

We showed Ali the cash—£25,000, which we had in a holdall in the boot of our car—and then discussed with him how the handover was to be done. Ali's suggestion was that we go to his house to hand over the money to him first, and that we would get the drugs later. We weren't about to agree to this, and for over an hour we argued with him about how the switch should be done. Throughout the conversation, Ali would frequently consult a mystery friend he called on the phone and to whom he spoke in a foreign language—we were fairly sure this person was Malik himself.

Eventually Ali told us that his friend was coming to speak to us, but that, as he was travelling from Manchester, there would be some delay. He suggested that the hotel was not the best place for this meeting and proposed that we go to his home with him. And so we followed him to his house, a reasonably sized semi-detached property in the Sparkhill district. Ali introduced us to his wife, who was in full Asian dress and didn't appear to understand much English. He began to try yet again to get us to hand over the £25,000, saying this time that we could stay with his wife until he returned with the drugs: this was, he said, proof that he was genuine, since if anything went wrong, we would always have his wife as security. This was hardly very gallant of him, and perhaps it was just as well his wife didn't speak much English, as I doubt she would have been very impressed with her

husband's generous offer to us! In any event, it wasn't a runner, and I
told him so. After some more phone calls, he said the main man had
agreed to meet us at a nearby restaurant in order to convince us that
they would not try to rip us off. I made the excuse of wanting to check
something in our car and took the opportunity to brief the
operational team as to our intentions. They confirmed that our covert
umbrella was in place and ready to move with us.

Ali then drove to a kebab restaurant in Stratford Road, Sparkhill,
where I hoped I would at last meet the elusive Malik. I was ushered in
to the room and, as usual, tried to weigh up the situation as quickly as
I could. I scanned the interior of the restaurant as if on automatic,
seeking out the doors, exits, windows and so on. I tried to pace the
distance from the door, and quickly realised I would have some way
to go if the wheel came off our plan and I needed to make a rapid exit.
Unfortunately for me, and not for the first time in a such a situation,
I was led right to the back of the restaurant and through a semi-
curtained area. Although it was obvious that there were a number of
harmless customers in the restaurant, the group I was led to join was
clearly made up of some of Malik's inner circle—but the man himself
was not yet among them.

I was shown to a seat on the inside of a table, but managed to sit
facing towards the door. My chaperones were seated around me.
Again, I was painfully aware that if things went wrong, there was a less
than even chance of me making it to the door without serious injury.
I had to content myself with the knowledge that Birmingham's finest
were watching my back—or I hoped they were anyway. We passed the
time waiting for the main man to arrive by making small talk and
sampling some Asian snacks which Ali had ordered. Sometime later, I
finally spotted our friend coming into the restaurant.

Although I had never met him, I knew it was Malik: the description
I had been given was extremely accurate. He obviously thought he was
God's gift and dressed accordingly. He sauntered up to me, acting the
Don and holding out a hand bedecked with some of the most
outlandish jewellery I have ever seen, including, on the second finger
of his left hand, an enormous brown oval ring with a streak of yellow
through it. His watch was equally outrageous and his designer clothes
were finished with a flamboyant waistcoat. Despite his apparent
confidence, it was obvious to me that Malik was extremely tense and
keyed up. It was his eyes that gave him away, darting back and forth,

continually checking out the room, as if he was expecting the police to crash through the door at any moment. He got up from his seat a number of times, moved quickly towards the door and looked out anxiously. Ali exchanged glances with me, and explained that Malik was merely checking his car, as it was a bad neighbourhood. As if, I thought.

Although obviously born in the UK, and an articulate English speaker, throughout the proceedings Malik seemed to prefer to speak in another language through Ali, whose manner towards him was grovelling and obsequious. It was in fact rather uncomfortable to have to watch this middle-aged man, crook though he was, bowing and scraping in the presence of this thug, articulate or not. Through Ali, Malik indicated that he had drugs he was more than willing to sell to us, in lots of up to a kilo at a time—on condition that we hand over the £25,000 for this test kilo up front this time. Only the most trusting of criminal associates would have agreed to this, and even then, never on a first deal, so I argued that I would do a boot-to-boot operation only, for obvious reasons.

As the meeting progressed, Ali asked several times, on instruction from Malik, whether I knew a person called Alan from Belfast involved in the dealing world. Each time the question was put to me, Malik would stare into my face, looking for some reaction, it seemed. At the same time, I was watching out of the corner of my eye as a number of strange looking individuals came into the restaurant. Perhaps I was imagining it, but they appeared to be receiving certain instructions and then approaching to observe me closely, as if sizing me up somehow. One in particular, an elderly Asian with a long white beard and in full Afghan dress, hobbled towards me on his stick and stood staring at me so intently that I began to feel very uneasy. The old man's face was lined and weather-beaten and his intense green eyes flashed me a look that seemed to penetrate my very soul. This was unnerving, to say the least, as it slowly became clear that, rather than Malik being the one to find himself under scrutiny, it was I who was now being made to feel like a suspect in an identity parade.

I was becoming more uneasy by the second, and felt my body starting to tense up with the adrenalin rush that only comes when you are faced with a possible critical situation. The human body is a wonderful machine in a crisis. Like those of an animal cornered in the wild, your senses pick up the slightest movement and part of you is instinctively primed, ready to hit out at any aggressor. I found myself lightly moving a fork which was sitting on the tabletop into my grasp, ready to use it if need be—that would do the guy on my right. The ashtray at my elbow was for my neighbour on the left. In the mayhem which might ensue, I might just get to the door, provided I was the one who struck first.

The instinct for self-preservation is a wonderful thing. My mind was racing through all the possibilities: they were obviously thinking that I was or could have been Alan, the individual they kept asking me about so insistently. They must have come across him on their travels, and whether he was a criminal who had ripped them off, or another undercover officer, I didn't know. I surmised it was probably the latter. I didn't however know of any other Irish undercover officer who had been in against these targets before: all of the intelligence I had been given at my briefing had confirmed this. I did though know an undercover officer from Belfast who used the alias 'Alan' on occasion, and I was beginning to have a sneaky suspicion that he was the man they were after. I watched the old man with the white beard intently for some sign of recognition.

To my intense relief, the crisis seemed to blow over as suddenly as it had arisen.

I noticed the elderly Afghan make eye contact with Malik and give a slight shake of his head. Thinking that the best line of defence was attack, and also, it has to be said, to release some of my nervous tension, I began to rant and rave, 'What the f***'s going on here, anyway?', demanding to know who all these people were. 'Do you know who I am?' I exclaimed indignantly, and began making all sorts of dark threats. Malik knew exactly where I was coming from, and moved immediately to try to calm the troubled waters. Through his mouthpiece Ali, he said he was sorry, but that they had had a bad experience with an undercover cop on a previous job and that they couldn't be too careful. Again, outwardly, I raged with indignation. Inwardly however I breathed a huge sigh of relief: obviously something somewhere had gone awry, but this time I was lucky, and right at that moment that was all that mattered to me.

I was later able to confirm that Alan, the officer I had been thinking of, had in fact been in against Asian targets in the past, and that it was most likely him they were after. Someone somewhere on the background team had missed the connection. This incident reminded us, if indeed we needed reminding, that it was vital for the Operational team to research all of the people involved or concerned as fully and carefully as possible, in order to ensure that there was no crossover. As I had so nearly experienced to my cost, your life itself could depend on their degree of competence. Then again, there is always the slight possibility that they in fact did know, but that someone had made the decision not to tell me, for whatever reason. It wouldn't have been the first time.

Thankfully, on this occasion I left Malik with only my pride hurt, promising to contact them again. As I left, I could see Malik's top-of-the-range sports car parked nearby. He and I would keep in touch over the following months, but it was down to the professionalism and hard work of the Birmingham Crime Squad team that Malik would eventually fall. Our meeting had provided the vital evidence the Crime Squad needed—the proof that Malik was dealing in large quantities of heroin. They put him under round-the-clock surveillance and this, combined with other good detective work, would lead to him appearing at Birmingham Crown Court on 24 February 1998.

In court, Malik did his best to keep up the pretence that he was a watch and car dealer and had amassed his massive fortune through these businesses by relatively legitimate means. His story didn't wash with anyone, however. He had spent £22,000 on an Aston Martin, £44,000 on a Nissan Skyline and £20,000 on designer watches, and had been observed spending thousands in cash at casinos. More importantly of course, police operations had led to the recovery of some six kilos of heroin from members of his gang, and gathered additional evidence that would tie him to the importation of a further 5.8 kilos. Malik would find himself with a very hefty sentence to serve—as would our friend Ali, who was put away for at least five years. Despite all his earlier protestations about what another prison sentence would do to him, I couldn't bring myself to feel sorry for him. He knew exactly what he was getting himself into and had had a very good idea of what the possible consequences would be.

I was to deal with the Asian community again on two other anti-drugs operations, both of which involved Class 'A' drugs and focused on the Birmingham and Liverpool areas. In April 1998, I was asked by the Birmingham Crime Squad to back up one of their undercover officers, Joe, in a meeting with an Asian group who were supplying large quantities of heroin in and around Birmingham. The meeting was set to take place in the Novotel at Birmingham Airport. Joe and I had arrived early and were drinking coffee in the bar area, from which we could observe the CCTV camera at the entrance. A short time later, Joe confirmed that our contacts had arrived. We were approached by a tall black guy accompanied by a slightly younger Asian man, in his late twenties or thereabouts. The Asian introduced himself as 'Pops'; his companion was 'Sammy'. Pops went on to explain that he would be happy to supply heroin to us by the kilo, but that we would have to collect it on the mainland: he wouldn't deliver to Ireland. If we preferred, we could even pick it up in Holland. He'd give us a discount in this case, he said, as long as all the dealing was done through him in advance. Joe was the lead undercover officer on the case, and so I let him do most of the talking.

The gist of what Pops was saying was that he would expect the money to be delivered to him a few days before the actual trade: only then would he deliver the drugs. A very unlikely scenario indeed, and one we knew that the Crime Squad would never run with. However, this was only Joe's second meeting with this particular pair, so we said we would meet them again sometime soon, and walked them out to the car park. We were not however to have the pleasure of seeing Pops and Sammy again after all: they were arrested during a drugs deal in a conventional Crime Squad operation a few weeks later.

My last dealings with the Asian gangs occurred a few months after this. The operation in question had originated in Ireland, but we had been able to progress it by means of an introduction through a colleague who worked for the Liverpool Undercover team. At the time, the scene was dominated by two main drug dealing gangs in Liverpool, who were fighting out a major turf war. The Asian gang into which we had managed to gain an introduction were major suppliers of large quantities of cocaine, which, unfortunately for us, was now starting to appear on the streets of Dublin and Belfast with monotonous regularity.

Once we had consolidated the relationship with the Asians, we were able to negotiate the purchase of five kilos of high grade cocaine at £44,000 a kilo. We subsequently travelled to Liverpool for the handover, liaising with the team there to collect a hire car and the flash money. We had arranged to meet the gang in an old and formerly majestic hotel near the railway station. No doubt a splendid hotel in its heyday, it was now the haunt of pimps and prostitutes, its once sumptuous carpets and magnificent staircases worn and shiny, like skid pans for the unwary.

We hired a room, and then John contacted the gang and arranged to meet them outside so that they could come to check the money. He returned about twenty minutes later with a serious-looking young Asian guy who kept a hood pulled up over most of his face and barely spoke or raised his head the whole time he was with us. John showed him the money, which he checked in a cursory way. He then left again quickly, telling us that we would do the handover in the street outside the railway station. John went to check on their parcel and was able to confirm that they had the drugs in a car parked just inside a building site in the vicinity of the station. The Crime Squad's operational plan, now that the stash had been identified, was to take the courier out as he made our way towards us, and before the money changed hands.

For once, things went according to plan for us. The Crime Squad pounced on the courier with the drugs when he was only about 150 yards from us. As the strike went in, there was general mayhem, and the young Asian courier with us was now too preoccupied with his own survival to worry about which direction we went in. Later, when we all regrouped, it was confirmed that five kilos of cocaine had been successfully seized and one arrest made. Our target later pleaded guilty to possession with intent and received 10 years imprisonment. A finger in the dyke perhaps, but it was still a major victory nevertheless and one more avenue closed down for the dealers.

Chapter 16

Entente Cordiale and the Spanish Enigma

By the middle of 1997, our confidence in our abilities as an undercover unit had grown enormously, and we were beginning to make a very significant impact on the drug scenes on the mainland and throughout Ireland. Excellent undercover work by all our team and highly effective collaboration with our counterparts throughout the UK and Ireland meant that the success rate of our operations was very high, and we had the criminal gangs reeling from one *coup* after another. More often than not, we managed to distance ourselves so far from the actual strike when it went in that the gangs didn't have a clue as to what had gone wrong, never mind who was responsible.

The effects of our successes went beyond the immediate seizure of drugs and the arrest of the perpetrators: there was also the knock-on effect on the morale of the other dealers. We knew from our sources that the gangs were becoming increasingly mistrustful, not only of other groups, but of their own members, and this atmosphere of suspicion was causing more and more in-fighting—which could only be good from our standpoint. Sometimes we were regarded as so far beyond reproach that we had been able to take out two or three consignments from the same gang in separate operations…In truth, we were perhaps sailing a little too close to the wind on occasions, but such was the nature of the undercover game. Often it would be the person who blinked first who would fall.

By this stage, our anti-drug operations were taking us further afield too, onto the Continent and into Belgium, Holland, Spain, France, and beyond. It was exciting and enlightening to broaden our horizons in this way—even in terms of experiencing the different ways in which our European colleagues operated. The degree of help we could expect in different countries was really down to how progressive the police authorities in question were. We found the Belgian and the Dutch authorities to be very helpful as a rule. In Belgium, this was down to the quality of the relationships we were able to build within the Judicial Police. Many of these grew into important personal friendships. I am thinking here in particular of my friend Jeff and his partner Ann: I owe a great deal personally to them both. Jeff, now retired, was to pay a serious price for his undercover work on dangerous long-term deployments, and suffered deep psychological damage, from which he has worked hard to recover. Thankfully, he has now come out the other side.

The Dutch, on the other hand, while always accommodating, tended to keep their distance. They were good about keeping in touch by phone, but clearly didn't want to be tied up babysitting me while I was on their patch, and so I would find myself spending days and weeks on end between operational deployments and active work literally pacing the streets of Amsterdam and Rotterdam on my own. Even today, I can draw a map freehand of virtually all the main thoroughfares and individual shops in the centre of Amsterdam! The French were undoubtedly the hardest work. They trusted absolutely no-one and were fanatical about paperwork and procedures. They would have no qualms about locking you up on the spot if you were caught in their jurisdiction on undercover operations without the required judicial umbrella. There were many times when we literally had to drive for the border and trust in God!

The Spanish however were magic. While sometimes they could have reduced you to tears, there were other times when you could have kissed them. There didn't seem to be any middle ground with them: they were either amazingly proficient or mind-numbingly incompetent. From my point of view, perhaps their biggest fault was their apparent inability to grasp the seriousness of the situation at times. As I shall relate, there were times when this flippant attitude seriously jeopardised important operations and nearly cost us our lives. However, there were certainly some lessons we could have learnt from our Spanish colleagues. They took each day as it came and they certainly knew how to enjoy themselves. They were the most hospitable of hosts. Some of the happiest memories I have from my career in the undercover world was in their company.

Operation Ambitious illustrates very well what I mean about the maddening inability of the Spanish at times to realise the seriousness of a situation. It was the autumn of 1997 and, through the underground networks we had been carefully cultivating, we had been approached to provide a driver to bring a consignment of cannabis in from Spain. The amount initially discussed was some 150 kilos. We weren't exactly sure which group was behind it, but strongly suspected the involvement of certain individuals in the LVF/UVF in the Antrim and Bangor areas.

On the evening of Sunday 14 September 1997, I drove to the car park of Harry Ramsden's fish-and-chip restaurant in York Street, Belfast, for a meet. I was accompanied by Jim, another undercover officer who had already made a number of deliveries for this particular group, but whose integrity was still intact—i.e. his cover was not yet blown. Jim, who had his left arm in plaster, had been asked by the contact we were to meet with to do a drugs run from Spain to Northern Ireland. He had actually already been given £2,000 as a retainer for doing the job. Jim had his arm in plaster for a very specific reason: we had decided that we couldn't risk him doing another run to Spain as the front man in the operation because of the possibility that he would likely be recognised by some of the principals. I was to do the work at the coal face in this job instead, both here and abroad.

Anyway, once we had found a suitable parking space outside the restaurant, Jim went to fetch our contact. He returned a short time later with a guy he introduced to me as John McCooke. Jim told McCooke that I was a lorry driver who also did the European runs, and we shook hands. He then gave McCooke back the £2,000 in an envelope, and told him that he was sorry that he wouldn't be able to do the run to Spain after all: as he could see, he was in plaster. Jimmy said that I was however more than happy to do the Spanish job in his place, if that was any help. McCooke said that he would need to run this past 'the man in Bangor'. He went on to talk more generally, warning us about the need for caution in this game, but talking of the rewards also, insisting that if we were to do six runs, we would make enough money to be able to retire. McCooke told us that we would get £300 a kilo for cannabis and that they never brought in more than 500 kilos at a time, in case the load somehow went astray. He then promised to be in touch again soon, and left.

The next morning, McCooke contacted us and we arranged to meet in front of the B&Q store in Ballymena. Jim and I drove there and were sitting in the car park when, shortly after 11.00 am, I observed McCooke come into the car park, with a woman and a child in his car. He pulled up beside us and looked about him furtively. Removing a white envelope from behind the sun visor on the driver's side, he got out of his car and came over to us, throwing the envelope on the front seat of our car. The job was on, he said: they were holding the drugs for us to pick up at a relative's house in Spain. Again, he gave us the same pep talk: if we were able and willing to do six runs for them, we could easily make enough cash to retire, as long as we were very careful. McCooke then drove off. The first thing I did was to check the envelope: it contained £1,000.

We then returned to our Headquarters, where a hurried meeting of all the interested parties was called. As with any importation in these circumstances, the assistance of HM Customs was required. Thankfully, we had a great working relationship, on the frontline anyway, with the specialist unit of Customs who dealt with such operations. The necessary approvals to enable us to pass through the UK under a covert protective umbrella were obtained from both the police and Customs high command. Then there was the task of contacting the British Embassy in Madrid to enlist the help of the Spanish police. There was never really a problem, although it would generally involve a mountain of paperwork for our back-up team. The exchange of the drugs and money was to take place in the Valencia region in southern Spain, and we would be driving the whole way.

A few days later, with 90 per cent of the paperwork completed, Jim and I set off on our road trip. We drove down through Dover and via Santander and the Basque country into Spain. The north of Spain, the dairy farming region of the country, is very like Northern Ireland, with green fields and high ditches. This part of the drive was pleasant enough, but the route through central Spain consisted of mile after mile of monotonous concrete motorway. The ring roads on the outskirts of Madrid were a nightmare, and we missed our turn-off three times before being forced eventually to stop in a side street. If you have never driven in Madrid, take a tip from me: don't even consider it, unless you think you would enjoy something like a cross between the Wacky Races and Armageddon! Our street maps were useless, and in desperation we decided to ask a passer-by. Lady Luck must have been smiling on us that day, however. The first person we approached turned out to be a young American business executive who was greatly amused by my pidgin Spanish and immediately enquired as to what two Irish men were doing lost in Madrid! I explained that we had to report an accident at the British Embassy for insurance purposes.

'Right,' he said at once, 'stick close to me, do everything I do, and don't stop, or we will never get there. Got that?' he said. 'Right oh,' I exclaimed, and with that our new-found friend climbed into one of the smallest cars I have ever seen and roared off, his arm waving through the sunroof, with us in hot pursuit. There followed what can only be described as a rollercoaster drive through the centre of Madrid. Traffic lights meant nothing to these people: you just had to drive into the centre of the junctions and beep your horn, like all the other drivers—and then join in the chorus of abuse which everybody seemed to be screaming in every direction. A short time later, virtually crying with relief, laughter and terror all at the same time, we were outside the Embassy. We thanked our American saviour profusely as he took his leave.

At the Embassy we made arrangements through the liaison officer to meet the Spanish police the next day in Valencia. It was a long drive, but we got there eventually, and reported to the police headquarters there—a battered but still operational building, otherwise known by the grand title of *Cra Fuerte Jefatura Superior Policia Es Type Facientes*. I still don't have a clue what this means, but it seemed like a pretty fancy name to give to such a ramshackle place! The Spanish were having their own problems with the Basque ETA terrorists at this time and were on a pretty high state of alert. All the doors to the station at the headquarters were guarded by mean-looking guys with pump action shotguns and bullet proof vests. I suppose it made us feel at home, anyway.

We were contacted that day by McCooke's people who instructed us to meet up with a guy called Mick, who would have the drugs. When we told the Spanish of our proposed arrangements, they agreed to arrange the necessary permissions and cover for us. A meeting was called and it seemed that half of Spain had been invited along. They seemed to talk mostly amongst themselves and occasionally with our interpreter too: we just nodded wisely when it seemed like the right thing to do.

It was now Wednesday and we were eager to get on the road again as soon as possible, as we had two or three days of hard driving ahead of us. Well, that was our plan anyway. The Embassy liaison officer told us however that we wouldn't be able to move until the Friday: we would have to wait another two days! I could scarcely take it in and let my feelings be known, but there was absolutely nothing to be done about it. The next day—the Thursday—was, it seemed, a holy day: a day to honour the patron saint of policemen. Therefore, they would all be going on the piss! I couldn't believe it, but there it was. I guess however that there was a part of me wishing that work could be treated like this at home—although I'm not sure how we would ever have got anything done, as our lives were so hectic at the best of times. A further meeting was set for the Friday morning, but in the meantime, the Spanish had a night's festivities arranged for us, and that meant all night! They took us for a late dinner at a nearby restaurant, where it seemed the whole barracks was in attendance. We had a fantastic meal with so many courses I lost count of them. Everything was washed down with the best of Spanish wine. After the meal, we all headed off to bars near the port, where it seemed that the whole town was enjoying the festivities. The next day—the holy day— the custom was apparently that anyone who had received a commendation or promotion would be officially recognised in a formal ceremony, and then afterwards there would be a great party for them and all their family members. Maybe they had something to teach us after all. At home, our families were treated more or less like lepers by our own authorities.

In the meantime, and after a number of phone calls to our dealer friend Mick, it had been decided that we would meet them on the Friday between 4.30 pm and 5.30 pm at a motel/restaurant which was some distance outside Madrid, and about 15 kilometres from Valencia. Mick said that I would recognise him, as he would be on crutches.

On the Friday morning, we met the Spanish operational team at police headquarters. These guys seemed to have brought every gun in the armoury with them! We discussed our plan of action, and all seemed in order—or so I thought. On the Friday afternoon, Jimmy and I drove our hired Corsa to the Hosteria La Carreta on the main road to Madrid, and parked in a side road near the motel. When we called Mick, he informed me he was awaiting my arrival in the café attached to the Total garage beside the motel. When I went to meet him, I saw a guy sitting with crutches in the company of three or four other people. I immediately recognised the one with the crutches as Michael Cahillane, a wanted criminal, formerly a resident of Northern Ireland and now known to be domiciled in Spain.

Cahillane called me over to join him, and introduced his companions as his brother, his girlfriend, and his Spanish business partner with his wife. He explained that he had smashed his leg in a motorcycle accident and it was certainly in a bad way. Apparently the injured leg had become infected, and as a result, a cage had been put around it, with a large silver bolt through the bone holding the limb together. One thing was for sure, I thought: Cahillane wasn't about to run away, anyway. As per my training, I had a good look at the company, memorising what details I could. Cahillane's hair was receding, and his left ear was pierced but held no ear ring. His girlfriend seemed older than he was, an English woman with dyed hair. Her teeth were badly stained, and although she was bedecked with jewellery, particularly many rings, it looked as though she had never worn a wedding ring. The brother was younger, with very dark hair, and wore jeans and heavy leather cowboy boots. Cahillane's Spanish 'business partner' was in his 40s with heavy stubble: his wife was Spanish also and dressed completely in black. She ate food from her plate constantly and never made eye contact.

Cahillane said he had been living in Spain for seven or eight years now, and could speak the language more or less fluently, due largely to the time he had spent in a Malaga jail on various charges. We then discussed the drug scene and Cahillane began to boast about how much money there was to be made. As far as the present consignment went however Richardson, the 'man in Bangor' whom the drugs were for, would be slightly disappointed, Cahillane observed, as there wasn't as much as he might be expecting. He also mentioned that he and his friends had taken the long way to meet me, in order to avoid police checks, and that they would be returning via the coastal route. He motioned towards a blue BMW which was parked nearby. It was good to see the drugs business was paying somebody well, I reflected. It would however be payback time very soon.

The Spanish business partner, Juan, wanted to take a look at our car, saying that he would stow the drugs in it while I waited in the café with Cahillane. As I walked him to our Corsa, I attempted to make conversation with him, but he pretended he couldn't speak English, which was rather silly really, since he had been nodding in agreement to everything Cahillane had been saying in English a few minutes earlier. What happened next however made it clear that in spite of all his supposed precautions, Juan was every bit as stupid as he looked. To my utter horror and disbelief, all I could suddenly hear was the unmistakable whirring sound of the electronic motor drive of a camera! The sound continued for what seemed like an eternity, but was probably in reality no more than a few seconds. I frantically scanned the area to see where the whirring was coming from. Literally a few yards from us, in the driveway of a nearby bungalow, sat an old battered van with, it was now obvious, the finest of Spanish covert operatives sitting in the back of it. 'Jesus', I thought, 'the wheel is well and truly off now'.

Almost as incredible as the fiasco itself, it seemed that my friend Juan, the seasoned drug dealer, hadn't heard the whirring of the camera either—or if he had, he obviously hadn't recognised the sound. I still have trouble believing this, but it was the case. Juan was clearly not the pro he thought he was. I breathed a sigh of relief and silently cursed the 'agente'. Unfortunately, it wouldn't be the last time my life was put in danger by these lunatics and their amateurish antics!

Anyway, Juan and I returned to the café a few minutes later. I asked Cahillane how much cannabis he had with him. Twenty-five kilos, came the reply and, not for the first time, I was incredulous. We had been promised something in the region of 150 kilos! I told Cahillane in no uncertain terms that if he thought we were driving from Valencia to Belfast for so little, he must be off his rocker. Although 25 kilos was still a fairly big consignment in Irish terms, we were used to transporting one to two hundred kilos at a time. Cahillane tried to smooth things over by saying that there would be a bigger load for us the next time, and that he would make sure we got the full fee which we had been promised—£15,000—for the load. He went on to offer us all sorts of other scams in an attempt to placate us. We argued for a while longer, but it was fruitless in any case, so we bade farewell and Jimmy and I went back to our car. I opened the boot, and there were two large cardboard boxes, which contained the 25 kilos in nine bars.

I had barely opened the boot when up came the Spanish back-up squad with our support officer from home. Wielding sawn-off shotguns and God knows what else, they jumped out without a word, grabbed the drugs, transferred them to their car and careered off again.

Sometime later, we met up with the entire Spanish team in their headquarters, and we examined and photographed the drugs. And early the next morning, we started on the long drive back under escort towards Santander and our ferry home. The Spanish weren't finished with us quite yet, though. When we got to Santander, the pantomime continued. The Spanish Magistrate who had accompanied us was now insisting that he proceed onto the ferry in front of us with the warrant, so that no one could obstruct us in any way. I have rarely seen such a farcical sight. According to Spanish law, which in many ways is very different from our own, you must have the written authority of a magistrate to be in possession of illegal goods such as drugs or guns etc. as part of an undercover operation. The majority of these 'magistrates' are quite young: they are in fact more like judicial employees than judges—perhaps something equivalent to our own DPP staff. Anyway, as we were boarding the boat at Santander docks, this particular young magistrate insisted in walking solemnly in front of our car, holding the said warrant aloft, for all the world as if he were part of a funeral possession. And this in full view of everyone on board the boat or standing at the docks! It was just as well for us that the majority of these bystanders would most likely have thought that we were being deported or something of the sort. We, for our part, were completely mortified. In defence of the Spanish however, I should add that I was later to learn that this small side show did serve some kind of purpose after all. Apparently, by walking in front of us until we got on the boat in this fashion, the magistrate was simply ensuring that, by indicating so clearly that we were under the protection of the Spanish Judiciary, no one could interfere with us, not even the captain of the boat.

At Dover, we were to be met by our own Customs and a Crime Squad escort, and escorted back to Belfast via Stranraer. On our return to Belfast, I spoke to McCooke and arranged to meet him at Harry Ramsden's diner the next day, 8 October 1997. When we met, we discussed the shortfall in money and then, on his instruction, I left to deliver the drugs, which were now in the boot of my car, to the 'man in Bangor': Richardson. I met him near the Marina in the seaside town. When he got into my car, he immediately asked whether I would do another run of between 60 and 70 kilos. After a short conversation, I began to help Richardson transfer the drugs from my car to his. He was of course completely oblivious to the fact that he was now under the cover of a massive covert umbrella of both surveillance personnel and uniform support. Richardson made his way straight home and was arrested a short time later as he was dismantling the parcel. A short time later, our other friend, McCooke, who had been shadowed since my meeting with him, also found himself in handcuffs.

On the other hand, it was to take nearly ten years for Michael Cahillane to be brought to justice. He was finally arrested by HM Customs when he made the fatal mistake of returning to Northern Ireland. He appeared at Belfast Crown Court in March 2007, charged with possession with intent to supply. Although this operation ultimately had a successful conclusion, it was more down to the grace of God than anything else. It wouldn't be the last time either that our Spanish colleagues would put us through the mill.

Chapter 17

Fatal Attraction: The Dublin Mob and the Loyalist Connection

There is no better illustration of the basic principle that in the criminal fraternity, particularly in drug dealing circles, greed truly does conquer all, than the strange alliances which began to spring up between the Dublin mob and the loyalist paramilitary groups in the North in the mid to late 1990s.

The insatiable greed which now existed amongst the criminal warlords in Dublin in what was becoming an increasingly 1920s mafia-style environment meant that those gangs working for the Dublin Godfathers John Gilligan and George Mitchell aka 'The Penguin' had been forced to look to the northern Loyalist gangs, who could provide new sources of drug income for them. Ultimately of course, and thankfully, such associations would more often than not turn out to be a double-edged sword for the Dublin gangs. In the case of 'The General', Martin Cahill, it was his contacts with various loyalist groups which would attract the attention and ultimately the censure of PIRA Brigade staff, and lead to his eventual demise. The other Dublin Godfathers were risking the same fate by cultivating such frowned-upon associations. And of course, the existence of such links opened up new avenues for our unit in the North to infiltrate the Dublin gangs, enabling us to work together with our Garda counterparts to hit the drug dealers hard and often. We couldn't stop every consignment from the Continent and other parts of the

Republic getting to Dublin, but we were able to intercept a number of million pound loads of various types of drugs destined for Dublin at this time. It should go without saying of course that the Garda had been carrying out raids by conventional means very effectively for years prior to these joint operations with us, and were achieving particularly impressive results in this area in the mid to late 1990s.

By late 1997, our unit had infiltrated the upper echelons of the criminal gangs in Dublin and Cork to such an extent that we would be meeting various members of the gangs on a regular basis in different locations throughout the UK and Ireland to discuss shipments of drugs. As I have said, the Dublin gangs working for John Gilligan and his ilk were now collaborating with a variety of notorious Loyalist paramilitaries from our part of the country, and in particular with a Northern criminal who went by the name of 'Speedy'. A twenty-year-old punk who loved fast cars, Speedy was known to police on both sides of the border. He had a reputation for frequently informing on rivals and associates as a means of removing them from the scene as opposition or of settling private scores, particularly if they owed him money. Such behaviour—together with the lethal mix of contacts which he cultivated from various opposing factions, such as the Dublin gangs, splinter Republican paramilitary groups such as the IPLO and INLA, and Loyalist organisations such as the UDA and the LVF—was no more than a ticking time bomb waiting to explode. No-one was to be particularly surprised when, in the final event, Speedy got more than his fingers burned.

By 1997, Speedy had been working with the Gilligan gang for over three years and was often spotted in trendy Dublin nightspots in the company of various gang members. He was a close associate of Brian Meehan aka 'The Tosser' (who was strongly suspected at the time of having driven the motorcycle in the Guerin murder). Speedy also ran with a number of other high-profile gang members who were now in hiding in Holland and Spain and wanted by the Garda. These ex-pats were still active however and were sending over large shipments of drugs to Speedy from their foreign boltholes. He in turn was distributing the drugs in question to all and sundry, across the board, regardless of their criminal pedigree or political affiliations. There is no doubt that Speedy had a death wish which he seemed in a great hurry to fulfil: for, apart from being a wanted man by police on both sides of the border, he was, by virtue of slagging off their members, also high on the current hit list of the PIRA, who were beginning to regard the Dublin gangs' associations with Loyalist organisations such as the UDA and UVF with growing alarm.

Speedy would on some occasions prefer to drive the consignments himself—just for the hell of it, as acts of pure bravado. On one such occasion, we had been tipped off that he was coming North, over the border, with a load of nearly a quarter of a million pounds' worth of drugs which he had just collected from the Dublin gang. Accordingly, a road block of the elite HMSU (Headquarters Mobile Support Units) had been set up to intercept him as he approached Belfast. Apparently undeterred by what must have been the intimidating sight of the HMSU reception party, Speedy simply drove his high-powered car at full throttle straight into the police blockade, ramming it with such force that he set one of the police cars on fire in the process. He made good his escape by abandoning the damaged car in West Belfast—but not before burning the contents, thereby ensuring that he did not give the police the satisfaction of seizing the drugs. Unfortunately for us at the time, Speedy's erratic, nomadic lifestyle, whereby he would sleep in a different location every night, meant that he was extremely difficult to keep tabs on. He was however to get his comeuppance not too much further down the line.

Ironically enough, the Veronica Guerin murder and its aftermath was one significant development which enabled the exiled members of the Gilligan gang to get a foothold into the importation of drugs into Dublin from Europe. The Garda's massive witch hunt for Guerin's murderers had resulted in a temporary blip in the supply of drugs from Europe into the Dublin market through the usual channels. The subsequent shortage in supplies meant that exiled gang members such as The Tosser would now be able to step into the breach and become direct conduits for the dope runs from their European boltholes. Luckily for us however, the fact that these guys were becoming increasingly dependent on Speedy and his associates would prove to be their Achilles' heel. Speedy was now not only distributing the merchandise on their behalf, but also collecting the corresponding cash payments: in effect, he was now their cash lifeline as well as their mule. Had he been a more stable and mature individual, as opposed to a crazed, virtually psychotic lunatic, things might have gone more positively for the crooks. Over and above the fact that he was basically a self-destructive madman, Speedy was now himself using increasingly large quantities of coke. Many drug dealers suffer a similar and self-inflicted fate, and end up becoming addicted to the filth they are trading in. In Speedy's case, the result was that any semblance of stability he had began to unravel altogether. His behaviour became ever more irrational, with him being arrested on one occasion in one of The Tosser's flats in Dublin, naked and out of his head on coke. As if this wasn't bad enough, it quickly emerged that the naked female in whose arms he had been found was in fact the girlfriend of one of the Dublin gang members who was currently slammed up on remand.

The environment in which Speedy was now operating was nothing more than an increasingly messy pool of suspicion and recrimination. Even many of the ordinary, so-called decent criminals at the time were beginning to noticeably distance themselves from the murderous antics of the Dublin mob, making any excuse not to deal with them. As a result, the same mob were finding it nigh on impossible to get any lorry drivers or other couriers to deliver their shipments for them—which tied them even more to Speedy, and him to them.

Unfortunately for Speedy, by this time the PIRA Command had had enough of his antics and those of the Dublin mob. Apart from any other consideration, these activities were now attracting the spotlight of the Republic's Asset Recovery Agency and the scrutiny of the North's security services, and both agencies were beginning to look more closely at a number of areas which the IRA would have preferred to be left alone. Speedy would finally meet his end, gunned down in a hail of bullets in a Newry public house. Responsibility for the murder would later be claimed by the PIRA's associated unit, DAAD (Direct Action Against Drugs). It is a sad reality that very few—friend or foe—would grieve the demise of Speedy.

In spite of it all, the connections hewn by the Dublin gangs with the renegade Loyalist groups dealing in drugs would remain intact, with others taking the place of Speedy and his like. At the risk of sounding like a broken record, it was avarice—sheer greed—which would do the trick every time. In that sense, our work was never done.

I should take the opportunity, when talking of the Dublin mob and the drugs scene in Dublin, to say something about the Garda and what a privilege it always was to work with them. Sadly, it was only very late in my career that I was to get the opportunity to work closely with the Garda Síochána, for I was to greatly enjoy the experience and make many friends among their number.

It had always been my perception earlier in my career that there was a policy on both sides of the border, supported by the antiquated element of both forces, to stage-manage any supposed co-operation. There was some localised operational co-operation, but this was mainly between individuals who had formed good working relationships at ground level: any more formalised relationships at border level had not really worked out, due to the politics of the day. They were no doubt set back too by such tragedies as the murder of Superintendent Harry Breen and his RUC colleague in 1989, ambushed and butchered by PIRA murderers on their way home from a working trip to Dundalk. There have been enquiries set up and talk of collusion. Regardless of any such possibilities, I always personally thought that both forces were too blasé about the security arrangements for such visits.

I can remember the first time I visited Dublin Castle and the Headquarters of the Garda Drug Unit. As I walked into the main squad room, I was definitely a little nervous. I was introduced to the squad, and the majority came forward readily to shake my hand. I was aware of a slight coldness on the part of some of the younger members of the team, but I believe this was very likely because they had never actually met someone from our Force personally before: in any case, any coldness I had detected in their manner would later completely evaporate. The senior officers welcomed me in a genuinely friendly way and I knew from the very start that these people were true professionals, like the majority of Garda officers I have had the privilege to serve with since. As I have said, we would go on to forge important friendships: these were colleagues on whom I would literally depend for my survival in some operations. After that initial meeting, I can remember feeling slightly embarrassed, and in a strange kind of way, upset, when I discovered that the Garda had a full-time liaison officer from the Liverpool Crime Squad attached to them. I can remember thinking there was something ironic about it— here was a Brit with a permanent posting in Dublin Castle, part of the set-up, so to speak. Meanwhile we ourselves, literally up the road, were still obliged to communicate with our Garda colleagues through our respective Headquarters. It was, to put it mildly, completely hopeless.

Clearly, our co-operation with the Garda Síochána was shrouded with secrecy for reasons relating to the undercover nature of our work and all the security implications which went with it. Undeniably too, however, there were a number of politicians on both sides of the border who for a very long time saw any kind of co-operation between the forces as evidence of some kind of sinister plot, the aim of which, depending on your point of view, was either to subvert the Irish state, or to hoodwink a Northern majority into a united Ireland with that first crucial step: an all-Ireland police force.

For me, the practical truth of the situation is that the border only exists in the minds of politicians: criminals have no such problems. In the fight against drugs, terrorism and organised crime, real, lasting success will not be possible until an all-Ireland body of law enforcement officers are free to pursue this criminal scum from Derry to Cork.

I will not take the liberty of naming and perhaps embarrassing some of my closest friends in the Garda, but they know who they are: they became more like brothers and sisters to me than work colleagues. They and their senior officers were experienced, hard-nosed detectives who weren't afraid to speak plainly when things hadn't been done to their satisfaction—but they were always as honest and genuine as they were blunt and straightforward. I have been honoured to work with such colleagues, whose professionalism, dedication and courage was second to none. At the risk of repeating myself, I have to say that I consider it a privilege to have served with them.

Chapter 18
The One that Got Away

I have recounted many of our victories in the fight against the drug dealing gangs in Ireland, the UK and further afield. It would be unrealistic of course to give the impression that we had only successes, as there were of course occasions when mistakes would be made which would result in the parcel actually getting through. In our defence, such mistakes were rare, and our success rate was very high. But even the best-laid plans are open to human error on occasion, and we undercover cops were human too, of course.

One such job was an operation involving the Dublin mob and a consignment of ecstasy tablets to be delivered to Dublin by our old friend Speedy and his associates in the North. I had been contacted by some of Speedy's mates in the North with whom we had already done business. Despite the fact that on that occasion they had lost their parcel through us to a drugs bust, they obviously had no notion that it had been anything to do with us, and so our cover as lorry drivers who were not averse to doing the odd illicit run was still intact. The contact was asking whether we would be able to bring in a parcel from Holland for some friends of his in Dublin. These 'friends' were, we knew, the remnants of the Traynor gang, which was now controlled by The Tosser and Speedy. The contact was telling us that they had a relatively small parcel, about the size of a large holdall, waiting to be picked up in Holland. He said that they had had a scare recently with one of their own drivers and didn't want to use any of their usual couriers.

We already knew that these guys were getting paranoid as, together with the boys from the Castle, we were causing them serious problems at that time. They didn't know which way to turn or whom to trust. Speedy and the gang were obviously hoping that, by switching to a Northern driver for part of the route, they would be safe.

We checked our intelligence with the Dublin Castle Headquarters team, and agreed to keep them informed of any developments. After a few further phone calls with Speedy's chum, I drove down with another undercover colleague to meet the Dublin mob in a pub on the main Dublin Road, near Dundalk. Prior to the meet, we met up with the Castle team for a briefing. I would need their armed cover for the meeting with the contact, since the law dictated that I couldn't go into the South armed or for that matter with any other kind of back-up. Even my being in possession of a radio could have been construed as illegal in some quarters, such was the farcical world we had to live in. In any event, I was very happy to put my safety completely in the hands of the Garda team. Apart from anything else, they would be as interested as I was to see who would turn up to meet us.

My undercover colleague and I went into the pub in question and ordered a pint. After about a half an hour, I saw a guy whose face I recognised from the Dublin mob, enter the bar. He appeared to be looking around for someone, and I knew that he had recognised me, but he did not approach us and left almost immediately. I don't know whether he had a genuine reason or not for such behaviour or whether this little bit of theatre was supposed to impress us, but he came back in almost immediately and came up to us, waffling away about how you couldn't be too careful these days. I recognised him as having been involved in a major shipment from Belgium a few years previously: he went under the name of 'Matt'. He had a shaven head and was wearing black from head to toe, including a small black, commando-style woollen hat. This garb gave him a far more sinister appearance than his slight frame warranted, as was no doubt his purpose in wearing it. Anyway, we got down to business straight away, and I told him that we could have a driver for them the following week, but didn't want to be messed about by having to wait around. Matt assured us that the stuff was waiting for collection, and had been for over a week already. He added though that he could very well ring us to tell us he didn't need us after all, as they had been trying to move it on themselves. I asked where he wanted the parcel delivered to, adding that anywhere in the South was out of the question, as our driver wouldn't go down there. Our guy would however be willing to meet somewhere in the North, or anywhere they wanted in England. I was hoping that they might go for that, as it would mean we could extract our man from the equation as early as possible.

We needed to wind this first meeting up quickly now: I didn't want to hang about in Dundalk any longer than absolutely necessary, in case I was recognised by any other miscreants in the area I might come across on my travels. I also knew that our Garda friends would be waiting to take Matt away under surveillance, so I bid him goodbye and we all left together. As my colleague and I gunned our car towards the border, I was able to contact the Garda, and they confirmed that Matt was a well-known drugs dealing target and that they were babysitting him all the way.

A few days later, Matt was in touch with me again, asking if we could be in Holland the next week, as their parcel was there and ready to go. I arranged the necessary authorisations to travel through Holland. On this occasion though, I decided that there was no need for us to take a HGV the whole way to Holland to pick up what was after all just a holdall, and I arranged to rent a lorry there with which we could do the pick-up. We could then fly the gear back into Belfast with the help of our Customs friends. Once everything was set, we flew to Holland, and made our way to the Rotterdam area where by this stage we had a well-established base, about which I will explain more at a later point. We made contact with the Holland Operational team and they were able to rent a suitable vehicle for us.

Once we were ready, we got in touch with Matt and gave him our exact location, asking him to pass our number to his people so that the pick-up could be arranged. Later that evening we were contacted by a guy with a Southern Irish accent, who told us that his people would be in the Rotterdam area the next day, and asked where we would meet. We told him that we would specify a place to meet whenever he rang the next day. We then informed our back-up teams of our plans, and briefed the Garda as agreed. As far as we could tell, the drugs would be brought into Northern Ireland, but it seemed that they were destined for the South, and our Garda colleagues would have to be ready at their end.

The next day, we had our driver park our vehicle as planned in one of the many lay-bys leading up to Rotterdam port. We contacted the gang to give them the details of our truck. As dusk approached, the surveillance teams reported that a Dutch registered Citroen had cruised past our vehicle three times, and was now parked about three hundred metres away. There were two men in the car. We told our driver that he should expect visitors shortly, and within a few minutes the Citroen closed in on our lorry. Our Dublin friends however parked about three vehicles away from our truck, and called our driver from there, asking him to alight from his lorry and walk down towards them. With some degree of satisfaction, we noted that they seemed to be getting increasingly paranoid with everyone they met: the seeds of suspicion and distrust amongst their ranks were now well and truly sown. This was exactly what we wanted.

Our man got out of his truck and walked down towards the car, but as instructed by us, stood well back from it. One just didn't know how far the paranoia of our targets would push them. We closed our surveillance umbrella tighter around them and waited. The guy in the front passenger seat got out of the Citroen, pulled a medium-sized sports bag from the back seat, and cautiously approached the undercover officer, who recognised him as being an associate of Traynor, whose gang had boasted about being involved in the murder of Veronica Guerin. The undercover officer had seen the same man on a previous job involving a large shipment of cannabis. The target's eyes lit up in recognition, as he handed over the bag to our man with a smile and mumbled, 'See you later mate,' then strolled back to his car, which immediately hurtled out of the car park. As soon as they had gone, we examined the bag which had been handed over and found it to contain 8,000 'E's. Our surveillance team were able to confirm later that the Citroen had crossed the Dutch-Belgian border.

We returned to Belfast the following day to organise the reception committee for our targets, along with back-up at our end. We had of course been keeping the Garda informed throughout, and we drove down for a briefing with them. A day or two later, allowing a suitable length of time for a lorry to have done the return journey from Holland, we contacted the Dublin mob to inquire where they wanted to meet us for the handover of the drugs. Their first suggestion was that we could bring the parcel down on the Belfast to Dublin train, but I said that there was no way we were about to risk travelling any further. We had kept to our part of the arrangement, and it was up to them to pick up the goods and pay us: we didn't want to be messed about. The contact said that he would have to consult the others and rang off. About an hour later, he rang back, saying that they would drive up to Newry to collect the bag. In hindsight, we should probably have drawn them deeper into the North, but we were confident that we could control the parcel no matter where it was, and we had been proved right hundreds of times before. A few hours later, the Garda were in position and we were ready and waiting for our criminal friends to arrive to collect the bag.

You can allow for many eventualities in an operation, but there is one element you can't always cater for, and that is human error. When the gang made contact again, they suggested a rendezvous for the handover at a place in the North, on a small road just about a hundred metres over the border. We knew that this would have been too difficult for us to cover with conventional surveillance, and proposed instead a filling station on the busy main route between Belfast and Dublin, just over the border in the North: they agreed to meet us there. In order to make sure that we had the whole area covered, I had deployed a number of surveillance officers on foot in and around the garage, as well as numerous operatives in cars. Shortly after 2.00 pm, the targets contacted the UC, who was sitting in his vehicle in the front of the garage, to announce their arrival at the garage.

By this stage we were like coiled springs, waiting to pounce on the gang as soon as we got the word that they had collected the goods. A black v6 GTI Volkswagen spun into the car park and drew level with our man's vehicle. Within seconds I had confirmation that the handover had taken place. The Volkswagen tore out of the garage, but wrong-footed everyone by heading North instead of South. I gave instructions to my team to close in on it at once, but just as I spoke, the bad guys wrong-footed everybody again, pulling up beside a southern bound car in the middle of the road and throwing the bag of drugs into it, after which it took off towards the South at speed. There would, in fact, still have been no problem with this new development, if only everyone had been alerted to it. Unfortunately however the surveillance operative who was the only one to witness the switch, which had only taken about three seconds to complete, wrongly assumed that others had seen it too, and she didn't alert the rest of the team.

The rest is history. By the time the operative in question had decided to share this crucial piece of information with the rest of us, the gang members had slipped the net with the drugs. Absolutely sickened, and embarrassed to the core, I brought my car to a screeching halt beside the Garda control car to relay what had happened to them. They roared off at once in hot pursuit of the criminals with the drugs. I returned to base, completely dejected and dismayed.

These things happen in life, but in our game you couldn't afford to make the same mistake twice. I had learnt my lesson, and this would in fact be the only time I would let our target and the parcel get clean away. I had learned the hard way that: 1) being overly self-confident was fatal, and 2) one should never depend on any one person alone.

As it turned out, in the long run the Garda, fortunately enough, were able to spare me some of the embarrassment and sense of personal responsibility which, rightly or wrongly, I felt so keenly. Some days later, they were able to recover most of the haul in a raid in the Dublin area. I was very glad to hear of their success. On the positive side, I suppose the cock-up on this job did have some advantages in the long-term, in that it meant that our cover was still intact with the Dublin mob in question, none of whom had had any idea of what had actually happened. And so we were free for another crack at them whenever the opportunity arose, which luckily it did. This next time, we left nothing to chance.

Apart from all of the hassle and frustration generated by this incident and our mistake, one thing which it did highlight once again was the absurdity of a situation where two forces with separate command structures and using different radio frequencies were trying to police a border which only existed in the minds of extremist politicians and bigots.

Chapter 19

Operation Metro: All's Well that Ends Well

It was autumn 1997, and our sources were indicating that the Dublin gangs were desperate to get drugs into the city for the upcoming Christmas and New Year period. The word was that the Dublin and Cork gangs, who at the time were starting to collaborate in a number of ways, were now working closely with each other to bring a major consignment in from the Continent. Our intelligence was confirmed by the fact that various approaches had been made by contacts we had in these gangs to me and other undercover officers in our unit, in our guise as transporters and HGV drivers who were more than open to the idea of making extra cash by bringing in a few extra boxes of illicit goods.

Since the revamped unit had been in operation, we had spent some considerable time consolidating this particular 'legend'—that we were in the haulage game with ready access to truck drivers of a criminal mindset who were prepared to work with the drug dealing gangs. We had quickly become aware that most of the gangs on both sides of the border had for quite some time been exploiting the huge lorry traffic which is part and parcel of any island's trading activities, and Ireland's in particular. Criminals had of course been making use of such traffic for years in terms of bringing in contraband alcohol and cigarettes: bringing in drugs was merely the next step in a sense. There were literally thousands of HGVs commuting between Ireland, the UK and Europe every week. The majority of the associated haulage companies were fully legitimate operations. Such businesses face one major problem in terms of keeping control of the service they provide, apart from the normal day-to-day problems associated with the maintenance of a massive fleet of haulage vehicle: that of employing reputable drivers. The fact is that, due to the huge volume of activity and associated work, there is a steady market for temporary drivers, some of whom work for agencies, but the vast majority of whom are usually guys with other jobs, moonlighting to make a few extra pounds outside the system. In such circumstances, and because in a sense of this lack of accountability, there are likely to be individuals among such workers who will be prepared to take a one-off risk and the opportunity to make a small fortune by bringing in one or two boxes of illegal goods.

We had therefore decided at a very early stage that to plant our operatives into this milieu of 'ghost drivers', so to speak, would pay dividends, and so we set about building up a working backstop for our undercover operations within these circles. As it happened, I had a number of very good friends who were in positions of responsibility in some of the major haulage companies, and they were only too happy to oblige by giving some of our operatives legitimate runs from time to time. The fact that they didn't have to pay our men was of course an added incentive! The advantages of such an operation for us were clear: our unit could gain valuable experience in driving HGVs, make valuable contacts in the driver's fraternity, and build up invaluable backstopping legends. Once they were moving in these circles, they could make it known that they were open to doing the odd illegal job, and be able to offer their services when the opportunity arose. More often than not, once word had got out that they weren't averse to the idea of being involved in something dodgy, they would also be approached by other drivers to do runs.

And so when, a little later in autumn 1997, we were asked by Garda High Command to assist in infiltrating a conspiracy to bring an unknown but sizeable quantity of cannabis into the South, we were ideally placed to make interventions through the lorry-driving circuit. Garda intelligence was very much in line with our own: that criminal gangs from Dublin and Cork were intending to bring in a large consignment of drugs which had been already purchased in Belgium and would be brought as far as the UK mainland by the sellers. The crooks were looking for a lorry driver from home to bring the load into Dublin, but were becoming increasingly reluctant to approach any of the Southern Irish drivers due to the high loss of loads they had recently sustained. A Garda contact was now proposing to introduce one of our guys to the gang as a possible driver, with the cover story that he had met us on another operation and thought that we were Northern criminals.

We were more than happy for the Garda contact to pass our details on to the Southern gang, and Ronnie Flanagan, Chief Constable at the time, gave us verbal permission at once over the phone to progress the operation with our southern colleagues. Operation Metro would prove to be one of our most successful raids ever, in terms of the size of the seizure and the arrest of the principal players. It would also prove to be one of the most frustrating and infuriating operations we had ever been associated with, in terms of the number of twists and turns and false starts involved. Although the end results would be unparalleled, there was more than one point during the course of Metro when I seriously contemplated throwing in the towel altogether. I have never been so painfully aware of the extent to which this game was all about biding your time and never making your move too soon. It required nerves of steel and was definitely not for the faint-hearted or highly strung…

In October 1997, we received a call on our covert mobile from the Southern gang: they were keen to meet our man, the driver who had been recommended to them. The caller proposed a meeting at a well-known hotel near Dundalk a few days later. We informed our main Garda contact within the Dublin Castle Unit and arranged to go to the meet under their protection. At the hotel, our man met a guy called Richard who, judging by his accent, was obviously from Dublin and who asked him whether he'd be willing to do a one-off delivery of something in the region of 200 kilos of cannabis. Richard said that contacts would bring the parcel as far as the London area, if our guy could take it the rest of the way to Ireland. The undercover said that he would be very interested in the job. Two days later, they had another meeting at a bar in the same area, the purpose of which was for our driver to meet the main man behind the job. I had travelled down for this meeting too, to brief the Garda and lie in wait with their team near the venue of the meet, in order to see who would arrive. The undercover officer went into the bar and met Richard and his companion, who went by the name of 'Adrian' and was also Southern Irish. This meeting was confirmation indeed that there did appear to be a major criminal conspiracy in motion to bring a large consignment of drugs into Ireland. We agreed to continue to assist the Garda, and to await further developments.

A few days later Adrian called our man, who was now back in Belfast, asking if he would be in the South Mimms area of London within the next few weeks. When he was told this was a possibility, Adrian proposed a meeting in South Mimms with our driver on 30 October.

On the day of the proposed meeting, we all travelled to London. I had arranged surveillance cover from the London Crime Squad. After a series of false starts, our undercover guy eventually met up with two new contacts: Mick and Pat. Adrian however did not make an appearance. According to the other two, he had been involved in some sort of road accident on his way to the airport, but might be along later. Mick then turned the conversation to the business in hand: would our man by any chance be in Holland again soon? It seemed that there had been some communication problems between the crooks: Pat said that they had been told that our driver would be going the whole way to Holland to collect the gear. Our guy put him straight, saying that Adrian had never said anything about Holland: at a push, he would be able to go to Belgium, because that was a route he tended to do from time to time—but Holland was out of the question. (The reason for this was that it would be a logistical nightmare for us to have to operate over the two land frontiers on a live job. It wasn't impossible to do, but it was something we tried to avoid if possible.) Pat however kept insisting that their driver wouldn't cross the border into Belgium. This wasn't the first time we had come across this paranoia, but we could never really understand why it existed. Although Pat assured him that it would only entail having to drive 2 or 3 kilometres into Holland to collect the merchandise, our man kept stalling, with a number of different reasons and excuses.

After the discussion went back and forth for a bit longer, Pat eventually said he would ring the 'main man' to see if there was any way he would concede to a pick-up in Belgium rather than Holland. During the time Pat was outside making the call, Mick asked our driver if he would be willing to do runs from the mainland into Ireland, to which our man replied that he would be happy to do so. Pat returned to say that the boss had put a definite veto on the idea of a Belgian pick-up. Anxious to keep the crooks onside, our man then began to talk about ways in which a pick-up in Holland could be dealt with which might make things easier for him. The conversation was concluded with our driver saying that he would consider the Holland route, as he was keen to do the job, and that he might make a few 'dry runs' there in order to familiarise himself with the lay of the land. He agreed to keep in touch with Mick and Pat. Later that day, he got a call from Adrian, who said that he had been briefed by the others and understood the problems, but that they would, he hoped, be able to find a satisfactory solution.

That evening, our team made the journey back to Belfast. Straightaway, I set about briefing the Garda, our own authorities and Customs, and made a start on getting the required permissions to travel through Belgium and Holland, should we be required to do so. I was stretched to the limit at this time, working flat out on the paperwork for this operation, trying to keep on top of my other undercover jobs, some of which were at a very advanced stage, and keeping an eye on other operations that I was involved in, most of which were being run out of the UK.

Within the next few days, the word from Adrian, who was believed by the Garda to be from Cork, was that the arrival of the drugs at their holding area was imminent. Operationally, we were on immediate stand-by, ready to roll at a moment's notice. Given the considerable logistical back-up involved in covering the operation in the three or four countries, this meant that there was something in the region of five hundred officers standing by to assist this Garda operation. Everything was set for us to travel to Zeebrugge via Dover in or around 3 November, and be in position for 5 November. Time ticked by however, with not a word from the targets. Our operations were generally being disrupted across the board at that time, due to the lorry drivers' strike in France at the time. The blockades and chaos on the frontiers meant that everything, including of course illegal cargoes, had gone to ground.

Near the end of November, Adrian finally contacted our undercover officer to inform him now that the shipment was actually on the UK mainland, and would be ready for collection the following week! The designated place for the handover was to be the service area of our original meeting place, at the South Mimms services. My well-laid plans were completely up in the air now of course, and I had to start all over again to frantically try to put teams together to cover the lift, surveillance and so on. As usual, the South East Regional Crime Squad did not let me down, and quickly mobilised in close support. However, Adrian then contacted our man again and requested *yet another* meeting to discuss matters, at South Mimms on 28 November 1997. Yet *again* we travelled to Heathrow, and were in place to cover the meeting with the South East Regional Crime Squad Team. Adrian, this time with an unknown black guy with a Dublin accent, met our man at the airport and insisted that the load was still on, explaining that they were having problems moving it at present. It was left that they would get back in touch when they were finally ready.

We didn't have much other than courtesy calls from the Dublin gang until a fortnight before Christmas. At this point, they were desperate, it seemed, to get the shipment in before Christmas and the New Year: there was something akin to a drug famine on the streets. Two weeks before Christmas, and here I was again, off on what those around me, who didn't know the background, took to be junkets. I knew it would be especially hard for my family. Yet again, my children would be without a father. I needed this like a hole in the head. But I had no choice—and so once again I went through the by now well-worn channels, briefing all the agencies involved, and so on. In some quarters by this time, they were so used to me doing the rounds on this job that they barely acknowledged my making contact. The poor old Crime Squad were called on again and, to their eternal credit, even though it was so close to Christmas, they came up trumps.

On 17 December I accompanied the undercover officer to London to liaise with the Crime Squad. We had arrived in freezing temperatures, and as we made our way towards South Mimms, the weather started to further deteriorate. At South Mimms, our man met up with an individual known to me as 'The Dutchman' and Adrian, who were awaiting the arrival of the load. We remained on the site throughout the day, the whole team now struggling to even move in the atrocious weather conditions. Unbelievably, we would have to stand down yet again! The conditions anyway were such that, even if by some miracle the gang did turn up with their load, it was doubtful whether we would be able to keep it under proper surveillance. The Dutchman pleaded with our driver to stay until the snow cleared, but it was too close to Christmas. Sanity had to reign at some point in this job, and we all desperately needed a few days' rest. Our man told

Adrian and the Dutchman that he would be in touch when circumstances were more positive, and we started on the long journey back. You can imagine how we were feeling by this stage.

We weren't to get very much of a respite however as, early in the New Year, on 5 January 1998, Mick rang our undercover officer, inquiring if he would be in England again soon. They arranged to meet at 11.00 am on the following Thursday, near South Simms. Mick even rang again on 6 January, just to confirm that everything was online and that the Dutchman would be flying over to the UK that night to arrange the handover.

Given the nature of this operation to this point, no one was really very surprised when on the day of the meet, Mick contacted our man to say that, try as he might, he couldn't raise the Dutch end on the phone, and nobody knew where they were. Further attempts during that day were also fruitless and in the evening Mick announced that he was going back to Dublin to try and sort the mess out. Unbelievably, we had to stand down again…

The news from Mick the next day was that the Dutchman had been badly injured in a car crash and would be out of action for a few days. These guys were not the luckiest, it seemed, but before our suspicions about the frequency of road accidents in this operation began to run away with us, the Garda were in touch to corroborate Mick's story. I was at my wits' end with this job, to put it mildly, and we had a few serious debriefs on whether or not to bin the whole thing. Apart from the many thousands of operational hours which had been expended so far by all the agencies involved, the costs were spiralling out of control. Yet, on analysis of all the available intelligence and the evidence, it seemed clear there was something very big in the water: we just couldn't land it yet! All the Garda intelligence from contacts on the street was suggesting that the gangs were waiting for 'a very big one'. On top of this was the reality that the cupboards of the dealers were completely bare, and they were panicking. And then, there was the presence of the Dutchman on the plot. A big fish, who seldom risked leaving his home territory in Holland, his presence in London was attracting the interest of security agencies across the continent. We decided to ride out the storm.

So when Mick rang on 13 January 1998 to arrange the pick-up for the following weekend, we had no choice but to go with it. We were in the middle of a number of jobs but I informed the Garda to be on standby and moved all our available resources onto the operation. Adrian and Mick both rang our driver separately to confirm that the handover would happen at South Mimms at lunchtime on the Sunday.

By this stage I was rolling our battle team and wagons slowly towards London and had placed all the agencies involved on high alert —yet again. Mick was in contact on the Saturday to confirm that everything was on track for the Sunday at 12.30 pm. But at 11.30 am on the day itself, he rang our man to say that there was good news and bad news. The bad news was that—surprise, surprise—there might be a delay in doing the business. The good news however, he said, was that there would now be up to 400 kilos in the parcel. With trepidation, I broke the news to Crime Squad personnel, many of whom had been babysitting us now for over 72 hours. All credit to them, they just responded with a shrug, saying that it would be worth the wait anyway, and settled down to organising the further logistics involved with the delay in the convoy. In the meantime, Mick was insisting that our driver would meet them at South Mimms anyway: he and Adrian were waiting to take him by taxi to meet the main man. The lorry was only twenty minutes away and, on its arrival, the undercover officer joined the targets in their taxi, which took off for Terminal 3 at Heathrow Airport. We were forced to crash out other surveillance teams in our wake to cover this development.

Our guy met the Dutchman at Garfunkel's Restaurant in Heathrow Airport. The Dutchman turned out to be a well-known organiser on the Dutch end for the Irish gangs. A big fish indeed, and the fact that he had been prepared not only to come out of the woodwork, but to take the additional risk of travelling to the UK, meant that this wasn't going to be a usual load. It had to be a monster one. The Dutchman explained that they could only do the job first thing on the Monday. When our man explained that this would cause him real problems with his boss and that he would probably be sacked if he wasn't back on time, all three of the crooks attempted to persuade him to wait. Mick said that if he did, he would get another £20,000: surely this would cover any problems he might face back home?

I was apprised of the situation and decided we would have to run with it. The bird was up: we would just have to wait and see where it landed. We had committed too much time and effort, never mind money, to this operation for us to pull back now. I briefed the boys in the Castle about what was happening, and they left the matter completely in my hands. I think they too appreciated the fact that we had probably put the equivalent of the Garda national budget for the entire year into this operation so far!

And so our man told the trio that he could stay to do the handover at 4.00 pm on the Monday. The Dutchman said again that it was best to wait: he had lost sixteen and a half tonnes of gear in the last twelve months. I allowed myself a smile when I heard this later: in one way or another, we had taken out most of this—we must really have been busting their balls by this stage! This latest strike, if successful, would cripple them for good. And yet it seemed that our nerve was to be tested yet again on the Monday! That morning, the Dutchman rang our driver to say that job was off, but that he would meet him during the week to pay him the promised fee anyway. When he was told that this wasn't going to be possible, he said that Adrian would travel to Belfast to hand over the cash in person.

As you can imagine, I was pretty low by this stage. I had used up an awful lot of favours thus far. I could see by the faces of the Crime Squad teams that it was only their good manners, professionalism and perhaps respect for our Force which stopped them from telling me where to stick our job at this point. It was one of those truly lonely moments. I was at rock bottom, having crashed from an enormous high to an all-time low. Recriminations would come soon enough— for the time being we all retired to the nearest boozer.

The operation finally came to a head on 29 January 1998. It was almost an anti-climax when, in position yet again at the Services area at South Mimms, our driver got the call to say the parcel was on its way. A short time later, a Dutch registered lorry quickly pulled up, and in a matter of minutes the parcel had been transferred: a massive load of cannabis and skunk, to a street value of some five million pounds! We remained *in situ* for a period until we were sure the targets were well gone and then I joined our man the driver for the long haul home.

The stench in the cab was overpowering. The load had been far more than we expected, filling the sleeping quarters of the lorry completely, up to the roof. It quickly became apparent that among the consignment was some of the foulest smelling skunk we had ever come across. This stuff was so potent that we were forced to keep the windows of the lorry down—otherwise we would have been spaced out of our heads on the stuff. We were by this time under the surveillance umbrella of half of the UK's National Crime Squad. We reckoned our load was well in excess of 400 kilos. This was a big one by anyone's standards! The Irish mobs had invested a lot of money in this parcel, and heads would roll if they lost it and we and the Garda would ensure that they would. There was no doubt about it: this would be a crippling blow to the gangs responsible, who were eagerly awaiting its arrival. Apparently they had already sold a number of advance orders. In fact, celebrations in Dublin and Belfast were already well underway in anticipation of a big payday.

On leaving the South Mimms complex however, we hit a snag we hadn't really reckoned with, and I very nearly had a heart attack. As it transpired, the DOE Inspection service, Customs and the Police would frequently seal off this massive complex, looking for defective vehicles and customs offences. This, would you believe it, was one of those occasions! We were desperately trying to call in our close Crime Squad support in order to protect the integrity of our operation, when suddenly the passenger door of our lorry was yanked open. In jumped a rather elderly customs man with a clipboard who politely gestured for us to pull over to one of the rows of lorries awaiting a documents check. I looked at him in disbelief. He was sitting in a confined space, and actually *on top of* a 25 kilo box of one of the biggest consignments of cannabis to hit the UK, in an atmosphere where the stench of skunk was so overpowering as to make your head spin! To our utter amazement however, he didn't bat an eyelid. A short time later, I watched with incredulity as he jumped out of our vehicle thanking us and wishing us a pleasant journey...

Our driver and I sat motionless for some time after this, unable to speak, both from shock and utter disbelief. Eventually, we pulled ourselves together and set off on the long journey towards Ireland. By this time, everybody's heart had lifted, and the Crime Squad were certainly glad that they had persevered with us. It wasn't every day you got a hand in taking out a load this size! By this time, senior command of all the forces throughout the UK were only too glad to assist, and at home our colleagues in both the North and the South were determined that this massive load would not get into the wrong hands —for any length of time, anyway. It was crucial however that we take out the principal targets when they collected the load. To this end, I had never seen so many surveillance operatives in my life. It would not be an exaggeration to say that, of the 100 or so vehicles travelling in the same direction as the target lorry, at least fifty were transporting Crime Squad personnel of one sort or another. The vehicle was handed over from the surveillance umbrellas of one force to another in the trip from London, until it was seen to enter the Belfast-bound ferry. Even then, operatives remained in sight of the vehicle and its driver, should they decide to yet again change vehicles.

On arrival in Belfast, we took a short break, with the vehicle under armed guard and a virtual surveillance cordon, which by this time included planes and helicopters. The cavalcade then chaperoned the vehicle slowly towards the border. Our driver was going by the book, taking his time in order to ensure that he wouldn't be stopped for any traffic violation. As we drew close to the border, I transferred to the Garda's command car. Our Garda colleagues were awaiting our arrival with a similar display of surveillance talent, including their air cover and Armed Response Unit. We always got so much stick in the North for being an armed force, while people would contend that the Garda were effectively unarmed. I don't like to shatter anyone's illusions, but I had never in my life seen so many guns, from Uzis to revolvers. Like us, the Garda were determined that this consignment would never hit the streets of Dublin.

It seemed that the load was not designed for Dublin however, and for some hours we headed south, in the general direction of Cork. Our driver was taking it slowly. There had been a few phone calls from the bad guys—just enough to gauge the lorry's estimated time of arrival at various points. I had never been as far south as that before, and by this time was enjoying the sights. Our driver always seemed to choose old cemeteries in which to take his obligatory breaks. It was good to stretch your legs, have a smoke and study the history of whatever area we were in, which could be traced in the headstones, from Famine to Insurrection.

It was late afternoon on 31 January 1998 when things finally appeared to be coming to a head. Our Garda colleagues were getting more and more keyed up, and the chatter on the radios was now almost constant. Our driver had just reported that the crooks appeared to be calling him on to the slaughter destination. We were in Co. Tipperary, and the truck had entered a woodland area which was about four miles south of Cahir. The Detectives from the National Drug Unit, with whom I had worked for years, were quite confident that the lorry's final destination was Cork and that this was merely a drop-off of part of the consignment. The large surveillance umbrella had buried itself everywhere and anywhere in the surrounding area, including private driveways. I was amazed at the cooperative attitude of some people, who were only too happy to help the Garda and didn't seem to mind the intrusion at all: it would have been a different ball game in the North. The lorry was stationary now, and suddenly there appeared to be activity in and around the cab, with some of the boxes being unloaded.

Soon after, the lorry was on its way again, travelling towards Cork, with only the driver onboard. On the site in the woods, two cars, a Mercedes and a Toyota, appeared a short time later and the occupants alighted. The team now had to split, with one half keeping tabs on the lorry, and the other moving in for the strike before the cars left the scene. The strike team moved in and after a short struggle the culprits in the cars were arrested, as they loaded half the haul into their cars. With the team now split between this scene and the lorry, our priority had shifted to stopping any of the drugs getting out. It was decided to close the operation down at this juncture, and in a deliberate overt strike, the lorry was taken under control, as part of the team swooped on it, just outside Fermoy in Co. Cork. The driver melted into the countryside to live to fight another day.

The results were fantastic: drugs to a street value of £5 million had been recovered and four major arrests made. The crime lords in the south of the country had been dealt a body blow which would seriously set them back on their heels. Amazingly, they never suspected any involvement on the part of our undercover guy, and he was actually able to hit them again shortly afterwards, when they lost another load in the North. I think there must be something in those Kerryman jokes after all...

Chapter 20
Operation Hydra and the Turkish Mafia

My relationship with certain elements of the Metropolitan Police was to take a serious nosedive in 1997, when old enemies I had made resurfaced in a plot which itself would have been fit for a Stephen King thriller. The whole business certainly brought home to me yet again that there were really very few people in the circles I was moving in professionally who could be trusted— even among those who were supposed to be your friends. To this day, I still contemplate as to whether these people actually set me up from the beginning, or just exploited a golden opportunity for petty revenge. I must say that the considerable thought which I have given to the matter since has led me to the conclusion that with these particular individuals I was probably drinking from a poisoned chalice from the very outset.

The whole fiasco commenced innocently enough, with circumstances which were completely beyond my control in the first instance. In late 1996, a senior member of so10 from New Scotland Yard got in touch with one of my administrative staff to inform us that one of their officers had just opened a covert bank account within our area, as part of a major operation against a money-laundering gang in their jurisdiction. Such notification was in accordance with agreed protocols which were in effect throughout the UK, whereby an undercover unit in one jurisdiction would keep another informed of such activities within theirs. It was a matter of courtesy, but also a measure by which to ensure that operations would not be needlessly compromised. Under the same system, any deployment of undercover operatives outside their own immediate jurisdiction would require the authority of an officer of ACC rank or higher in the force area concerned. In Northern Ireland, this was usually the ACC Crime. In the case in question, no deployment or proposed deployment was mentioned to my staff, and so the matter of the covert bank account was simply noted in our records. We were alerted to the fact that an officer from the specific operational unit in question would be over from the Met to sort out the paperwork regarding the covert account.

What was not relayed to us however at any point was that a sizeable unit from the said operational team in the Met would actually deploy within Northern Ireland and embark on a course of action which consisted of basically doing their own thing. As it happened, two of these officers were originally from Northern Ireland and, although now members of a mainland force, for some reason best known to themselves had decided that our unit, and me in particular, wouldn't be informed of the deployment. Sheer arrogance was the driving force behind their unprofessional conduct, from what I could see. Unfortunately for these wayward officers, they managed to draw attention to themselves almost from the moment they set foot on our turf.

Northern Ireland is a small place, and that very day I got a phone call from a contact to the effect that these officers had booked themselves into the Europa Hotel in Belfast's city centre under false names. I didn't really give the matter much thought at the time, as they hadn't contacted me themselves, and I thought they were merely passing through. Within a day or so however, I was awakened in the middle of the night by a senior officer from Headquarters screaming at me down the phone, demanding to know on behalf of the ACC Crime what the f*** was happening: why hadn't I kept them informed about these people and whatever the hell it was they were doing over here, and so on? Apparently, the ACC's office had been receiving complaints from senior banking staff as to why these officers were not complying with agreed protocols—and I was getting the blame. There was nothing new in that, I suppose, but it was indeed the first I had heard about what these people were up to. They had definitely not followed proper procedures, and had simply bypassed the officer who was supposed to be assisting them at this end. It seemed that they had attempted to open a false bank account in one of the local banks, and had also tried to set up a covert company. Alarm bells had been pressed—literally!—by the official at Companies House where the formation of new companies is processed, and the matter was now a full-blown fiasco. I was told in no uncertain terms by the senior officer who had called me to bring these people to heel quickly, and,if the matter was genuine to make sure that we gave them the assistance they needed to despatch the matter as rapidly as possible, without any further trouble.

Since I knew where the rogue delegation was staying, I sent some of my officers to catch up with them and bring them back to our office. A few hours later, I was confronted in my office by the two undercover operatives. The junior officer, with whom I had always had a good rapport, apologised and told me he thought everything had been arranged in advance. The more senior of the two however was withdrawn, sullen and obviously hostile: 'I believe I have to ask your permission now to come to Belfast,' she spat at me, her face contorted with rage. I replied by telling her in no uncertain terms what I thought of her and her methods of operating, and that she shouldn't be so bloody cheeky. I was trying to help her, I said, and if she had gone about the whole matter in the proper manner from the start, this whole shambles wouldn't have happened. To be honest, I was also annoyed at the fact that the rest of the Operational team hadn't even had the courtesy to come to meet me face-to-face also, and had in fact simply gone back to London in a sulk.

I didn't realise the significance of it at the time, but the whole team happened to be from No. 3 Area in the Met. Professional as we were however, we offered to assist them with whatever backstopping they needed, and I subsequently reported back to the ACC that the matter had now been resolved. That was the last I ever expected to hear of the matter. I noticed that relations seemed a bit chilly after that for a while with certain members of SO10, but I wasn't overly anxious about it. After all, what happened had been of their own doing.

Almost a year to the day later, I was contacted by the Met to join a team whose mission was to infiltrate the Turkish mafia gangs operating in London. At that time, these gangs were urgently looking for someone to transport drugs into the UK on their behalf, and our unit had the necessary expertise to attempt this type of job. The targets were highly placed within the Turkish criminal fraternity and were known to be dealing in large quantities of heroin. We also had recent intelligence to the effect that they now had access to firearms.

And so it was that I found myself at Stansted Airport on a chilly October morning in 1997, preparing to meet one of the Turkish gang. I had stayed airside of the Arrivals gate until the Operational team had liaised with me, and attached a Nagra tape recorder to my back with surgical tape. I could never get used to the size of the Nagras, but at that time they were probably the best recording devices available for such purposes, and they did have the ability to pick up nearly 100 per cent of a conversation. Apart from the obvious clarity required for any subsequent court case, clarity of recording was essential for us to be able to transcribe the tape onto paper at a later point. Transcription was a painstaking task which could take endless hours at the best of times, and if the recording was of poor quality could nearly drive you to distraction. Anyway, as soon as I was ready, I went out through the Arrivals gate in the normal way, and went straight to a prearranged meeting place at a coffee bar right beside the gate.

A short time later, I was approached by my contact. He was a large Turkish guy of about thirty years of age. He looked very much like someone who worked out regularly in the gym, supplemented by a fair helping of steroids. I was quietly pleased to have these initial observations confirmed by my new friend, who said he was called Andy and went on to tell me, in broken English, that he had injured his shoulder in the gym about three months previously, and had put on about three stone since then, simply by eating normally. Andy said that he was a Turkish Cypriot, and that nearly all his circle of associates and friends were a good bit older than him. He also confided that he wasn't completely comfortable with the London Turkish fraternity, who, in his opinion, lacked respect.

Part of my cover story as Billy Craig—which wasn't too far from the truth—was that I was over in London to arrange other drug runs. I asked Andy what their requirements were, and he said that they were working on a load which might be ready to move soon, but that they were being very cautious at the minute. He said that they had about 100 kilos of heroin which would need transportation. I told him our fee would be £250 a kilo. Andy went on to say that the goods were in Spain at present. He then told me that he used to work for the Richardsons (one of the big London criminal gangs) as an enforcer. He suggested coming over to see me in Ireland with an elderly Irish man called Clarke before we did any business together: it would be important to meet me in my home territory, so that he could go back and tell his people—this would put them at ease. I said that this would be no problem, and we agreed to meet again to progress the relationship. At that point, Andy suddenly pulled a large bundle of cash from his pocket, asking me if I was alright for money whilst I was in London. I laughed, telling him I was okay, but thanking him all the same. He then told me that if I was ever passing through London again in the near future, I should ring him: he'd be happy to come to meet me and help me in any way he could. We finally parted company, with me taking a train into the centre of London, to clear my back just in case Andy had anybody watching me.

I kept in touch with Andy by telephone over the weeks that followed, ringing him once or twice from London. He kept asking me to call in and see them, and it was getting to the stage that he was becoming a little suspicious that I hadn't done so. In late November 1997 we were involved simultaneously in a number of operations targeting different gangs on the mainland. Some of these gangs were English and some Irish. On 26 November, I had meetings set up in London with two of these groups to discuss various shipments which were waiting for collection in Holland. These meetings had been arranged for that evening, so I thought this would be a good opportunity to catch up with my Turkish friends for a few hours that morning. I contacted a Detective Sergeant from the Operational team on this job, Hydra, ahead of my trip, telling him of my plans. He asked if I wanted any surveillance cover on my morning visit to the Turks, and I replied that there was no need: the meeting with Andy and his mates was for legend-building purposes only, and I wouldn't be discussing any specific drugs consignments with them. I would already be tying up two surveillance teams later for my live meetings in the evening, so there was no point in taking up any more of their resources. In hindsight, this was probably not the most intelligent decision I have ever made. I was probably becoming too blasé and self-confident. The Turks I would be meeting with were in reality very dangerous people who wouldn't hesitate to kill if they thought it was necessary. I was no doubt taking unnecessary risks, and if the wheel had come off the plan at any stage, I would have been without cover or protection. Hindsight can be a wonderful thing, of course.

On the day in question, I rang Andy from the airport on my arrival and suggested meeting up. He was delighted to hear from me and said that he would take me for lunch. We arranged to meet at Palmers Green Tube station. A short time later, I was standing leaning against the wall reading a newspaper as I waited for Andy to appear, when I suddenly heard a horn honking nearby. I looked up but didn't see any car. The horn sounded again, and I saw Andy waving from his vehicle. It was a hearse, one of those old-fashioned ones! Andy was killing himself with laughter. 'I thought you would like this, Billy,' he beamed. It was like something out of an Al Capone movie. I got into the car beside Andy, and we drove to Cypriot restaurant nearby. Over lunch, he seemed keen to impress all his friends, introducing me to everyone individually as his friend from Belfast. We had a great meal and a good chat, with Andy telling me all about a gambling house they had just opened, which was bringing in profits of between £5,000 and £6,000 a week.

After lunch, the conversation turned to business. Andy said that there was no powder about at present, and that they were waiting until Christmas to bring some in. I told him that that would be no problem from our point of view. He then told me that they were expecting a consignment of cannabis anytime, which I had gathered already, since Andy had taken a number of phone calls from potential dealers during our meal. Once our meeting was over, Andy left me back to the tube station and told me to keep in touch, and ring him any time I was over so that we could meet up again. It was obvious that I was being accepted into the gang's fraternity, and so I felt pleased with the way things were shaping up.

When I returned to Belfast, after the two evening meetings, I reported the day's events to the Operational team through the usual chain of command. I heard nothing for some time, and then one day I received a strange phone call from a friend at Headquarters. He told me that someone was making trouble for me at the Met, and that my superior officer, a Detective Superintendent, and his henchwoman had flown to London for a meeting. I was completely mystified, wondering what I could possibly have done wrong—but all I could do was wait and see what would transpire. A few days later, I was summoned to the Detective Superintendent's office in the Criminal Investigation Department's Headquarters in Belfast. The said Detective Superintendent was a smarmy bastard and one of those people who had never seen a shot fired in anger in their entire life. In fact, he and I hadn't really been on speaking terms for some time, as I had told him I believed that he was protecting a senior officer whom I strongly suspected of criminal behaviour. I had a feeling that what was unfolding now was connected in some way with the issue of this bent officer.

The Detective Superintendent was sitting at his desk with a file marked 'Secret' open in front of him. He started asking me pointless questions in a grave tone of voice, trying to pretend that he was a detective…I told him that I didn't understand why I had been summoned: I had done nothing wrong. I then asked what the file sitting in front of him was about, saying that I knew he had been in London with his underling. He replied that it was for him to know what was in the file. This childish behaviour lacked all professionalism, and I told him I suspected that he and his henchwoman were trying to fit me up because of my earlier allegations against his friend. At this, I jumped up and simply grabbed the file. His mouth just fell open in disbelief. I however turned on my heel and walked out of the room with the file under my arm. I went downstairs to copy its contents, and then went back up to his office. He was still just sitting there, as if dumbstruck. 'That file's confidential,' he whined. I simply threw the file at him, saying that we would see who was in the shit now. It turned out that the file contained correspondence relating to a complaint by the Operational team commander from Hydra, that I had needlessly endangered my life and risked compromising others by visiting the Turks in London without cover. The team commander went on with a series of venomous allegations, the main purpose of which, it seemed clear, was to wreck my reputation with the Met utterly and completely.

To say that I was stunned by this turn of events is putting it mildly. The allegations were vindictive and petty in the extreme, and none of it made any sense, particularly given the fact that, just a few weeks previously, I had been presented with a gallantry award by the Metropolitan Police and had of course received numerous commendations from them on a regular basis over the years…Why in God's name would they do this now? I had in hindsight and on my own admission taken a risk, of that there is no doubt. But it was hardly the end of the world, and surely didn't necessitate the lengths they had gone to. Then it hit me: this was the same team that had been caught with their pants down in Northern Ireland on that occasion a year or so earlier, when they were found to be operating in our jurisdiction without permission and had bolted back to London. Their conduct had doubtless caused them a lot of grief at their end, and they had probably been hauled over the coals for it, that was certain. It seemed now that they hadn't been able to just let the matter go, but had taken this opportunity to get their own back.

I made a formal complaint about the whole incident and demanded that it be investigated, not only by our own senior command but also that of the Met. But the report I had submitted on the matter was simply buried: ignored and then forgotten about. It all just seemed to confirm to me yet again that in the dark shadowy world in which I now had to operate, no one was to be trusted—not even my colleagues. I would later report the whole matter again to the ACC Crime, along with my conviction that I was being victimised because I had voiced my suspicions concerning the senior officer to my immediate superior. As it transpired, the whole issue was simply covered up, including my allegations in relation to the bent cop—but I shall relate more on this presently.

Chapter 21

Operation Waverley and the Drugs Barons of Dundee

1999 was drawing to a close and Hogmanay festivities were in full swing, but the Scottish Drugs Enforcement Agency (DEA) had other things on their mind than seeing in the New Year. They were instead becoming increasingly alarmed at the activities of gangs of drug dealers based in Dundee. An ancient University city, and one of the true flowers of Scotland, Dundee was unfortunately at this time becoming as notorious as Glasgow as a centre for drug dealing activity. A further cause for grave concern which was confirmed by all intelligence was the increasing propensity of the members of these drug dealing gangs to carry firearms and resort to violence with little provocation. At least one recent shooting which had taken place just over the Scottish border on the English side had direct links to the Dundee mob. Operation Waverley was a highly organised and focused attempt to infiltrate the gangs in question and disrupt their activities.

My alias for this job was to be Sean Murphy, and I was 'referenced in' to the criminals' circles by John, another undercover colleague who by this stage had already done sterling groundwork in terms of infiltrating the gang. Posing as a representative of the Irish criminal fraternity, John had been actually living with the Dundee crooks in their own environment for some months, taking a flat in their neighbourhood and frequenting their social haunts. Thinking that he was an Irish criminal with good connections in the criminal underworld in Northern Ireland, it wasn't long before our crooked pals brought him into their confidence. Yet again, it was that old ally of the detective, sheer greed, which enabled us to get still closer to them. When John intimated to them that Sean Murphy, one of his Irish mob contacts, would be interested in discussing the purchase of drugs with them, they quickly smelt yet another avenue for increasing their own profits. They were particularly keen to sell the speed which they were churning out in increasing quantities from their underground factory.

And so it was that on 12 January 2000, suitably briefed and accompanied by my undercover colleague John, I found myself outside one of Dundee's finest eating and drinking hostelries. We had been summoned there to meet some of the gang, to discuss the first of what they doubtless hoped would be many drugs transactions with them. John left me straight away to meet a high-ranking member of the gang, while I went into the bar and ordered a meal for myself. Sometime later, I was joined by John and a middle-aged man, whom he introduced as Joe. No doubt in an effort to impress and intimidate, Joe confided in me almost at once that he had spent some time in the British Army's Parachute Regiment. He then proceeded to pull a small plastic bag from his coat pocket and handed it to me, saying that it was a sample of their latest batch of stuff and a lot better than the last lot. I passed the bag to John, who put it away. The bag contained about £50 worth of pure speed. We were aware that before Christmas, this gang had been peddling rubbish, which had been well 'chopped down'. I told Joe that it had better be good gear, and he replied that they had five kilos of it and hadn't received any complaints as yet. This new batch was top notch: according to Joe he had tried it on the previous Sunday, and his tongue was still nipping.

The conversation then turned to prices and terms. Joe told me that he could supply five kilos of base speed at a time, and could guarantee that it would be of the same standard as the sample he had just given us. He was looking for £3,800 for a kilo of speed and £1,200 for an ounce of coke. I asked if he could do me a deal if we ordered a kilo of coke, and he said he would do his best to come back to me with a good price. Incredibly, given how high up Joe seemed to be in the chain of command, he admitted that he'd be prepared to rip off his own courier, suggesting that he could keep the price down by letting his runner believe that it was a kilo of speed he would be carrying (as opposed to a kilo of coke)!

Joe said that he wanted to visit us in Belfast, as he had heard there was a good scene there. He then asked if we would be interested in any Sweeties ('E's). I told him to talk to John about that, as I only really dealt in powder. Joe went on to boast that it was he who was supplying all the coke in the area and controlling most of the drugs scene in Dundee. During the time we sat talking, he was making and receiving numerous phone calls, which were clearly related to various drug deals and the movement of other illicit goods. I noticed that a large bundle of cash was clearly visible from the pocket of his coat, which was hanging over the back of the chair. When I advised him to be careful not to lose it, he laughed, boasting that there was £5,000 there and plenty more where it had come from. There was no doubt about it: we were in the company of a very industrious individual who was deeply involved in the Scottish drug scene. Unfortunately for him, we were recording every word he was saying on a covert recorder. At the end of our meeting, Joe asked us for a lift up to his house in the Ann Street area of Dundee. At the debrief later, I was surprised to find out that he did indeed live very close to where we dropped him off. I was sometimes amazed that these people would go to extraordinary and often ludicrous lengths to exude a fog of secrecy around themselves, and yet let you take them to their own homes! On the drive across Dundee, no doubt in an attempt to further impress me, Joe kept trying to sell me his Porsche—but I declined on the grounds that such a car was too noticeable—a fact which didn't seem to bother him.

Joe and I kept in touch over the following few weeks. Our next meeting took place on 7 March, at the same venue as the last time. This time, Joe was accompanied by an older man, who appeared to be higher up the chain of command. Dan, as he called himself, was between forty and fifty years old, with a good head of wavy hair. Both his arms were heavily tattooed, and he had the general demeanour of an ex-soldier. We again discussed buying a kilo of coke from them. Yet again, they seemed also very anxious to offload their base speed, which seemed to be still in plentiful supply. It was becoming increasingly clear that their factory was located somewhere in the Dundee area, and they were obviously going full-pelt at producing their speed. We knew that they were quite happily mixing it with rat poison and every other toxic substance they could lay their hands on: it was lethal stuff which would do untold damage to kids. Dan seemed a lot more security conscious than Joe, insisting on moving tables three or four times—each time, in fact, that anyone who came into the bar sat anywhere in our vicinity. Little did he know that every word he uttered was being recorded in full stereo! We parted with arrangements to proceed with the deal as soon as they had the coke.

Our next meeting was at the end of April, and again at the same venue. We were now trying to bring the operation to a head as soon as possible. Up until this point, we had been playing for time as we built up more and more evidence on the case from a number of different sources, including other undercover officers and conventional surveillance. The reason we needed to hurry things along now was the mounting evidence in recent months that this gangs' inclination to use violence and firearms was growing as their influence and power in the drugs scene was becoming greater. There was at least one instance we knew about in which it seemed that they had tried to murder or seriously injure someone. John, our undercover officer, had been awakened in the dead of the night by Joe, who was in an utter panic and was begging him to come and pick them up at a roundabout on the road to Glasgow. Eager to gain further access to the gang, John had hurried to the scene as Joe had requested. It seemed that Joe and a companion had ditched their car, apparently after having dumped firearms they had had in their possession. All John could elicit from them was that they had been on their way to teach someone a lesson for withholding money on a drugs deal. What was obvious to us at that stage was that allowing the operation much longer would mean running the ever-increasing risk that these cretins would shoot or murder someone.

At our penultimate meeting with the gang, we again met Joe and Dan. We made the final arrangements for the purchase of a kilo of coke and 10,000 'E's for a sum of £47,500. We agreed to meet to do the deal some two weeks later, at one of Scotland's finest hotels with beautiful views over the rolling picturesque Scottish hills. This hotel would prove not to be the ideal location we had assumed it would be. While it was some distance from the road and therefore easily controlled from a surveillance point of view, subsequent events would prove that a quieter and perhaps more discreet location would have served our purpose better. Hindsight however is always a great gift after the event. (I have deliberately avoided identifying the various premises we used as meeting places in the actual operation: it would not be fair to risk damaging the public reputations of the fine establishments concerned by suggesting any kind of association whatsoever, no matter how tenuous or innocent, with the murky world of drug dealing.)

I entered the hotel with my colleague John. With me I had a holdall which contained the £47,500 in used notes. I had a further £2,500 in notes in my pocket, for any last minute deals that might arise. The entrance to the hotel bar was on the ground floor, while the entrance to the main bar and function area was up quite a steep set of stairs near the main door. When we entered the main bar, it was pretty busy. As it turned out, we had unfortunately picked a day on which there was a Scottish National Social Workers' conference. In any case, we made our way to two settees near the window and waited. At one point, one of the delegates from the conference joined us. We were some of the few people there who were smoking like trains. This guy, who told us he was a local Labour councillor, was, it seemed, quite the nosey parker. I think he was suspicious as to our real purpose at the hotel, as he launched on a series of searching questions. We told him we were car dealers, which I don't think he fell for. Eventually though, when he realised he wasn't getting any answers to his many questions, he became bored and went back to his conference.

We sat on in the function area, consuming gallons of coffee and several trays of sandwiches, for which the charge was absolutely outrageous. Finally, we were joined by Joe, who told us that two other gang members would be coming to check the money we had before the drugs were handed over to our courier, who was some miles away. One of these guys was referred to as Chuck. The DEA's plan was that as soon as the handover of the drugs had taken place, the strike teams would move swiftly, first on the couriers and then on the gang members who were with us. Not for the first time on an operation, we would know that the strike was imminent, but wouldn't know that it was going in until they hit us. We continued to make small talk with Joe for a while. Apparently he was hoping to go on a trip to Florida in the not too distant future, financed of course by his numerous drug deals. At one stage in the conversation, he asked me if I could get him a 9mm Browning pistol: this was the model he had preferred to carry when he was in the military. Most likely as a result of his cocaine-fuelled paranoia, Joe seemed convinced that his partner Dan was trying to muscle in on his business and was actively planning to take him out soon. He, Joe, was determined however to get the first strike in. I reflected that it was indeed fortunate that the DEA were going to close these guys down. If they didn't, the whole scene was going to get very messy, that was clear.

At this point, Joe got another call on his mobile: it seemed that now Chuck would only be bringing 5,000 of the 10,000 'E's that we had been promised. I was not happy, telling him what I thought of their organisation and the fact that we were now being messed about like this. He came back with a lot of waffle and excuses, saying that it was out of their control. We would actually find out later that the greedy buggers had sold the rest to another dealer in Glasgow the night before! John and I then had a hurried discussion about how much money we would need now: we were carrying the full amount in the holdall. We decided for safety's sake that John should go out and leave the rest of the money in the boot of our car, which was alarmed and under our surveillance umbrella. He came back with £27,500 in the holdall, which he deposited in against the wall beside the sofa we were sitting on. We were still waiting for Chuck and his companion to get there. It was around tea time at this stage and we were getting weary: we thought the whole matter would have been done and dusted by this time.

At last, Chuck and his companion, whom he introduced as Terry, arrived. They were two of Glasgow's sorriest specimens. Covered in bling—gold chains, signet rings and earrings—with matching tattoos, their pasty faces bore the scars of a lifetime's failure on the streets of Govan. Their Glasgow battle dress of denim jackets and jeans, which stank to high heaven, stood out a mile in the salubrious trappings of the five-star hotel. Judging by the smell emanating from their clothes, I suspected they had both stayed overnight in some kind of drinking den. I observed that their arrival hadn't gone unnoticed by the hotel management, who were now casting anxious glances over in our direction. I am sure by this stage in any event, even before the arrival of Chuck and Terry, they had been wondering what this group of Irish and Glaswegian hoods were doing, encamped in their front lounge all day.

We showed Chuck the money in the holdall at his feet, and he went through the motions of counting it. Satisfied that it wasn't counterfeit, he got to his feet, slinging the bag over his shoulder. 'Hold on just a minute, squire,' I challenged. 'Where d'you think you're going?' When he replied that he was going to take the money out and then make a phone call to get the drugs delivered, I told him that he was dreaming if he thought he was leaving before the gear was on the plot. I told him that they could leave with the money as soon as our man had the drugs, and not before. At this, John and Chuck left to get a better signal on the mobiles and to arrange the handover with our other half of the team some miles away.

I knew the strike was getting close now, because I had observed a number of people who were obviously Crime Squad come in to that part of the hotel, anxiously scanning the bar area to locate us. They were now positioning themselves around us, exchanging furtive glances. As per usual in such cases, I knew that it was highly unlikely that any of the strike team would know we were undercover cops: in this sense, there was always a time just prior to the strike when you would be wondering if you were going to end up in hospital!

John and Chuck came back and we sat chatting about future drug deals and so on, until Joe got the call to confirm that the handover had taken place. At this point, I got up and we all shook hands, as John handed over the money to Chuck and Terry, who left us, disappearing in the direction of the stairs and front door area. We sat on with Joe chatting for a few minutes, until all at once the Crime Squad officers appeared out of nowhere for the arrest. Doing things by the book, they donned the usual checked baseball caps, and with cries of, 'Crime Squad, don't move!' they rushed us at the table. We were all pushed onto our faces and I had the good fortune to be handcuffed, on one hand anyway, by a beautiful young blonde officer. I have a funny feeling it may have been her first arrest. Because of my size, she was having great difficulty in getting the other half of the standard issue handcuffs onto my other wrist, and she was getting slightly exasperated, to say the least. I wasn't being deliberately awkward, but my arms are not the longest and just wouldn't meet close enough behind my back for her to be able to snap the cuffs on. The more she struggled to bend my arms up my back, the funnier it seemed to me, and I started to laugh. This was a mistake, as she momentarily lost it and, calling me for everything under the sun, then started to bash me over the head with a slipper baton. With the help of some other Crime Squad cops, she managed to get me down the stairs and to push me into the glass of the foyer window. Still pretty annoyed, she was working out her frustrations by banging my head against the glass.

Through the window, I could see that a battle royal was taking place in the lawns outside. Chuck and Terry had been ambushed as they were leaving, and had taken to their heels across the lawns, hotly pursued by the Crime Squad. They were giving as good as they got and were rolling around among the flowerbeds. To add to the general entertainment, it was at this very moment that a Government minister arrived in his official limousine with accompanying entourage: there, no doubt, for the Social Workers' Conference. The minister's minders, obviously unsure of what was happening and thinking perhaps that the pandemonium was something to do with a possible attack on him, proceeded to bundle him unceremoniously into the back of the car, which took off at speed back down the driveway again...

As my young blonde captor escorted me to a waiting police vehicle, two DEA cars swung into the forecourt in front of us. The occupants of the car jumped out and, identifying themselves to my escort, they grabbed me and propelled me into the back of their car. My young blonde friend, resisting their efforts, kept holding on to me for grim death, vehemently protesting that I was *her* collar. Thankfully, for my head's sake, they pulled me away from her and got me to safety!

Later John, the other undercover officer, and I met up for the normal debriefing and to make a start on the usual mountain of statements and paperwork relating to the operation. The DEA had had a good result, and John and I were taken along later that evening to a function to meet the rest of the Crime Squad team. We were of course still introduced to the team by our aliases, and I can still recall the look of horror on my young blonde friend's face when she saw me and realised what had happened: she just couldn't look me in the eye! I forgave her for trying to bash my head in, but I don't think her colleagues did, and they kept her going the rest of the evening, holding their hands up to their heads every time they walked past her...

All in all, we had had a great result. Not only had five arrests been made, but the DEA had been able to recover a substantial supply of drugs and firearms. Often the operational team would be able to take out the targets on the basis of our intelligence alone, with us well distanced from the actual strike, so that the bad guys would never knew what had hit them. On such occasions, we would obviously not come out of the woodwork, so to speak, to give evidence in any subsequent court hearing, although the Judge would have been briefed of our involvement. In Waverley however, the DEA case against the gang in question was to include evidence from all wings of the operational team, including the undercover element. And so, we were part of the operational plan until the very last moment, to ensure maximum damage to the criminals on the plot and add the final bow to the evidential package. Joe, Chuck, Dan and friends would receive their just rewards: that was certain.

Chapter 22
A 'Little Bit of Theatre'

The opening sequence at the very beginning of this book recounts a key moment in a major operation we became involved in early in the year 2000: Operation Long Island. Based near Nottingham in the UK, the team I was working with on Long Island were very good. The undercover unit there was run by a very bright young Detective Sergeant who had a natural instinct for the work and was prepared to put in whatever time it took to get the results. Believe me, such officers are a rarity. I have worked with some real losers over the years.

The target, Briggs-Price, who, among many other things, was a major player in drug dealing circles, had a penchant for heavy gambling and it was this that was to provide the chink in his armour which enabled undercover officers to infiltrate his group and gain the confidence of his henchmen. When it came up in conversation that Briggs-Price was looking to import hundreds of kilos of heroin into the UK and needed someone who could provide reliable transport, our guys took the opportunity of mentioning that they had some Paddy connections who would be up for that sort of job. They were careful to protect themselves from future allegations of acting as 'agents provocateurs' by warning Briggs-Price's henchmen that these Irish guys were a bad lot and that it would probably be best to steer clear of them after all. We then waited for time and our old friend greed to do the rest.

This case turned out to be no different from any other. As usual, the prospect of lining their own pockets still further was enough to blow any concerns or fears out of the water, and no-one was surprised when, having got my contact details from my undercover colleagues, Briggs-Price himself, under the name of 'Robert', got in touch with me. I went live on the job on 11 February 2000, after signing, as per usual, the 'Instructions to Undercover Officers' (Appendix B). It wasn't until Valentine's Day that I received the second call from Briggs. Unfortunately however I was driving at that moment, and my tape recorder was in the back seat of the car, so by the time I had stopped and retrieved it, Briggs-Price had rung off. He had left a number on my answering service, but in fact it took quite some effort and persistence on my part to raise him again. The Operational team were over the moon that he seemed to be taking the bait.

When I did finally get to speak to Briggs-Price, he was very shrewd and wouldn't say very much—other than that he had been given my number by a mutual acquaintance and also told that I might be able to assist him with some transportation. He referred to the merchandise he was wanting to move as 'ponies', and I in turn told him that I would have to discuss the 'insurance cost' with him— meaning of course the transportation cost.

Briggs-Price said that he was offering a new jeep as part down- payment for this first job, but that the rest of the details on the job would be dealt with by one of his people, a guy he referred to as 'a wee kid' called John, who would be in touch with me very soon. This 'wee kid' was in reality a man of about 45 years of age and one of Briggs- Price's top lieutenants. He must in fact have been with Briggs-Price when he had called me, because he rang me back almost immediately Briggs-Price had hung up.

John Barton fronted as a carpet importer and was from Caunton near Nottinghamshire, and not far from Newark. At first sight he certainly did not seem like the stereotypical villain. Softly spoken and quite articulate, he had a smart dress sense and his manner in some ways was rather effeminate. After his initial contact with me, Barton and I would subsequently make dozens of coded phone calls from nearly every phone box in Belfast. For security reasons, I had a rather elaborate tradecraft as regards having telephone contact with such individuals. I would not make calls from a particular phone box more than once in two weeks; in order to prevent all my conversations being traced or overheard by either side, I would break up a specific conversation over three or so calls. The first time Barton and I talked,

I told him to write down the numbers of around eight different call box phones, from which I would be ringing him in a specific order. After that I would merely tell him to ring number 2, number 4, or whatever, according to whichever box was the nearest or most convenient that I went to, and he would refer to his original list. It was a primitive but very effective ploy. At this time, I was actually involved in a number of operations and would sometimes find myself in the ridiculous position of carrying three covert mobile phones, my own mobile phone and at least two pagers. As well as this array of communications equipment, I also had to carry a tape recorder, telephone coupler and a number of tapes. This made socialising difficult on some occasions: if, for example, you happened to be out for a meal, or in someone else's house, you would sometimes have to excuse yourself from your companion or host and disappear for half an hour at a time. When you also consider that you wouldn't be able to tell any of these people what you were doing, the sort of bizarre explanations they might come up with for your behaviour can only be imagined! Thankfully, my wife, friends and acquaintances had long ago given up asking questions anyway.

John and I continued our acquaintance through frequent phone calls over the weeks which followed. We always took care to speak in code and sometimes these protracted calls were taking me hours to physically translate and transcribe for evidence purposes. From our discussions, it was emerging that the group wanted to move a considerable quantity of gear, and the countries of Holland and Turkey were mentioned. John was still attempting to organise transportation at his end, and it was clear that he was having problems doing so. As our conversations progressed, he was becoming more confident in our relationship, and was very keen to meet me in Belfast. I discussed this possibility with the operational team: could we pull it off, and bring him over to Belfast and back again without a compromise? We decided that we could, as long as the whole thing was carefully planned and we put the necessary resources behind it.

We devised a plan whereby I would meet Barton in Belfast airport with a discreet surveillance umbrella. I would have a wired car and would aim to get the whole job on tape on the way into the city. We would take him for a drink in Pat's bar in the docks area, just to make it all the more convincing. As I have explained, Pat would often help us on such jobs and, I think, got as big a buzz from being involved as we did. Pat agreed to put on a Céilidh band and it was planned that we would take over the whole back bar with our people. We would have a couple of guys on the doors, who could keep an eye on things. Should anyone turn up who might risk blowing everything—a cop, for example, out for a sly pint—they would quite simply be told to piss off. We decided that, for legal reasons, we would not initiate any real talk with the target in the bar: anything revealed during the course of such an exchange would not have much legal weight, largely because alcohol would no doubt have been consumed by him at that stage. Over and above this, the chances of us capturing a clear recording in the bar would be almost impossible anyway. A tape in the car would be the best idea. Getting John to talk in private would be far easier anyway: we could cite security reasons for this, which he would be certain to go along with.

On the night of Barton's proposed visit to Belfast, things had been going reasonably well. I had however had a bit of a bizarre call earlier in the day from the Detective Sergeant in the English Ops team. As it turned out, there was a certain conflict between them and the guys from the local Customs authority, who had been fighting for joint authority on the operation. There would be lots of brownie points to be had if this operation came off successfully, and Customs were going to make sure they would be up for a share of the glory too, if there was any to be had. This kind of conflict happened all the time between the police and Customs: sometimes it would seem that more time was spent arguing with one another than actually on the job, locking up the crooks. The problem I always found with Customs set-ups was that you could count on one hand the number of them who had any real brains, or balls either. In Northern Ireland, for example, there were only two officers I ever encountered who could have been described as in any way competent. The rest of them were in my experience a bunch of tossers, who were nothing short of a liability. This instance was to be no different.

The English Ops team told me that one Customs guy in particular —whom they had christened 'Agent Starling', after the film character of that name (Clarice Starling of *The Silence of the Lambs*)—had been spotted hanging about near the airport our target was flying out of. It appeared that Agent Starling had decided to do his own thing and was obviously working to his own agenda—this despite the fact that he had been warned that there was a live operation ongoing. Nervous that our friend Starling would end up compromising us in some disastrous way, we discussed whether or not to abort the job altogether. So much time and effort had been put into the operation, however, that we decided to go ahead with it. As I neared Belfast International Airport, I got another jittery call from the team: Starling had gone missing, and they didn't know whether he was on our side of the Irish Sea or still in England, or even possibly travelling on the same plane as our target! I continued regardless, parking at the short-stay car park and activating the recorder in the boot of the car. I had been told by our technical people that I should have four hours' tape time and I thought that that should be more than enough for what I needed.

I locked the car and made my way to the Arrivals hall. I was about thirty minutes early, but that would give me the time to vet the area for any possible baddies sent over in advance, and possibly intercept the unexpected opposition from Customs—something I should not have had to worry about in the first place. The Arrivals hall was full by this stage. You can be taught the rudiments of people-watching in a classroom, but refining it comes only with years of living off your wits and reading others' reactions. It might just be a cough, or a glance that lasts too long: only experience can teach you the telltale signs that will betray someone's true purpose. I glanced around the hall, but everyone seemed engrossed in their own business. As I looked around again however, I noticed someone who made direct eye contact: a small, weedy-looking guy with a goatee beard, hat and scarf, who was trying hard not to be noticed, but was somehow strangely conspicuous. I continued scanning the room and then turned my gaze back to my creepy little friend: his eyes were still darting around but regularly glancing in my direction. His very physical appearance seemed out of place, somehow. I continued looking around and then back to my new friend. Yes, there was the eye contact again. 'Good evening, agent Starling,' I mused. By now he was on his mobile phone, and his eyes were dancing between me and a fixed point to his right. I followed the direction of his gaze. Lo and behold, there was another one on a mobile telephone too, staring fixedly at Starling and then glancing at me every so often.

Now, what were two people doing, talking to one another by mobile telephone when they were just a few yards away from one another, I pondered. This was too painful for words: their tradecraft and training—or lack of it—was lamentable. This wasn't a training run—it was a live operation against one of the biggest criminal gangs in the UK!

I was brought back to reality by the ringing of my own phone. I recognised the caller's voice at once: it was Matt, a trusted friend from our own Customs. 'What are you doing, mate?' he enquired. 'Matt, you know perfectly well what I'm doing, or you wouldn't be ringing me,' I laughed. 'I need to speak to you urgently,' he pleaded. Matt was a good guy and was clearly embarrassed at having to make the call. It was obvious that one of his supervisors was holding a gun to his head, so to speak, so I decided to make it easy for him. 'Can't talk now, Matt. Ring my base—I've to get on here,' I rattled off, and hung up. I then rang our Ops room straight away and told them that I was aborting the meeting at this location and would ring the target from outside.

Once I got outside, I contacted the Ops team again to apprise them of the situation in the terminal building. As I had predicted, they went ballistic. Leaving them to fight it out with Customs, I went back into the Arrivals hall. Running my gaze over the crowd again, I saw my two amateur spy buddies looking agitatedly at me. God, they really hadn't a clue. I shouldn't have, I know, but I just couldn't resist the temptation to play them at their own little game and make my point. Anyone who knows Belfast International will recall that just as you leave the main Arrivals hall and walk about five yards down the one-way exit corridor, there is a large pillar, just beside the chapel of rest entrance. I walked down the exit route and as soon as I passed the pillar, I stepped smartly in behind it. The two clowns hurried past and then suddenly realised that I wasn't in front of them anymore. Panicking, they both swung around sharply, ending up staring directly into my face. I stared back at them. There was no need for me to speak—the look of incandescent rage on my face said it all. The two fools scuttled off down the one-way system as quickly as they could, looking suitably humiliated.

Now that my point was made, I was finally able to concentrate on the job in hand. I nipped back into the Arrivals hall and then, walking quickly and against the pedestrian flow, made my way out back towards the car. As I did so I could see the two losers from Customs, running frantically for their cars. Once I had stopped the recorder in the boot of my car, I drove quickly out of the airport grounds, but instead of travelling towards Belfast which anyone following me would have expected, I took an immediate left and headed into the country in the direction of Crumlin. I was amazed but not at all surprised somehow that the Customs surveillance team hadn't this break covered: there wasn't a car in sight. I turned off my lights and, after driving about a mile, turned into a field. A few minutes later, cars roared past in both directions: obviously my friends playing catch-up, but much too late in the game.

I waited until all was quiet and then drove slowly by a circuitous route towards Belfast. All hell had broken loose at Headquarters, it seemed, with our team and the English Crime Squad threatening all sorts of retribution against the English Customs guys. Anyway, I was now finally able to get on with the job in hand. I contacted Barton, of the Briggs-Price contingent. He was still waiting at the airport for me. I made up some story about having spotted some Customs people there: I recognised them as the people who had busted me some years ago for counterfeit fags and now they were on duty at the airport waiting for a flight from Tenerife to come in. I concluded my story by saying that I had thought it best not to meet John at the airport in full view: if they had spotted us together, it would have piqued their interest in him. This was professional behaviour which would impress him and would also cover me if the gang happened to have any friendly faces planted at the airport who might have spotted the Customs fiasco, which wouldn't have been possible to miss by anyone halfway vigilant.

I arranged to meet John at the side of the Europa Hotel in Belfast's city centre. As I got nearer to the city, it seemed that I was still not shot of our Customs pals. In hindsight, I had made the mistake of speaking to both my Operations room and the target, John, on my mobile phone and Customs must have been able to monitor John's phone, if not my own as well. As I cruised around the area in the vicinity of the Europa, I became aware that I was being followed. These guys were straight from that TV show 'The Knock': the only thing they didn't have was flashing blue lights on their heads! I took them on a bit of a mystery tour of the city centre, and through the pedestrian areas which didn't seem to deter them. When I deliberately drove up one-way streets the wrong way, they followed me. At least I knew the level of expertise I was up against. I was actually embarrassed that these people were supposedly on my side of the law. I decided to go ahead with the meet in any case, as our target was standing waiting for me by this time. I needed however to start the tape in the boot before I picked up Barton, so I pulled into nearby Bridge Street and, fumbling about in the darkness, attempted to switch on the recorder. As I did so, I was startled by the arrival of an estate car which abruptly pulled right up in front of my car. You've guessed it: it was my old friends from Customs! Driver and passenger both jumped out and it was obvious that, as I was bending down over the boot of my car, they hadn't seen that I was there. I stood up and when they saw me, they jumped about a foot in the air! At this stage I was just standing staring at them in disbelief, now even beyond anger or frustration. They didn't know what to do or where to put themselves, and so they both just turned around and stood staring at the brick wall. Confronted with this utterly ridiculous situation, all I could do was laugh loudly and jump into my car, taking off at speed. As I did so, I could see the two fools scrambling to get into their car again. The evening's events were approaching a level of farce which Brian Rix would have marvelled at.

As I finally made my way to the rendezvous with Barton, I was informed by the Ops team that Customs had at last admitted defeat and stood down. Thank Christ, I thought. I spotted John at once, recognising him from the description he had given me on the phone, and went up to introduce myself to him. He had hawk-like features and was dressed in an expensive leather coat. With his immaculately groomed hair and expensive eau de cologne, he was clearly someone who took pride in his personal appearance. I drove around the greater city centre area for some time, just to be completely sure that I had indeed lost my more obvious followers.

I told John that I had arranged for us to join a number of the guys from my organisation for a bit of relaxation, suggesting that it would be better to have any business discussions now, whilst we were alone. He agreed that this was a good idea and I then began to drive in the general area of the hotel we had booked him into: The Hilton, which was just newly opened around that time. As we drove, we discussed my fee for transporting the gear, as well as possible dates for the job. Little did I know that the tape machine had failed to function: I had obviously pushed the wrong button or connection in the dark, no doubt partly at least due to the pressure of the Customs' antics. The defence counsel later would not be immediately sympathetic as to this explanation for my error, but on a live operation these things were bound to happen from time to time. I would have to rely later in court on my memory of the conversation only.

It was obvious from what John was saying that his organisation was involved in the illegal trade of virtually every illicit commodity in Europe, from counterfeit cigarettes to drugs. The only problem they had was the usual one experienced by such gangs: a shortage of trustworthy drivers. John said that they had 100 kilos of heroin in Holland which they wanted to move in 30 kilo lots. They were willing to pay me £2,000 a kilo for transport. This wasn't really a great deal, in terms of the risk involved. Anyone found with anything like these amounts of heroin would be liable to get life and would be very lucky not to get a stipulated sentence too. I knew however that the details could be negotiated at a later point and, anxious to progress things quickly, I told him my terms were £10,000 up front now and that I was prepared to accept the Land Cruiser that they were offering, which was worth £40,000, as part payment. John told me he specialised in top-of-the-range vehicle theft: the paperwork was perfect and the Jeep in question had a full spec., including leather seats and air-conditioning.

John then asked if I could also move drugs from Spain as well as Holland and if I was willing to move cigarettes too, and so on. I didn't however want to be sidetracked from the case in hand, and I told him we could discuss such matters at greater length after the deal in question. He seemed happy enough with the deal, so I then took him to the Hilton, where I had booked him in under my alias. We gave him a few moments to book into the hotel and freshen up, and I then drove with him to Pat's Bar. I ditched the car with the back-up team and we went into the bar.

The whole team were really getting into the swing of things in the bar, with the Céilidh band giving it all they had in the corner. Barton was in his element. Everybody bowed and smiled in his direction as if to the Don, and he was lapping it up. Here he was in the Irish gangsters' lair: everything was roses! Pat the bar owner was clearly enjoying the whole charade as much as we were. In many ways he was a closet cop, and I am sure if he hadn't been a publican he would have made a great detective. He was a gentle and truly amicable giant of a man, in moral as well as physical stature. He shared my hatred of anybody dealing in drugs. He was afraid of no one and, since he had once boxed for Ireland, very few people would ever dare to argue with him.

The team and I had discussed evidence-gathering at the pub, but we had decided that it wasn't really necessary or indeed potentially very useful, since there were associated difficulties such as the problem of trying to record anything audible over the din in the bar, as well as the legal issues concerning alcohol. It was really 'a bit of theatre', as we referred to it in the business: a valuable opportunity to consolidate our cover and bond more closely with the targets. In fact, John and I had a good conversation in the bar: at the bottom of it all, he was really quite an articulate guy. His wife was one of the top dog breeders in the UK and they both spent a lot of their time showing dogs. Like me, he had a keen interest in Irish horseracing, and had been to Cheltenham for the Gold Cup meeting, etc. Such was his mindset, however, that he very shortly turned even this conversation to the issue of race fixing: criminality was clearly a way of life to him.

All in all, the night was a great success. The highlight of the evening was without a doubt Pat's rendition of *Danny Boy*, which he sang especially in John's honour. Would you believe it, this hardened criminal was so moved by Pat's performance that he started to cry! We shed a tear ourselves, but not for the same reasons. Sheer relief and more than a little merriment at the evening's proceedings had something to do with it in our case. Later, we took John back to the hotel. He was as happy as a sandboy and had clearly swallowed the whole thing, hook, line and sinker. The game was well and truly on. The whole charade of that evening had been aimed at winning their confidence and it had worked a treat. We went back to Pat's and celebrated into the wee small hours.

Over the following few weeks, John and I kept up our daily clandestine phone calls, with the same routine of using a different phone box each night and changing mobile phones frequently. For our part, it was a measure to keep agent Starling at bay more than anything else. Finally, I got a summons from the Big Boss himself, Briggs-Price: he wanted to meet me and discuss the arrangements. I agreed to travel over to Newark in the UK to meet him.

The night before our meet, I got an early evening flight and attended a full briefing with the Detective Sergeant in charge of the operational team and the senior officers running the job. Everything seemed to be going according to plan and the next day at 10.30 am, once the team were deployed as planned, I put a call in to John to tell him I had arrived and was ready to meet him. Everything seemed on track, except that I didn't get John on his phone, but someone called Brian instead. This Brian then informed me that John had been detained on a job in Holland, but was hurrying back to meet me. Unfortunately, we had to spend most of the rest of the day on a series of back-and-forth phone calls between me and Brian, who didn't seem to be able to give any idea of when John was likely to appear. Eventually, as evening approached, I rang Briggs-Price directly, and he suggested that I come on my own to meet him straight away. And so, there I was, sitting in the Mercedes in that leafy layby, contemplating my imminent encounter with the main man...

I started the Mercedes and gunned towards Newark. It wasn't every day I got to drive a new Mercedes, and I decided I might as well enjoy it, even if just for a short time. Newark is a picturesque little English town which looks like something from a typical picture postcard. As I approached Briggs-Price's hotel, I pulled into the car park and parked the car. I then strolled into the bar, trying to look as nonchalant as I could. I could see a couple of people at the bar giving me the once-over, but it was perhaps just the novelty of seeing a stranger.

I ordered myself a drink, and had a good look around the bar and out of the large patio doors through which I had arrived a few minutes earlier. The hotel was doing good business and the restaurant and bars were full of locals and holidaymakers alike. Obviously these legitimate proceeds weren't good enough for my criminal friend, but then of course for people of his ilk, they seldom are. Very soon, I caught sight of a person answering the description of Briggs-Price talking to someone outside. A few minutes later, the man himself came into the bar from the patio area, an Asian guy in tow. Briggs-Price was a big man, with the physique and generally windswept appearance of a traveller. He was carrying a young girl of about nine effortlessly in his huge arms. The child was obviously recovering from chemotherapy treatment: her skin was pale and washed out looking, and she had a scarf tied around her head. She had the face of an angel though, and greeted me with a smile to match. She was hugging Briggs-Price as only a daughter would do. I have a beautiful daughter and I momentarily thought of her and wondered what she was doing. When dealing with people while in an undercover role, you have to be aware of the possibility of developing tendencies which are related to 'Stockholm Syndrome'—i.e. beginning to identify too closely with, or even empathising with, those you are working against. I had no

problem with Briggs-Price and any of his hangers-on, and as I have
said already, I didn't generally suffer greatly from pangs of sympathy
for any of the many drug dealers and other criminals I have been
instrumental in putting away, often for many years of their lives. I
must however admit that that little girl's face has haunted me to this
day. As she gazed at me with her lovely child's eyes, I was suddenly
acutely aware that I was a key part in an operation whose sole aim was
to lock her father up for a very long time—albeit because of his highly
criminal and immoral drug-dealing activities.

Briggs-Price and I recognised each other from the descriptions we
had been given, but I suspected that he had been watching me arrive,
as he was right on my heels. He introduced himself, and the Asian guy
who was with him, Tyre. Tyre was a small, chubby guy wearing a
leather jacket and jeans. Briggs-Price didn't want to hang around and
suggested I follow him in his BMW jeep: Tyre would bring up the rear
in his Jeep. A short time later, we left the hotel in convoy. We drove
through the countryside for no more than ten minutes or so, until we
came across a substantial house and grounds, surrounded by a
massive wall. We gained access through an impressive set of large
electric gates, and pulled into the courtyard of the house. As the gates
closed behind us, I became aware of the presence of a number of
attack dogs, Dobermanns with slashed ears, which quickly
surrounded the vehicles, snarling and slobbering over the windows. I
couldn't help thinking that it was like a scene from some gangster
movie. My musings were cut short abruptly with the cold realisation
that I was now very vulnerable indeed. Although I had been fully
briefed that an attack and intervention force was on standby to extract
me should I be compromised, I was acutely aware that I was now
enclosed within a tight ring of security which would mean that in a
crisis situation the strike team would have great difficulty in getting to
me before my throat was cut.

I waited until the dogs were locked away and the road was clear
before alighting from my vehicle, noticing that Tyre had the good
sense to do the same. We then walked through a very large and ornate
metal cage and on to the front door of the mansion, which also had
an electric lock. As the door ominously clicked closed behind us, a
further inner door was opened by a beautiful blonde girl carrying a
crying baby. She smiled in Briggs-Price's direction, but she had a
haunted look in her eyes. I was later to learn that she was a former

Miss UK contender—what she saw in Briggs-Price, other than his money, I do not know. This was truly a case of Beauty and the Beast.

I followed Briggs through the house towards the rear of the premises, until we came to a large bar and games area beside a swimming pool. This was a Pool, with a capital P. Completely indoors, it looked to me to be about the same size as the public baths in our part of Belfast. Every few metres around the pool were larger than life-sized statues of Greek gods and goddesses. Yes, it seemed that until now, crime had certainly paid as far as my host was concerned. But all that was about to change drastically. We sat down at the card table and Briggs-Price ordered Tyre to open some wine. I was offered a wide choice of wines from his substantial stock, the majority of which would have cost at least £25 a bottle.

Briggs was able to confirm that John was definitely coming in from Holland shortly, and would be joining us later. Sitting opposite my host, I could see that he was weighting me up, just as I was him. He was being very guarded in his speech and was watching me closely. His piercing eyes were as cold as ice and I felt a shiver go through me. This was undoubtedly the most difficult time in any operation. If you lose your nerve at this point, you're f***ed, to put it bluntly. I reminded myself yet again of the fact that the intervention unit was close by, ready to storm the place if the wheel came off the plan, but the reality, I knew, was that I would be at the bottom of the pool long before they got to me.

Briggs was showing off big-time, referring to Tyre as his 'Paki', and other derogatory names, which Tyre didn't seem to mind in the least. Both men talked incessantly about the police bugging things and being able to listen to conversations through someone's mobile telephone, even when it was switched off. I noticed both had taken their batteries out of their phones, and I did the same, to make them feel at ease. The whole time Briggs was gazing at me with those cold, piercing eyes. All at once, he got up and went over to a cupboard. 'Wait until you see this, Sean,' he exclaimed. For an awful moment, I thought he was going to produce a gun but instead he pulled a large expensive-looking briefcase out of the cupboard, and set it on the card table. Snapping the case open, he took out from its interior something which looked like an incredibly sophisticated and expensive scanner. This marvellous piece of apparatus, my host informed me, was capable of detecting any kind of bug, and was the very best that money could buy. Nonchalantly but very deliberately, he ran the device over me and particularly around my private parts, and I could see that he was watching the dials intently. After a few very tense moments, he seemed satisfied and finally put the thing away. Thank Christ I wasn't sitting there with a Nagra taped to my back this time, I thought, inwardly breathing a huge sigh of relief. The operational team had decided not to go down that route on this occasion, but instead we had had the cover surveillance boys plant various bugging devices all over Briggs-Price's mansion some time before.

After this, Briggs' mood seemed to relax slightly, but he would continue to refer constantly to bugs and phones, stating that he never kept a mobile telephone longer than three weeks. At last, John arrived and joined us, at which the boss seemed to visibly relax further. We got down to business then, and discussed how we could transport the heroin. John's idea was to move the whole lot in one go, but I told him that this would be far too dangerous, and proposed that we collect it in lots of 30 kilos. Briggs-Price agreed with me, then went on to openly boast that he had already been responsible for bringing thousands of kilos of cannabis into the UK. He said that he wanted to diversify into other products now: the cannabis had been a good earner, but now a lot of people knew about it, and there were too many questions being asked. It was not only the law you had to watch out for, he continued, but your own lads as well, who might be only too willing to rip you off. Briggs-Price was a very greedy man indeed and was obviously keen to expand his seedy empire and trade in other things too, such as large quantities of cigarettes, for which there was always a steady market. At times, he seemed to be talking more to himself than to anyone else, and every now and then, he would launch into another mumbled rant of jumbled half-sentences. Part of me didn't care what he was saying by this stage anyway: I knew every word of our conversations was being picked up by the multitude of bugs hidden around the house and, as far as I was concerned, I had by now achieved my objective: to get confirmation beyond all doubt of Briggs-Price's intention to import large quantities of heroin into the UK.

Not too long after, I said my goodbyes to Briggs-Price and Tyre, and drove back towards Nottingham. John Barton had scrounged a lift with me, and as we drove he made small talk: Briggs, he said, was a mad man and had once been caught with a semi-automatic shotgun but had been able to get off by hiring a solicitor and paying her a small fortune. The solicitor in question was a woman, it seemed, and the best money could buy. John also let it slip that Tyre was in fact knocking off Briggs-Price's wife, and that if the boss found out he would probably literally skin Tyre alive. I knew he was more than capable of it. The Operational team were later able to confirm the story about Tyre and Briggs' wife: apparently, they had known about it all along, and had in fact had to spend many a cold night and morning listening to them at it! Their preferred place, by all accounts, was Briggs' favourite armchair. It is said that when Briggs was eventually told about the affair and these details, he went absolutely apeshit. The unfortunate Mrs Briggs-Price and Tyre would later pay a heavy price for their indiscretions...

Before John got out of my car, he suggested meeting me for breakfast. At first, I thought he was joking, but apparently not. It was just as well that I was still in character and on my own the next morning, for at 7.30 am precisely, John came into the dining room of my hotel to join me for breakfast. Over the following weeks, he and I would speak many times. As far as the heroin went, it was obvious that they were having problems getting someone to bring the gear to a location within range of our transport. As it transpired, the investigative team in conjunction with HM Customs ultimately decided they had enough evidence before the job went ahead, and moved to arrest Briggs and his cohorts and seize their assets.

On a high note, some two weeks after my retirement from the police service, I was to see Briggs-Price and his fellow conspirators found guilty at Nottingham Crown Court, after a long and hard-fought case, in which I had spent three days being screened in the witness box. In the final event, HM Customs had actually taken the lead in the prosecution as they had primacy in importation charges. On 12 April 2003, the Judge, commending the police for their professionalism and bravery, recommended that Briggs-Price not be considered for parole for at least ten years of the twenty-year sentence he had just been given. John Barton, however, is to this day, still at large and a wanted man. As Lech Mintowt-Czyz was to comment in his column in *The Mail* on 16 April 2003: 'Almost three years after he was caught trying to set up a £10 million heroin deal, a long jail sentence was almost certainly ahead. But in his search for an escape route, Barton had no need to hatch a masterly plan. He simply asked the judge for his passport back and the authorities willingly obliged.'

Unlike the rest of his co-accused, Barton was an articulate, astute individual. He had diligently observed his bail conditions in the pre-trial period. He had been granted his passport to make several trips abroad, allegedly to collect evidence for his defence, and had returned on each occasion to report back to the police. With his personal Doomsday rapidly approaching, on a final trip to Holland in the company of his solicitor, Barton simply disappeared. In his absence, the learned judge who had earlier released him on bail, sentenced Barton to 22 years in jail. There was word on the street however that Barton's punishment for in effect introducing me to the inner sanctum was death, and that he had met an untimely end. This may be true, but I have a funny feeling he is studying the racing form from the bolthole he had taken so many months to prepare before his trial. Who knows? Perhaps I will meet him at Cheltenham on some future occasion, or maybe simply bump into him in the street some day? Stranger things have happened.

Chapter 23
The Dutch Connection

By the year 2000, we were carrying out a substantial number of operations in Holland and Belgium, as well as in Ireland and the UK. This was in large part down to the fact that we had over the years managed to establish a very effective backstop which centred on an establishment called the Ski Hut in Rotterdam. This bar/restaurant was to become a base for us, a place which we used for meals and socialising, as well as meetings with all sorts of contacts, from the drug dealing criminal fraternity to the Dutch police to operational teams of units from all over the United Kingdom and the rest of Europe. Although to the uninitiated it might have seemed like this life of spending our days and nights in bars, restaurants and clubs was nothing more than a never-ending junket, the crucial importance of building a credible, functioning backstop should never be underestimated in the world of covert operations. This 'legend building' would go a very long way to enhancing our profile and credibility with the gangs of drug dealers and other criminals we were so keen to infiltrate. A 'little bit of theatre', as we sometimes called it among ourselves, could mean the difference between seizing the drugs and arresting the bad guys and an operational non-starter.

The staff and regular clientèle of the Ski Hut believed that our crowd dealt in 'white goods'—household ceramics such as baths, toilets, sinks and tiles, and furniture—and we soon became accepted by them as part of the furniture on the premises. As part and parcel of our legend-building, we would get our own and other drivers to pull up outside the Ski Hut in their large articulated lorries and sound the horn. Those of us sitting at our usual table in the bar would then get up and rush outside to offload two or three boxes of cigarettes or wine from the lorry: we would then sell these on to some of the punters in the club at knockdown prices. To them and anyone who happened to witness the scene, we were clearly willingly dealing in suspect gear. This, together with the fact that we also obviously had access to large transport vehicles, meant that it wasn't very long before we were being approached by members of the criminal fraternity and their friends and associates, asking whether we would be interested in getting involved in the transportation of illegal goods of other kinds...

At night, an adjoining nightclub to the restaurant opened for business and this too was a centre for all types of activity. Our group were so much of a regular fixture there that the management granted us free VIP entry to the club. In true Irish tradition, we became adopted by punters and staff alike, and were close friends of the doormen, who were pretty scary guys. Again, it all helped the impression we were trying to create: to outsiders and casual observers, these friendships no doubt gave us the appearance of having a large degree of influence generally: we seemed like important people on the circuit. This backstop became a very valuable one, not only for our team, but also for other undercover units who would come and spend time with us as part of their own legend building and cover stories. Criminals are everywhere, and I'm not being flippant when I say that they seldom have a swag bag by which you can identify them! More often than not, it is the quiet unassuming person who is the contact you are trying to attract in the first place.

I should make it clear that while to it might have seemed to some that the time we spent in Rotterdam consisted of nothing more than a constant round of clubbing, partying and eating out, this certainly didn't mean that we spent our days drinking. We had a job to do and we could never lose sight of that. On operational jobs, alcohol was a complete no-no. As I have said earlier, the Dutch police were very friendly and accommodating, but they had no intention of spending their time on babysitting duties, and so we were often left to our own devices for long periods. To pass the time during the day, I would walk the streets of Rotterdam and Amsterdam and before long I knew every shop, museum and café in both city centres. Being a bit of a war buff, I also occupied myself by seeking out all the museums and related places of interest, and became an expert to the extent that I would often find myself giving the Dutch directions to their own landmarks and monuments!

It didn't take long before our legend building in Rotterdam began to reap rich rewards. By the year 2000, we had successfully infiltrated the criminal fraternity's network of drivers and couriers to the extent that they literally didn't know what was hitting them, or who on earth was responsible for the continuing major seizures of their illegal cargoes throughout Europe. In order to further muddy the waters and add to this confusion, on some occasions we would, as I have mentioned, take out the drugs before they were even delivered to us, intercepting them in France, Holland or on the mainland UK.

However, by the beginning of the millennium, operations were becoming increasingly dangerous, as it was more and more frequently the case that we would find firearms, either on the plot or concealed in the consignments we were delivering on behalf of the criminal gangs. This created a number of problems over and above the obvious threat to safety and security. There were many legal problems connected to the transportation of illegal firearms through foreign states, meaning that any operational plan had to be doubly insured to make certain that these weapons would never fall into the hands of criminals, and terrorist hands in particular. This was another reason we would be keen to have such consignments taken out at the earliest opportunity. As soon as firearms were introduced into the mix, quite rightly, the security services of both the host country and our own would have to be involved in some shape or form: thus on many occasions, cargos with such goods were stopped at source. The problem with the international drugs world was, and still is, that the huge revenues which can be generated will always attract the involvement of terrorist organisations, as a means of financing their activities. Groups such as the PKK will get involved because they have easy access to the poison at source. Other terrorist groups will work at the delivery end, dealing directly themselves, or extorting local drug dealers in order to raise the money for their various causes. There was also however for us the unavoidable reality that modern criminals and the drugs fraternity in particular were increasingly inclined to both carry and use firearms. The simple fact was that, whether we liked it or not, our job was becoming more and more dangerous as time went on—and there was very little that we could do about it.

One of the very many operations in which we were able to make valuable use of our Rotterdam backstop was Operation Elapse. It was January 2000, and one of our undercover officers had recently been contacted by an Irish criminal who was known to have extensive international connections and was strongly suspected of being involved in major drugs importations into Ireland. This crook, who had introduced himself as Mickey from Cork, had asked Allan, our undercover officer, if he would be able to bring over a consignment of drugs on his behalf the next time he was doing a Dutch run. Mickey wanted the gear to be brought into Cork and at this initial stage in the proceedings, Allan told him that this would be no problem. We could deal with where the handover would ultimately take place: for now, Allan was keen to draw Mickey in as soon as possible.

Our first move was to check, as per usual, with the National Drug Unit in Dublin that we were not cutting across any of their operations: they confirmed that we weren't. They did however have quite a bit of background on this guy Mickey: it seemed that he was a member of a mob in Cork who was heavily involved with the Dublin gang. There was also intelligence to the effect that Mickey's team had been hit badly by anti-drugs operations during recent months, and that this was most likely a last desperate attempt by him and a few of the Irish dealers to recoup their losses. As would have been usual with all cases involving the importation of drugs into the United Kingdom, it was decided that from an early stage we would mount a joint operation with the assistance of the National Investigation Service wing of HM Customs. We would also be keeping the Garda fully informed of all developments: as can be imagined, they were also extremely interested in the activities of our friend Mickey and his associates, and would be keeping close tabs on him too.

Mickey went ahead to confirm final arrangements with the undercover officer regarding the collection of the drugs. Allan was told that the consignment would be waiting for him in the Rotterdam area—which of course suited us down to the ground. The base which I have spoken about was there, and also very much in the vicinity of the Euro port. As I have said, we had a close working relationship with the Dutch Special Operations Unit, in the Rotterdam area in particular.

Very shortly thereafter we moved over to our base in Rotterdam and waited for the call to let us know that the gear was ready for us. A few days later the call finally came, and as before we moved our lorry out to a lay-by near the Euro port. After a short wait, a Dutch registered car approached and delivered a holdall to our driver. It was as simple as that and it is as easy as that. The journey back to Belfast via Scotland went off without a hitch.

The holdall we had been given contained in fact 18,000 ecstasy tablets, with a street value of approximately £200,000. As it transpired, for legal reasons, Allan our undercover guy couldn't comply with Mickey's initial request that the drugs be delivered to Cork. The sticking point was that Mickey had instigated the offence by contacting Allan in the North, and therefore the whole operation had been authorised through UK channels. We couldn't just dump the drugs in the Republic because it happened to suit us better!

Allan told Mickey he was having problems getting the package to Cork, and our criminal friend finally agreed that he would send someone up to the North to fetch it. Mickey however turned out to be a very greedy boy indeed, arriving in Belfast in person the night before the proposed pick-up date. He immediately contacted Allan, who told him that he would get the gear to him the next day, at a meeting place near the Europa Hotel. Mickey was mixing business with pleasure on this trip, it seemed: he had brought a girlfriend with him to Belfast, and was asking Allan about a suitable Bed & Breakfast. This was more than helpful of him, as we were able to ensure that he was kept under constant surveillance from the moment he booked into the Bed & Breakfast Allan recommended, in the City's University area. A true gentleman, Mickey had obviously decided that he was not going to take the risk of going to the handover the next day himself, and he sent his unfortunate girlfriend to collect the drugs from Allan. After picking up the drugs on the day in question however, the girlfriend was followed to where Mickey was eagerly awaiting her or, more likely, the drugs.

Mickey was arrested a short time later by the uniform support units that had been shadowing him. He was subsequently charged with the importation of a class 'A' drug and possession with intent to supply a class 'A' drug. He subsequently appeared at Belfast Crown Court on 23 November 2000 and pleaded guilty to the offences charged. He was sentenced to five and a half years' imprisonment. When he was granted bail however he made a run for it. Mickey remains at large but, should he ever turn up in a British jurisdiction again, he will be forced to serve the rest of his sentence.

Chapter 24
Drawing the Line

There comes a point in everyone's life when they feel that they have run the race to the best of their ability and the time is right to withdraw from the battlefield while still reasonably unscarred. In terms of my own career, a number of factors and incidents were to coincide, leading me to the ultimate conclusion that such a time was rapidly drawing near for me.

As the years passed, the revamped surveillance unit at Castlereagh had become more and more successful, and the remit and scale of our operations had broadened and escalated to a degree that we would not have been able to imagine in our first year. Success in many other fields brings such rewards as recognition, accolades and promotion. In the twilight world in which we undercover officers moved however there were seldom any of the aforementioned rewards on offer. All too often the only recognition we would get from those among our own authorities who even knew what we did was a 'Well done' scribbled at the bottom of a report. Unfortunately, the nature of our work did attract notice from some of our colleagues in other unwelcome ways, bringing to the surface all sorts of petty jealousies and trivial professional rivalries within the police establishment. The negative power of such influences should never be underestimated, and I personally witnessed how they could contribute to, or even be completely responsible for, the downfall of some very gifted and promising officers.

Recognition of professional success was not a given—neither, I realised as the years passed, was an adequate level of psychological support for undercover officers and the particular set of problems which the nature of our work can give rise to. In police units such as the Metropolitan Police and the National Crime Squad, they had senior officers in place who were forward-thinking and had considerable experience themselves of the difficulties that the undercover operative will face. As a result, in these forces the back-up at all levels—from organisational to fiscal and professional support—was of a very high quality. Such units had dedicated psychological support and counselling strata in place at a very early stage. The RUC and subsequently the PSNI, on the other hand, only set up the so-called Recreational Health Unit relatively recently. Although the staff there was supposed to help us, the reality was that they were very reluctant to do so in any truly constructive way, and we were denied any structured support at all, other than that which we organised externally for ourselves.

To give an example: I was the Force's representative at the ACPO (Association of Chief Police Officers) Undercover Working Group, and at a meeting of same in London, we were informed that the doctors and medical representatives of the forces and agencies present would be meeting in Italy to discuss medical and physiological support for undercover operatives. When I returned to Northern Ireland, I rang our Force Medical Officer and advised him of the meeting, thinking that he would be interested in and perhaps even enthusiastic about this opportunity to compare notes with and learn from his counterparts in other forces. I couldn't have been more mistaken. In a very cavalier and abrupt manner, the individual in question told me that there was nothing to be gained by the likes of him attending such a gathering. The same guy also subsequently refused to meet us individually for counselling purposes, but said he would only agree to meet us in a group. How it was imagined that anyone could unburden themselves of some very real anxieties and fears in such a suggested environment was beyond me. There was much talk about the opportunities available to officers to talk about problems such as heavy drinking, post-traumatic stress symptoms and so on, with the insistence that conversations of this kind would remain confidential. The actual truth of the matter, as every operational police officer knows and common sense will tell you, was that the opposite would be the case. My own opinion is that, in relation to all such matters, the exercise in the RUC's and latterly the PSNI's case was firstly a 'keep yourself right' one.

Ever since an incident in the late 1980s, when a deranged officer suffering a mental breakdown had gone berserk in West Belfast and tragically murdered people before taking his own life, the unacknowledged policy in the RUC was to disarm an officer showing any signs whatsoever of mental pressure at the first opportunity. Domestic incidents, heavy drinking, even certain types of conflict with colleagues could be seen as such signs, and if there was a perceived risk to either the subject or anyone else, then his or her gun would be removed at the first opportunity. This was and is, of course, the proper course of action, but to try and argue that it would be done in confidence flies in the face of reason, if not practicality. Every officer around any such individual would know immediately that he no longer had his gun: in a specialist unit, he would also, for his own operational safety and that of his companions, be taken off the ground altogether. The incident would be recorded on the officer's file, and I did not witness one instance of any such officer being able to successfully apply thereafter for a specialist position.

All of these considerations and circumstances would contribute to my own decision to hang up my career as an undercover officer and indeed to eventually leave the Force. There were other very pressing practical reasons too. Operationally, we were becoming increasingly aware that firearms were now appearing as a matter of course on the plots of our jobs, particularly those in foreign territories. The presence of firearms represented an obvious physical danger to the operatives concerned, but it also meant that operations which had to date been within the sphere of the criminal investigative agencies of the countries in question now had to—quite rightly, of course—include the various security services as well. These organisations of course would have their own particular agendas too. This in itself never really caused us many physical obstacles, but we had no desire or intention to start crossing over into their particular fields of operations. The fact that these demarcation lines were now becoming increasingly blurred was unsettling, to say the least, and added another serious risk factor to every job. Even more worryingly still perhaps, was the reality that in more and more instances, there seemed to be a direct crossover between terrorist groups from both sides of the fence in our criminal operations. In some cases it was nigh impossible to decipher one from another, all of which meant that we had to proceed with more caution than ever before. Until someone actually tries to kill you, you never really sit up and smell the coffee. There were many occasions when terrorists would have attacked you in the past, but you innocently or not placated yourself with the notion it was the uniform or the organisation which was the target and not you as a person.

When any of the above factors impinge directly on you or those you are responsible for, you tend to focus very quickly on the realities of life and where you are going in it. I experienced the consequences of such factors more than once later in my career, and it's not something I would recommend. A case in point concerned one of our operations that was based in Holland and that involved us in discussions with a gang of Dutch drug dealers about us providing transport on a shipment which we believed was intended for Ireland, most likely Dublin. I contacted our friends in Dublin Castle to keep them fully briefed, as we had no intention of cutting across one of their operations or walking into a 'blue on blue' situation. On our next trip to Dublin, I was taken aside by our Garda colleagues, who told us that they were in fact already working against these people, and that there was a strong terrorist connection. That was enough for me: I took that decision to close down our operation without any further prompting. I was later informed that the Dutch police had subsequently raided some of the addresses of these individuals in Holland and been able to seize a large number of firearms, which had been more than likely Ireland-bound. A brilliant result, but one which demonstrated very clearly the extent to which the topography of our operational landscape was now being muddied by criminals who were now involved in both drugs and firearms, and associating with terrorist organisations as well.

In late 2004, we had once again been able to infiltrate a major criminal conspiracy to bring a large shipment of drugs into Ireland, set up by the Dublin mob we knew to be responsible for supplying most of the drugs being brought into the country. Our role was to provide transport at the Dutch end. The job was at the stage where the delivery of the goods was imminent. All the necessary authorities and back-up support for the operation were in place, I had been in Rotterdam for a number of days. Everything had been going very much according to plan, and we had no reason to suspect that anything was wrong. It was the evening before the day the job was due to go down and, content that everything was set, we had taken the opportunity to travel into Amsterdam for a meal with our Dutch colleagues.

After an enjoyable evening, we were returning to Rotterdam on a late night train. All of us were in a good mood and eagerly looking forward to getting home soon. Then my official mobile phone rang: I could see it was a Dublin number. It was unusual to get a call so late at night, and I answered to find that the caller was a friend and colleague from the Garda Síochána. He asked me where I was, and I laughingly asked why he wanted to know, and what he was up to. Very quickly however I realised from the note of fear and intensity in my friend's voice that this was no normal call. I said that I believed that he knew where I was, or he wouldn't be asking. He told me he thought that it was me who was in charge of the operation at my end, and asked if I was doing a job in the morning. When I confirmed that this was the case, he told me that I should abort the operation at once, as the targets knew who we were. I was in a minor state of shock at this stage and said that I would ring him back. I sat staring at my travelling companions, who knew by my face that I had received grave news. They weren't far wrong. Even apart from the sheer level of organisation, number of man hours and huge fiscal cost to bring the operation to this stage, I would have to be extremely sure of my ground before I could call it off. In such circumstances, you find yourself suddenly in the grip of a powerful sense of paranoia. Simple things like the rat-tat-tat of the train's wheels, which only seconds ago you were oblivious to, suddenly sound like hammers in your brain. A million thoughts rush through your head: you find yourself glancing around you, freeze framing every face in case there is someone you recognise from the past, or you can spot one of those telltale signs by which suspect persons will betray themselves.

Gathering my wits, I rang back my friend. It was obvious that it was difficult for him to talk, but he told me that he had just received the news that we were in imminent danger. This guy didn't scare easy, and there was a cold sense of menace in the tale he began to relate. He told me that one of the Dublin contacts of the mob we were in against had received a message to the effect that we were 'British agents': this had been communicated a short time earlier to the Dutch end of their operation and they had decided that they would not be turning up at our meeting place the next day. Stunned, I confirmed with him again the exact words which he had used: 'British agents'. We agreed to talk later and he rang off.

Those words, 'British agents', kept repeating themselves over and over again in my head: it was such a strange choice of words and certainly not the usual turn of phrase that would have been expected. Anyone from home in the North wouldn't have used them. 'Cops' or 'black bastards': these would have been more likely, but not 'British agents'. It had to be someone from outside the North, and someone who wasn't sure of our real identities or what organisation we actually belonged to. If they had known with certainty, they would surely have said so.

I got off the train on autopilot, completely preoccupied with the news in hand. We had hardly reached our base when I got another phone call which told me that the targets at the Dutch end were now considering turning up at the meeting after all, and beating us up. Pickaxe handles as possible weapons had been discussed. It seemed that they still didn't know who we were exactly, but there was no doubt that someone had betrayed us and compromised the operation. Back at base we poured ourselves each a stiff drink and sat staring into the unknown, racking our brains as to what could have happened. All we could do was to wait for events to unfold.

As the night progressed, further updates from our sources informed us that the gang at the Dutch end were now discussing other options, such as kidnapping us or shooting us up in a drive-by attack: apparently they had settled on the latter course of action. We of course were only a cog in the wheel, and I didn't know how much the crooks actually knew. There were just too many unanswered questions at this stage and I didn't want to get anyone injured, let alone put in a situation where they could come under fire. We decided to call the job off, telling the Dutch contacts that we believed we were under surveillance and that it was too risky to do the handover in the morning. At least we would be gaining some sort of ground in that we had called it off and not them. This way, they would be unsure of whether their suspicions were justified, and in the meantime we could assess the problem properly. I advised our senior command that I was aborting the job. They trusted my experience and decision-making.

We returned home, somewhat dejected and troubled. Over the next days I called a war council with everybody involved and carried out an inch-by-inch and line-by-line examination of the operation and all those who had participated in it. This included a technical analysis of all transmissions by phone and other means which had taken place throughout the operation from the word go by every single person involved, even all of the administrative staff. I quickly zeroed in on one particular intelligence source in the chain who had been making strange calls to an unknown Dublin registered mobile around the time that things had started to go bad. There was now a strong suspicion that this individual might be a double agent. Unfortunately for us, as the story unfolded, it became clear that the leak had emanated not only from criminal elements, but also from a certain officer in the Garda Síochána who was in fact not involved with the specialist teams with whom we worked. In many senses, the Garda Síochána was no different from our own Force and they too had within their ranks a number of officers who were quite simply jealous of the successes of others. The agent had informed his controller in the Garda, the officer in question, that a controlled drug delivery was afoot. The officer in turn had either deliberately or by accident let it slip to his contacts in the criminal fraternity that a shipment coming into Ireland was under Northern security control. The words used, 'British agents', were indeed significant. Only a selected few in the Garda Síochána knew our actual identities and unit grouping: the mole obviously hadn't known who we were or where we were from, and this ignorance had led him to use the phrase in question.

My own superiors didn't have the balls to tell the Garda High Command the truth about what had happened and the implications, and so it was left to me to do so. While attending a major drugs conference with the Garda and other agencies in a Dublin hotel not long after the whole fiasco, I had a very frank discussion about the matter over a quiet pint with a senior Garda officer whom I knew well. The matter was dealt with and in the end I was happy that the wayward officer was now under control: his not-so-promising career in the murky world of crime-fighting thankfully came to an abrupt end. In this instance, the damage had fortunately been limited and the integrity of our operatives remained intact, thanks to some hasty repair work, but the whole debacle showed us that simple jealousies could cost us our lives. For me personally, this particular incident was just further confirmation of what I was feeling with increasing intensity: that the risks of the job were growing with each day that passed, and that, for me at any rate, it was soon time to withdraw from the fray.

Chapter 25
Time to Move On

The Garda weren't the only ones having internal problems, and at this point my own Force was causing me greater ones. For some time I had been having serious concerns about the fact that one of our senior officers was, or seemed to be, involved in inappropriate conduct of the most serious kind, involving drugs. When I raised these concerns with my line management, I had been greeted with derision and told to mind my own business.

For some weeks I had been unable to sleep with this knowledge. It finally got to the stage where my wife threatened to go to the Chief Constable herself if I didn't do something about it, as she was no longer prepared to stand my pacing the floors in the middle of the night. As I have said, I had tried to confide in my own Detective Superintendent a number of times, but my fears had been summarily dismissed. I felt I had no choice then but to go to a Detective Chief Superintendent in whom I had a lot of faith. He read my written report, and then said, 'I know what I would do, but I can't advise you what to do: it's your own decision. Just remember that if you put this in, you'll burn all your bridges behind you.' This didn't help me a lot, but I believed this man to be of sterling integrity and I was sure that he would have reported it—although maybe I was wrong. In any event, I finally rang the ACC's office and asked to see him urgently. His secretary realised by the tone of my voice that there was something seriously wrong, and arranged an immediate appointment.

When at this meeting I showed the ACC my complaint, I could see that he was visibly shocked, as the blood seemed to drain from his face. Looking me straight in the eye, he then told me that, on his word of honour, he would get back to me in writing within five days to inform me what his proposed course of action would be. In the days that followed, those words about burning bridges behind me continued to ring in my ears. Unfortunately, they would prove to be only too true. I thought I had seen most things by now in my service. Regretfully, this was not to be. Over time, I was treated as a virtual pariah. Senior officers avoided me like the plague. Colleagues and even former friends refused to speak to me. There were also serious attempts made to have me break off all relationships I had with the Garda, which I shall now briefly relate.

Around that time I had been asked by the Garda to attend a meeting with them which would also include officers from the Dutch Special Operations unit and the English Crime Squad. We were to discuss an undercover drugs operation which would be run at the highest levels against major Irish targets. I had attended countless meetings of the kind in the past, always without any questions asked by my own management. On this occasion however, when I requested permission to attend, it was suggested that I was on a junket and up to no good. It was only after intervention by a senior officer that I was backed to attend the meeting. There was worse to come however when Special Branch were used to take over my unit. Despite the fact that ours had been the only covert unit outside Special Branch control, and the most successful ever in the history of the Force, it had been decided by someone higher up the chain of command that we were to be amalgamated with their murky empire.

I have tried to come to terms with these decisions and actions: I have in fact spent hours trying to work out in particular the rationale behind the urgent rush to take over my unit and the decision to amalgamate it with Special Branch. Special Branch lackeys were actually assisted by my own CID Command in the takeover of my unit, excluding me from all meetings like the cabal they were. Tellingly enough, within two weeks of my leaving the job, they proceeded to burn every official record from my unit over the previous ten years. As a CID unit, we were bound by the law itself to preserve all of our records which consisted not only of masses of files on some of the country's top criminals and terrorists, but also of all our records relating to undercover operations in which we collaborated with the Garda. Other documents in our system were highly classified and contained what could be construed as highly controversial material concerning such matters as the activities of 'King Rat' (Billy Wright), taskings by Detective Sergeant Jonty Brown, who had by this stage also been classed as an enemy of the state in his own fight for the truth, as well as other inflammatory cases. All of these records could now be destroyed with impunity, by using a memo contained in *The Walker Report*, issued in 1981 by Patrick Walker, then Deputy Head of MI5 in the North at the time. (Walker went on to become Director General of MI5 between 1988 and 1991, before being succeeded by Dame Stella Rimmington.) Amongst other self-serving security suggestions, Walker had proposed in his memo that all records should be destroyed after operations. One can only presume he included in this records of national importance surrounding matters of national security. This directive was used by certain individuals to justify destroying all records of cases in which they might have left themselves or the establishment open to censure.

Although I had by that stage over thirty years in the police service, I could have worked on for at least another ten years had I chosen to. However, it was now becoming only too clear that my fanciful ideas of truth and justice—just as in the hair-cut incident so many years earlier in my career—were misplaced, to say the least. In the instance I have outlined, as unfortunately in so many others, the RUC's command would sadly go to any lengths to cover up and protect the wrongdoers. This time in my career was incredibly depressing: it nearly broke my heart to be treated in such an underhand and cowardly fashion after all the sacrifices, both professional and personal, that I had made.

My own conscience was clear however, and that was and is no small thing. I asked for a transfer out of the poisoned environment in which I now found myself. I was subsequently to retire from the Police Service as acting Deputy Head of Police Intelligence. I decided to leave with my head held high. I had spent over thirty years in the service of Queen and country and had, I hoped, done my bit in the fight against crime and in the undercover war against evil from whatever quarter. No one needs medals or their names in lights. I am proud of my service and of having had the honour to serve with all the many real heroes I was lucky enough to meet out there, from many different spheres of life.

There are of course many times when I have reflected in solitude on my service in the police, and on my time as an undercover officer in particular. The ghostly images of friends and colleagues who paid the ultimate price visit me from time to time, and I wonder if their sacrifice will ever be acknowledged by the ungrateful that now so easily forget them or malign their memory. In many senses we were indeed 'Ireland's Forlorn Hope' who, like many others through the centuries, were selected, or volunteered, to undertake extraordinarily perilous enterprises in the service of their country.

I have always tried to do my best and what I thought was right. There were obviously things I could have done better and I'm sure I may have inadvertently hurt some along the way, and for this I am truly sorry.

Have I regrets?

One evening during the time I was writing this account, I left my laptop turned on and open while I was taking a break. I returned to find that my son, who had read this chapter of my book, had added these words to the bottom of the page:

'Dad, this is from Patrick, your only son. I hope you know that I love you so much you can't even imagine. Thank you, Dad, for bringing me into this world.'

I have no regrets.

Appendix A

INDEX TO DRUGS

Heroin: Also known as 'smack', 'brown' and 'horse'.
Price: £70–£90 per gram (can vary greatly according to place of purchase and availability). Due to its highly addictive nature, some cartels virtually give it away to first time users.
Form: Street heroin usually has a brownish tinge to it, but can be white in its purist form. It can be injected, snorted or smoked pure ('chasing the dragon'). Most addicts prefer injecting.
Duration: Highs may last 1–5 hours.
Legal status: Class 'A'
Highs: An opiate, this drug creates an almost instant rush of pleasure. A feeling of cocooned warmth and sleepiness.
Lows: The use of heroin invariably leads to both mental and physical addiction. Withdrawal symptoms can include violent shaking, sweating, vomiting and possible coma. Pure heroin can kill and the shared use of needles by users and addicts frequently leaves the users open to the risk of infection and HIV. Addicts will frequently commit crimes in order to feed their habit.

LSD: (Lysergic acid Diethylamide): Also known as 'acid', 'trips' and 'tabs'.
Price: £8–£10.
Form: Generally available as squares of impregnated card about the size of a fingernail, which frequently bear a logo such as a joker, a clown or Batman.
Duration: Highs may last 6–12 hours.

Legal status:	Class 'A'
Highs:	Frequently causes severe delusions and hallucinations which are supposed to raise the user to a so-called 'higher plane'.
Lows:	A drug traditionally associated with the hippies of the 1960s era, a single dose of LSD can cause brain damage and severe side-effects such as fits and flashbacks, sometimes hours after use. The drug may make the user to feel that he or she is invincible and has superhuman powers, such as the ability to fly. This can often result in serious injury or fatal accidents.

Cocaine:	Also called 'coke', 'Charlie', 'white', 'Bolivian marching powder'.
Price:	£50–£70 a gram.
Form:	White powder which is snorted, smoked, injected or rubbed on the gums.
Duration:	One gram can produce a high lasting an entire evening.
Legal status:	Class 'A'
Highs:	Can lead to feelings of omnipotence and reduces the need to eat or sleep; fairly subtle changes in a person's behaviour can go unnoticed to the untrained eye.
Lows:	Regular use of this drug can quickly lead to addiction and can cause exhaustion, anxiety and weight loss. Severe damage can be caused to the nasal passages which can eventually collapse. Total heart failure can be another long-term consequence.

Amphetamines:	Also called 'speed', 'whizz', 'sulphate', 'poor man's cocaine'.
Price:	£10–£20 per gram.
Form:	Usually in wraps of powder, snorted up the nose or smoked in a cigarette. Occasionally available in pill form. Hardcore users inject it.
Duration:	Highs may last 6–8 hours.
Legal status:	Class 'B'
Highs:	A powerful stimulant which excites the central

nervous system. Elevates the mood and heightens endurance, including sexual stamina.

Lows: Lethargy and depression when the effects wear off. Psychologically addictive. Can cause panic attacks and occasionally heart failure. Those who usually peddle this particular drug are known to mix it with other substances in order to bulk out the volume. Substances used for this purposes may include anything from baking soda to talcum powder, but frequently rat poison is also used. A large number of deaths are cause by such additives.

Ecstasy: Also known as 'E's, 'XTC' and 'MDNA' (Methylenedioxmethamphetamine), as well as by various brand names. Tablets are generally stamped with a logo (Mitsubishis, doves, etc.)

Price: £10–£12 per tablet: can vary greatly however according to location of purchase and availability.

Form: Mainly in tablet form.

Duration: Highs may last 4–8 hours.

Legal status: Class 'A'

Highs: Euphoria and feelings of benevolence and great intimacy. Users often experience abnormal levels of energy, especially when dancing.

Lows: Can cause severe diarrhoea, nausea and sweating. Fatigue and depression can last several days and constant use can build up a resistance to the drug. There have been frequent deaths due to respiratory failure and overheating causing organ failure and heart attacks.

Cannabis: Also known as 'grass', 'weed', 'hash', 'dope', 'pot', 'skunk' and 'blow'.

Price: £25–£50 per quarter ounce for the more powerful 'skunk', which is usually grown on clandestine farms.

Forms: Most commonly smoked in a 'joint' or 'spliff', or using pipes and 'bongs,' which are sold in cannabis paraphernalia shops. Also eaten in cakes, known as 'space cakes'.

Duration:	Highs may last 1–3 hours.
Legal status:	Class 'C'
Highs:	Induces a sense of relaxation; enhances feelings of well-being and happiness. Users claim to experience greater intuitive insights. May occasionally cause hallucinations. Some users claim the drug can ease medical conditions such as Multiple Sclerosis.
Lows:	Continual use weakens short-term memory and may cause lethargy and paranoia.

Appendix B

INSTRUCTIONS TO UNDERCOVER OFFICERS

A Police Officer must not act as an 'agent provocateur'. This means he must not: either incite or procure a person or, through that person, anybody else to commit an offence, nor an offence of a more serious character, which that person would not otherwise have committed.

However, a Police Officer is entitled to join a conspiracy which is already in being, or an offence which is already 'laid on', or for example, where a person has made an offer to supply goods, including drugs, which involves the commission of a criminal offence.

If, during the course of an investigation into an offence or series of offences, a person involved suggests the commission of, or offers to commit a further similar offence (e.g. by offering to supply drugs unlawfully), a Police Officer is entitled to participate in the proposed offence. The officer must not incite such an offence.

Police Officers are entitled to use the weapon of infiltration of groups or organisations. In such a case it is proper for the undercover officer to show interest in, and enthusiasm for, proposals made even though they are unlawful, but, in so doing, he must try to tread the difficult line between showing the necessary interest and enthusiasm to keep his cover (and pursue his investigation) and actually becoming an 'agent provocateur'.

Police Officers must obtain confirmation that the information they are acting on is accurate and reliable before becoming involved in undercover operations.

Police Officers must bear in mind that, by virtue of Section 78 of the Police and Criminal Evidence Act 1984, a Judge may take into account the circumstances in which evidence was obtained in considering its adverse effect on the fairness of proceedings in Court.

Invariably, this means you enter a criminal conspiracy or become part of a pre-arranged offence.

Supervising Officer   ………………………………......

Date   ………………………………......

Time   ………………………………......

On ……………......   I was instructed by ……………..........
as to the 'Instructions to Undercover Officers' contained in this book.

Signed   ………………………………......
(Pseudonym)